English for Academic R<

Series editor
Adrian Wallwork
Pisa
Italy

This series aims to help non-native, English-speaking researchers communicate in English. The books in this series are designed like manuals or user guides to help readers find relevant information quickly, and assimilate it rapidly and effectively. The author has divided each book into short subsections of short paragraphs with many bullet points.

More information about this series at http://www.springer.com/series/13913

Adrian Wallwork

English for Writing Research Papers

Second Edition

 Springer

Adrian Wallwork
English for Academics
Pisa
Italy

English for Academic Research
ISBN 978-3-319-26092-1   ISBN 978-3-319-26094-5   (eBook)
DOI 10.1007/978-3-319-26094-5

Library of Congress Control Number: 2016933455

Springer Cham Heidelberg New York Dordrecht London

Printed on acid-free paper

Springer International Publishing AG Switzerland is part of Springer Science+Business Media (www.springer.com)

Preface

Who is this book for?

This book is part of the *English for Research* series of guides for academics of all disciplines who work in an international field. This volume focuses on how to write a research paper in English, though the majority of guidelines given would be appropriate for any language.

It is designed both for inexperienced and experienced authors.

EAP trainers can use this book in conjunction with: *English for Academic Research: A Guide for Teachers.*

How is this book organized? How should I read it?

The book is divided into two parts and the full contents can be seen in the Contents on page ix. This Contents page also acts as a mini summary of the entire book.

Part 1: Guidelines on how to improve your writing skills and level of readability.

Part 2: Guidelines about what to write in each section (Abstract, Introduction, Methodology etc.) and what tenses to use. Of course, not all disciplines use the same section headings, but most papers nevertheless tend to cover similar areas.

I recommend you read all of Part 1 before you start writing your paper. Then refer to specific chapters in Part 2 when you write the various sections of your paper.

Chapter 20 concludes the book and contains a checklist of things to consider before sending your manuscript to the journal.

How are the chapters organized?

Each chapter has the following three-part format:

1) FACTOIDS/WHAT THE EXPERTS SAY
In most cases, this section is a brief introduction to the topic of the chapter. Occasionally, the factoids are simply interesting in themselves and have no particular relevance to the chapter in question. However, they can be used by EAP teachers as warm-ups for their lessons. All the statistics and quotations are genuine, though in some cases I have been unable to verify the original source.

2) WHAT'S THE BUZZ?
This is designed to get you thinking about the topic, through a variety of useful but entertaining exercises. These exercises are designed to be done in class with an EAP (English for Academic Purposes) teacher/trainer, who will provide you with the keys to the exercises. The final part of each *What's the buzz?* section is a brief outline of the contents of the chapter.

3) The rest of each chapter is divided up into short subsections in answer to specific questions. These are either instructions (in Part 1) or in the form of FAQs (in Part 2). Each chapter ends with a summary.

I am a trainer in EAP and EFL. Should I read this book?

If you are a teacher of English for Academic Purposes or English as a Foreign Language, you will learn about all the typical problems that non-native researchers have in the world of academia. You will be able to give your students advice on writing quality research papers and getting referees and editors to accept their papers. In addition, you will generate a lot of stimulating and fun discussions by using the factoids and quotations, along with the *What's the buzz?* exercises.

You can also use the three exercise books (writing, grammar, vocabulary) that are part of this *English for Academic Research* series, plus the teacher's book that contains notes on how to exploit all the books: *English for Academic Research: A Guide for Teachers*. This guide contains keys to the exercises in the What's the buzz? sections.

I edit research papers. Can this book help me?

Certainly. It should clear up a lot of your doubts and also enable you to be a bolder and better editor!

Are the extracts in this book taken from real papers?

Most of the examples are taken from real published papers. In some cases the names of the authors and titles of the papers, plus where they can be downloaded, can be found in the Links and References section at the back of the book. Some examples are fictitious (and are indicated as such), but nevertheless not far from reality!

How do I know if the examples given are good or bad examples?

Example sentences are preceded by an S, e.g. S1, S2. If they contain an asterisk (e.g. S1*), then they are examples of sentences that either contain incorrect English or are not recommended for some other reason. Longer examples are contained in a table. This table contains the original version (OV, sometimes labeled *No!*) and the revised version (RV, sometimes labeled *Yes*). Unless otherwise specified, the OVs and sentences labeled *No!* are all examples of how <u>not</u> to write.

Useful phrases

A list of useful phrases that you can use in your paper can be downloaded free of charge at: http://www.springer.com/us/book/9783319260921.

Differences from the first edition

Each chapter now begins with Factoids and a *What's the buzz?* section. There is a new chapter (Chapter 9 Discussing Your Limitations) and around 50 new sections spread over a 100 new pages - particularly in the chapters on: *Highlighting Your Findings, Abstracts, Introduction, Discussion*, and *Conclusions*. The chapter on *Useful Phrases* is now a free download (see above).

The author

Since 1984 Adrian Wallwork has been editing and revising scientific papers, as well as teaching English as a foreign language. In 2000 he began specializing in training PhD students from all over the world in how to write and present their research in English. He is the author of over 30 textbooks for Springer Science + Business Media, Cambridge University Press, Oxford University Press, the BBC, and many other publishers.

Other books in this series

This book is part of a series of books to help non-native English-speaking researchers to communicate in English. The other titles are:

English for Academic Research: A Guide for Teachers

English for Presentations at International Conferences

English for Academic Correspondence

English for Interacting on Campus

English for Academic Research: Grammar, Usage and Style

English for Academic Research: Grammar Exercises

English for Academic Research: Vocabulary Exercises

English for Academic Research: Writing Exercises

Contents

Part I
Writing Skills

Chapter 1

Planning and Preparation

Factoids

Every day 7000 scientific papers are written, but not necessarily accepted for publication.

*****

At least two thirds of published scientific papers are written by researchers whose first language is not English.

*****

Approximately 20% of the comments referees make when reviewing papers for possible publication in international journals regard English language issues.

*****

A much disputed report drafted by the Organization for Economic Cooperation and Development found that only 12% of Italian and Spanish university graduates reached the top two levels on a standard literacy test, whereas around 13% of high school students reached these levels in Japan and the Netherlands.

*****

In the EU alone there are over 250,000 PhD students.

*****

China has nearly one million researchers, Japan 675,000, the Russian Federation 500,000.

© Springer International Publishing Switzerland 2016
A. Wallwork, *English for Writing Research Papers*,
English for Academic Research, DOI 10.1007/978-3-319-26094-5_1

1.1 What's the buzz?

Think of three good reasons for publishing your research in an international journal. The three quotations below should help you.

> *From note taking to publishing to teaching, language is the tool that gives sense to scientific activity. Whatever scientists do or observe, everything they come to know or to hypothesize, is mediated through language.*
>
> Robert Goldbort, Writing for Science

> *The writing of an accurate, understandable paper is just as important as the research itself.*
>
> Robert A Day, How to Write and Publish a Scientific Paper

> *Writing helps you to learn. Writing is not simply a task to be done once research or other preparation is completed - it can be an integral part of the work progress.*
>
> Nicholas Highman, Handbook of Writing for the Mathematical Sciences

****

This chapter analyses the benefits for you of publishing your research, and suggests various approaches for

- choosing the right journal and understanding what the editor expects from a paper in terms of content, style and structure

- deciding the order in which to write the various sections (Introduction, Methods, etc.)

- keeping the referees happy

1.2 Why should I publish? How do I know whether my research is worth publishing?

You will be more motivated to write a good paper, if you have thought about exactly why you want to have your research published. One of your reasons will probably be because you believe you can make a contribution to a gap in the current knowledge base of your field. It helps if you can write down concisely what this contribution is, and then double check that your proposed contribution really is original.

One of my students received the following comment by a referee as a justification for rejecting her paper:

> *Not acceptable. No new knowledge, science or discovery is presented.*

This kind of comment may reach you even six months after you have sent your paper for review. For you, it represents a considerable waste in time and energy spent on a paper.

So, before you start writing you need to have an absolutely clear idea of:

- what your research goal was

- what your most important findings are and how you can demonstrate that they are true

- how these findings differ from, and add to, previous knowledge

You know implicitly what the importance of your findings are – after all, you may have been working for months and years on the project.

But the reader does not know.

You must give the reader a clear message.

Discussing and presenting your findings to colleagues should help you to identify what your key findings are.

Make a list of your key findings and choose the most important ones to fit the space you have available (i.e. the total word count allowed by your chosen journal). For each key finding decide if there is another possible explanation for what you have found. You can do this by looking in the literature again. Make sure you have not inserted any bias in your explanation of your findings. Next, write an explanation saying why you think each key finding is true. However, write your explanation in a way that shows you are open to other interpretations.

The above suggestions should also help you to decide whether your planned paper really will have a contribution to make.

1.3   Which journal should I choose?

If you have never written a paper before and your supervisor has not indicated a specific journal where he/she would like you to publish, it is a good idea to ask colleagues in your research group what they read and what sort of publications they aspire to publish in.

Even if you are writing a paper for the first time, it does not mean that it will only be suitable for a marginal or not very well known journal. Your progress in academia very much depends on your ability to publish in journals that have a high impact factor.

An impact factor is a measure of how prestigious a journal is. The higher the impact factor, the more widely read the journal is, and the more likely other researchers will cite your paper. Tables of impact factors which rank all the peer-reviewed journals in the world are available on the Net, you can use Google Scholar to help you find them.

However, given the difficulties of getting published in a high impact journal (20.13), you might consider opting for a short article or a 'letter'. A literature review or a methodological text is often publishable. For instance, if you are studying medicine, you could consider writing a clinical review – a 2,500 word article which is essentially a review of the management of important and common problems. Many disciplines have such an equivalent.

When you have chosen three or four possible journals, look at their styles and think about their audience – what do the editors and readers expect from the articles (see Sect. 1.7)?

You could try to insert your paper into an ongoing discussion that is currently being covered in the journal. This approach may increase the chances of getting your paper approved by the editor.

The topic you choose to write about is obviously related to the journal where you want to publish. Occasionally it may be worth choosing the journal first (rather than your exact topic), and then deciding which angle of your research to focus on so that it will match the expectations of your chosen journal.

Note there are many online journals that advertise their services by sending emails to unsuspecting researchers – do not submit to such journals as either they are scams or at the very best have no impact factor.

1.4   How can I know exactly what the editor is looking for?

Read as many papers as you can from your chosen journal. This should help you to gain a clearer picture of what the editors of the journal are looking for to enable them to keep their readership levels high. Below are some of the typical things that editors hope to find in manuscripts.

TYPE OF PAPER	Original research, or a systematic review, or a position paper etc. (for more on the various types of paper consult Google Scholar or Wikipedia)
SUBJECT	Hot topic (contemporary issues), original and innovative; or controversial; or classic
AIM	Clarity of purpose, i.e. the research objectives are clear
RESEARCH	Well conducted, methodology clear, ethical, reproducible, no bias, limitations admitted
RESULTS	In line with research objective; entirely new or confirmation of other results already published in the same journal; not too broad as to be meaningless; can be generalized outside a very specific field
LENGTH OF PAPER	Short or long
STYLE	Personal (*we*, *I*), or impersonal (exclusively passive form), or mix (personal and impersonal)

Sometimes journals have themed or special issues on specific topics. These special issues are announced many months in advance of publication. Keep a look out for an issue that covers your specific area – it may be the perfect opportunity for you.

1.5   What preparation do I need to do?

Once you have chosen your journal, look at the most frequently cited papers to see how the authors rationalize the various steps of their research. Try to use papers that you will probably quote in your section on the review of the literature, and which are highly relevant to your topic and/or classic papers in your general field.

For example, you could create a table with some or all of the following headings:

* problem that the research addresses

* background information and relevant references

* elements that validate the level of innovation of the research

- conceptual model, methodology or procedure that the research takes into consideration

- materials, equipment and software used

- method used and the operational steps that the author carried out

- results achieved

- analysis and interpretation of these results

- strengths and weaknesses of the research, the insights demonstrated

- implications for further research

Then you can fill in your table with brief notes for each of the papers you have analyzed. This analysis should help you to:

1. write your own literature review, because after this analysis you will be very familiar with the literature
2. identify the differences in other researchers' approaches and results compared to your research
3. note down the strengths and weaknesses (including possible bias) in the work of others

These three points should enable you to understand in what ways your research is unique, innovative, interesting and useful, and how it extends what is already in the literature. Your aim is to find a knowledge gap to fill.

If you have done a very thorough literature search, then another publishing opportunity for you is to write a literature review.

1.6   How can I create a template?

Choose one paper that is close to your topic, that is written by a native English speaker, and that you enjoyed reading. Use this paper as a model into which you can 'paste' your own research.

Notice how your model paper is structured:

- how does the author begin?

- what points does s/he make in each section?

- how does s/he link paragraphs together?

- how does s/he connect the Results with the Discussion?

- how does s/he present the Conclusions?

As you read your model paper, note down some useful English phrases that the author uses. Such phrases will help to increase the readability of your text, as they will be familiar to your readers.

1.7   In what order should I write the various sections?

There is no standard order in which you should write the various sections of your paper. You should choose the order that suits you best. This may involve writing several sections simultaneously.

Many authors start with the Methods, which is often the easiest section to write because this is the part that will usually be clearest in your mind. Beginning with the Methods will also give you the confidence and impetus you need to move on to the other sections of the paper.

In reality, it is best to start with the Abstract as this will help you to focus / orient your ideas on what are the key aspects of your research. In any case, if you are going to present your work at a conference, the organizers will ask you to submit an abstract before you write the related paper – you can still change the Abstract when you have finished writing the actual paper.

You might find it useful to look at the scientific study protocol that you wrote when you outlined the aims of your research at the beginning of your PhD or before you began your current project. Here you should have written out your goals very clearly, and this will help you to write your Abstract.

The hardest part for most authors is the Discussion where you have to interpret your results and compare them with other authors' results. While you are writing the Discussion, you may find it useful to draft the Introduction, as some of the authors you mention will appear both in the Introduction and the Discussion.

A typical order for writing the various sections is thus:

Abstract (very rough draft)

Methods

Results

Discussion

Introduction

Conclusions

Abstract (final version)

It is a good idea to write the Results and Discussion before the Introduction. This is because you will only truly understand the significance of what you have done after you have written these two sections. Laying the background foundations on which you can highlight the significance of your research is a major part of the Introduction.

1.8 Should I write the initial draft in my own language before writing it in English?

Write directly in English rather than in your native language. This may be hard at the beginning. But with a model paper written by a native English-speaker in front of you, which you can follow step by step, it should be quicker than translating from your own language. From an English point of view, it should also be more reliable and accurate because you will be using some standard phrases that you have lifted directly or adapted from your model English paper.

Some researchers find it much easier to write a paper if they have already written notes in English throughout the research project. This means that you will already have much of the content you need when you finally start writing your manuscript. It also means that you will get a lot of practice in writing in English and may help you to discover any gaps in your understanding of your topic.

It might also be worth finding a native speaker to correct your written English for you whenever you write notes during the research. This might be a useful alternative to following a general English language course as it will be much more focused and also tailored to your particular needs. However, if your department or institute offers writing courses these are obviously well worth attending.

With your colleagues you could set up a writing group within your academic department. This would enable you to practice your own English writing skills and evaluate those of others in a mutual learning process.

One way of improving your writing skills and raising your profile in your area of expertise is to consider writing letters. Journals generally publish letters that offer a short critical review of the research of others. Such letters tend to be about 300 words long, so the same as or a little longer than an abstract. You can also write online rapid responses to letters in print journals.

1.9   How do I know what style and structure to use?

Each journal has its own requirements and style guide. These instructions tend to have different titles, for example: 'instructions for authors', 'notes for authors', 'author guidelines'. They often appear under a page called 'author resources'.

The guidelines include:

- types of titles that are acceptable

- structure of paper – for example, is the review of the literature near the beginning of the article or at the end? Are the Results included in the Discussion or in a separate section? Is there a Conclusions section?

- layout (including how the Abstract should be presented – one long paragraph, or 5–6 short paragraphs)

- structure of sections – some journals prescribe exactly how certain sections (most commonly the Discussion) are organized, and what subheadings should be included

- use of passive rather than personal style (*we, I*)

- how to make citations

- how to arrange the bibliography

- use of key words

- American or British spelling

It is vital that you rigorously follow your chosen journal's instructions to authors. So download these instructions from the journal's website before you start writing.

If you opt for a low impact journal, you will still find it very useful to look at the instructions of an equivalent high impact journal. Higher impact journals tend to have better author resources, which are useful for all authors, not just for those in the specific field of the journal itself.

If no journals in your discipline offer such resources, then I suggest that you look at the 'Welcome to resources for authors' page of the website of the British Medical Journal (bmj.com), one of the world's most prestigious journals. Even if you are not a medical researcher, the resources you will find there are very helpful.

The medical community has made a concerted effort to improve the quality of papers published in its journals. So reading one or two medical papers could help you learn techniques for clear structure and clear concise writing.

1.10   How can I highlight my key findings?

While you are planning what to put in each section, think of where and how you can highlight your contribution. It may help you to imagine that the reader has asked you these questions:

1. what problem are you trying to solve / investigate?
2. how did you solve / investigate it?
3. how does your solution / investigation differ from previous approaches?
4. what did you discover?
5. how do your findings differ from what is already in the literature, and what do they mean?

Readers generally read the Title and Abstract of a paper first, followed by the Discussion; though some may just look at your figures and tables! However, you cannot be sure at which section your readers will begin reading, so they need access to the answers to these questions in most or all the sections. Look at other papers in your chosen journal to see how the authors deal with such questions. Clearly, the emphasis you put on answering the questions will vary from section to section, and is likely to be greatest in the Abstract and Discussion, but consider covering it in the other sections too.

When you revise your paper if you think you have done too much highlighting, then you can always remove a few sentences. But while drafting your paper if you constantly try to highlight your contribution, this will give you extra focus.

Think of your paper as a product that you are trying to sell to the referee and journal. The clearer and more convincing you are, the more likely a journal will 'buy' your manuscript.

For more on underlining your contribution see Chapter 8.

1.11   Whose responsibility is it to ensure my paper is understood? Mine or my readers?

What kind of culture do you come from? Is there a power distance between you and your professors? Do your professors expect you to listen and understand by yourself what they are saying? Do they write in a way that requires effort on your part to decipher what they are saying? If so, you are in the majority on a worldwide scale. You are part of a receiver-oriented culture. It is your job, rather than the speaker's or writer's, to make sense of what you hear and read.

Anglo cultures too were once like this. But in the last 50 years or so, the roles have been reversed. It is the responsibility of the speaker or writer to ensure that their audience understand what they are saying.

Your job in your paper is to make the reader's understanding of your paper as simple and effortless as possible.

1.12   How do I keep the referees happy?

It is possible to write a paper in completely accurate English, but still have a paper rejected for poor writing skills – which is what happens even to native English-speaking researchers. On the other hand, a paper that is constructed well, and is easy to read, may be accepted (perhaps with some requests for minor revisions) even if the English is not totally accurate.

In my experience native referees tend to be more interested in how the paper flows and how easy it is to read. Non-native referees seem to focus more on grammatical and vocabulary mistakes, so very accurate English is important in order to keep them satisfied too.

All referees will appreciate it if you use simple language.

There are no journals, as far as I know, that are easier to write for in terms of level of English required.

When writing your paper bear the following in mind:

(1) A referee has no obligation to review your paper

Referees review manuscripts in their own time and have no direct financial reward for doing so. So do everything you can to make the referee's work easier and more pleasurable – clear English, clear layout, clear tables etc. By doing so you will increase the chances of your paper being accepted.

(2) Write in a way that a non-expert or less experienced person can understand

Research is becoming increasingly more specialized, so that even two people with the same degree may not be able to understand each other's papers. Also, due to the fact that research groups cannot always get the funding they need for research in their specific field, they may have to shift their interests to a related field where funds are available. This entails them reading the literature from this new field. The clearer the literature is, the more they will understand.

This means that when you begin the writing process, you need to bear in mind that your reader may not be as expert as you are.

(3) Make your paper interesting enough for an expert

Try to ensure that your paper has enough meat (i.e. scientific substance) for the experts. This does not mean you have to write in a more complicated way, but just that you include enough details to get experts interested.

(4) Look at the forms used in referees' reports

Every journal has a standard form for use by referees when writing their reports, which the editor then uses to judge whether your paper is suitable for publication or not. Through your professor and colleagues, try to find as many such forms as you can, and preferably the one for your chosen journal.

You can use the questions in the forms as guidelines for your writing. Here are some examples:

- Is the research novel and of international relevance?

- Does the article fit the aims and scope of the journal?

- Is the paper written grammatically and clearly?

- Is the writing style succinct and appropriate to the work?

- Is the title appropriate to the content?

- Does the abstract accurately describe the content?

- Are the conclusions borne out by the evidence and arguments?

It will help you considerably if you think about all these questions while you are writing your paper. Also, when you have finished, you should check that the answer to each question is 'yes'.

1.13 What role do search engines play in making a paper accessible to others?

A study carried out by James Evans, a sociologist at the University of Chicago, revealed that despite the fact more papers are available online than ever before (due to the digitization of older articles), it tends to be the most recent papers that are cited … again and again.

Search engines determine what we are likely to read. Our tendency is to click on what is presented to us on the first few pages of what the search engine returns. This narrows the scope of what we read and exaggerates in a self-perpetuating manner the importance of the articles that are ranked higher in the search.

This has implications for the way you approach the writing of your paper:

- key words are essential in order for the search engines to identify your paper

- no amount of key words is going to help you if readers are not immediately able to understand your paper, and cite it in their own

1.14 Summary

➢ Consult with your professor and colleagues about the most appropriate journal where you can publish your research

➢ Match your topic to the journal, or vice versa

➢ Download the guidelines for authors – these will tell you about the style and structure of your paper

➢ Choose frequently cited papers in the journal to see how other authors construct their argumentation, and note down ways in which your research is different and innovative with respect to theirs

➢ Choose one paper as a model onto which to map your research, imitating the style and organization. This model should be written by a native English speaker

➢ Note down useful / standard phrases from your model paper which you can then use in your own paper

➢ Decide on the best order to write the various sections of your paper. It is generally best to start with a very rough draft of the Abstract, and then whichever section is clearest in your head (generally the Materials and Methods)

➢ Consider having separate documents for each section. This enables you to work on several sections at the same time

➢ Make sure your unique contribution to your community is very clear in every section, not just in the Abstract

➢ Write in a way that even a non-expert can understand

➢ Referees work for free and often outside working hours – never submit a carelessly written manuscript

➢ Access referees report forms to understand the ways that referees will evaluate your work

➢ Write directly in English, and use every opportunity for improving your writing skills

➢ Use online resources

➢ Learn how search engines index your paper

Chapter 2

Structuring a Sentence: Word Order

Factoids

In Old English, the language spoken in English over 1000 years ago, a word could be placed almost anywhere in a sentence, and often with no change in meaning.

*****

Word order differs massively from language to language, even to say a simple concept such as 'I like you': *like to me you* (Croatian), *you like to me* (Estonian), *you are liking to me* (Irish), *I you like* (Korean), *to me you like* (Spanish), *you me I like* (Wolof).

*****

The English sentence *This is the rat that lives in the house that Jack built* would be rendered in Japanese as: *this Jack-built-house live-in-rat is.*

*****

Even when expressing extremely basic concepts different languages put the words in different orders. For example, many languages say *men and women*, but *mother and father*. However in China, they say *father and mother*. This probably has nothing to do with putting one sex in front of another, but simply that in cases of pairs of words we tend to say the word with the easiest sound first. This explains why around half the world's languages say *black and white*, while the other half say *white and black*. For English speakers it's easier to make the sound of *b* rather than *w*, for the same reasons a Spanish speaking person says '*b*ianco e *n*egro' rather than '*n*egro e *b*ianco'.

*****

When we scan results from a search engine, our eye rapidly goes vertically down the left hand side of the page, before starting again to read horizontally. This means that you need to think carefully about what grammatical subject to place at the beginning of the first sentence that begins a new paragraph, otherwise there is a chance that browsers and readers won't spot the key information that you want to give them.

© Springer International Publishing Switzerland 2016
A. Wallwork, *English for Writing Research Papers*,
English for Academic Research, DOI 10.1007/978-3-319-26094-5_2

2.1 What's the buzz?

1) How could these sentences be improved?

   S1. Finding a candidate with all the right qualifications, with a high level of communications skills, a good knowledge of at least two languages and a friendly personality is a rare event.

   S2. It is advisable that a foreign language should be learned at a young age.

2) Which is better? S3 or S4? Why?

   S3. You are doing this course in your own time but at the expense of your department in order to learn English.

   S4. In order to learn English you are doing this course. The course takes place in your own time but at the expense of your department.

3) Which sentence is the least readable? Why?

   S5. English, although currently the international language of business, may one day be replaced by Spanish or Chinese.

   S6. Although English is currently the international language of business, it may one day be replaced by Spanish or Chinese.

   S7. English may one day be replaced by Spanish or Chinese, even though it is currently the international language of business.

   S8. English is currently the international language of business. However, it may one day be replaced by Spanish or Chinese.

4) Decide if the following statements are true or false.

   • People want key information first. On CVs people put their most recent achievements first. They don't put what primary school they went to.

   • If you put the most important element at the beginning of sentence, it forces you to think what the most important element is. This will also help the reader understand more.

   • By putting subject and main verb at the beginning, you will be forced to write more concisely and probably with shorter sentences.

****

This chapter provides rules for deciding where to put various types of words within a sentence. For further details see Chapters 16–18 in *English for Research: Grammar, Usage and Style*.

2.2 Basic word order in English: subject + verb + object + indirect object

The order in which you put information in a sentence (or paragraph) conditions the weight that your reader will give to each element of information.

Native English-speaking readers have a clear expectation regarding the order in which information should be given to them.

English has a strict order in which words can appear in a sentence. Below is an example of this order.

The researchers sent their manuscript to the journal.

This order is rarely altered. It is:

- subject (*the researchers*)

- verb (*sent*)

- direct object (*their manuscript*)

- indirect object (*the journal*)

The key is to keep the subject, verb, direct object and indirect object as close to each other as possible:.

Last week *the researchers sent their manuscript to the journal* for the second time.

The sentence below does not follow the correct order:

The researchers last week *sent* for the second time *to the journal their manuscript.*

The position of *last week* and *for the second time* is wrong, and the indirect object comes before the direct object.

2.3 Place the various elements in your sentence in the most logical order possible: don't force the reader to have to change their perspective

Readers expect words/phrases that are closely related to each other, to appear next to each other within the sentence.

NO!	YES
Several authors have evaluated the possibility to minimize the levels of background compounds, both those released from the bag material and those from the previous sample collection *using a cleaning procedure.*	Several authors have evaluated the possibility *of using a cleaning procedure* to minimize the levels of background compounds, both those released from the bag material and those from the previous sample collection.
All PCR-amplified products were visualized on 2% agarose gel containing ethidium bromide, *under ultraviolet light.*	All PCR-amplified products were visualized *under ultraviolet light* on 2% agarose gel containing ethidium bromide.
The figures show, for each observation time, the average values of the peak areas of the compounds present in the dry gaseous standard mixture.	For each observation time, *the figures show* the average values of the peak areas of the compounds present in the dry gaseous standard mixture.
Overall the match between the aggressiveness of season-based inoculations and the capacity of the fungus to be active in vitro as a function of the temperature, *appears strict.*	Overall *there seems to be a close* match between the aggressiveness of season-based inoculations and the capacity of the fungus to be active in vitro as a function of the temperature.

In the NO! versions of the first two examples, the information in italics is key to the readers' overall understanding and should be placed earlier in the sentence closer to the elements it refers to. In the third example, the YES version avoids the need to break up the flow of the sentence. In the last example, the verb in the NO! version is almost at the end of the sentence - this is extremely rare in English and should be avoided.

Below are some more examples:

NO!	YES
It is important to remark that our components are of a traditional design. *However*, we want to stress that the way the components are assembled is very innovative.	*Although* our components are of a traditional design, the way they are assembled is very innovative.
Working in this domain entails modifying the algorithms as *we are dealing* with complex numbers.	*Since we are dealing* with complex numbers, working in this domain also entails modifying the algorithms.
Therefore, the rescaled parameters seem to be appropriate for characterizing the properties, *from a statistical point of view.*	Therefore, *from a statistical point of view*, the rescaled parameters seem to be appropriate for characterizing the properties.

The YES sentences all provide signals to the reader about what they can expect next.

The NO! sentences are confusing:

- In the first example, readers initially think that *traditional design* is the key information that the author wants to give them. The author then introduces new information that completely contrasts with the preceding information. In such cases, you need to forewarn your readers of such contrasts by using a linker that introduces a qualification, such as *although*, at the beginning of the phrase.

- In the second and third examples, the key information is only given at the end of the sentence. On the other hand in the YES examples, the author immediately tells readers the point of view he wants them to assume.

2.4 Place the subject before the verb

The subject (in *italics* in the sentences below) must come before the verb.

NO!	YES
In the survey participated *350 subjects*.	*Three hundred and fifty subjects* participated in the survey.
Were used *several different methods* in the experiments.	*Several different methods* were used in the experiments.
With these values are associated *a series of measurements*.	*A series of measurements* are associated with these values.
Once verified *the nature of the residues* ...	Once *the nature of the residues* had been verified ...

The key rule is: Say what something is before you begin to describe it.

In the NO! versions below, the authors have delayed the subject until the end of the clause. They have used an introductory subsidiary clause to stress the importance or evidence of the subject before telling the reader what the subject is.

NO!	YES
Among the factors that influence the choice of parameters *are time and cost*.	*Time and cost are* among the factors that influence the choice of parameters.
Of particular interest *was the sugar transporter*, because...	*The sugar transporter was* of particular interest, because...
Important parameters *are conciseness and non-ambiguity*.	*Conciseness and non-ambiguity are* important parameters.

A verb can come before a noun, if the verb is in the imperative, or if the sentence begins with *there + to be*.

NO!	YES
Noteworthy *is the presence* of a peak at ...	*Note the presence* of a peak at ...
	There is a peak at ...

The verb in the infinitive form is also found at the beginning of a phrase:

(In order) to learn English, a good teacher is required.

2.5 Don't delay the subject

As mentioned in the Factoids, when we scan results from a search engine, our eye rapidly goes vertically down the left-hand side of the page, before starting again to read horizontally.

This means that you need to think carefully about what information to place at the beginning of the first sentence that begins a new paragraph. If you misplace the key information, there is a strong chance that browsers and readers won't spot it.

In the following sentences, the parts highlighted in italics occupy the key left-hand position. They delay the subject, with the risk that readers may not even see the subject.

S1. *It is interesting to note that* x is equal to y.
S2. *As a consequence of the preceding observations*, x is equal to y.

To avoid this problem:

- delete or reduce the part before the subject

- shift the linking expression to later in the sentence

S1 and S2 thus become:

Note that x is equal to y. // *Interestingly*, x is equal to y.

Consequently, x is equal to y. // X is *thus* equal to Y.

Putting *it* in first position (S1) often delays the real subject. Instead, use modal verbs (*might, need, should* etc.) where possible (5.12).

OK	IMPROVED
It is probable that this is due to poor performance.	This *may / might / could* be due to poor performance.
It is possible to do this with the new system.	This *can* be done with the new system.
It is mandatory to use the new version.	The new version *must* be used.

2.6 Keep the subject and verb close to each other

The verb contains important information: keep it as close as possible to the subject. Anything that comes between the subject and the verb will be read with less attention, and readers will consider it of less importance (see next subsection).

S1 and S2 force the reader to wait too long to find out what the verb is and thus delay important information.

S1. *A gradual decline in germinability and vigor of the resultant seedling, a higher sensitivity to stresses upon germination, and possibly a loss of the ability to germinate *are recorded* in the literature [5, 8, 19].

S2. *People with a high rate of intelligence, an unusual ability to resolve problems, a passion for computers, along with good communication skills *are generally employed* by such companies.

S3 and S4 shift the verb to the beginning of the sentence and make the meaning / direction of the sentence immediately clear.

S3. There is generally a gradual decline in germinability and of the resultant seedling, followed by a higher sensitivity to stress upon germination, and possibly a loss of the ability to germinate [5, 8, 19].

S4. Such companies generally employ people with a high rate of...

S3 and S4 use active verbs. But sometimes you may need to use the passive and you may have several subjects for the same verb. In such cases, locate the passive verb after the first subject (S5):

S5. People with a high rate of intelligence are generally employed by such companies. They must also have other skills including: an unusual ability to...

2.7 Avoid inserting parenthetical information between the subject and the verb

If you insert more than a couple of words between the subject and the verb, this may interrupt the reader's train of thought. Readers may consider this parenthetical information to be of less importance.

Sentences are much easier to read if they flow logically from step to step, without any deviations.

NO!	YES
The result, after the calculation has been made, can be used to determine Y.	After the calculation has been made, the result can be used to determine Y.
This sampling method, when it is possible, is useful because it allows....	When this sampling method is possible, it allows us...
These steps, owing to the difficulties in measuring the weight, require some simplifications.	Owing to the difficulties in measuring the weight, these steps require some simplifications.
	These steps require some simplifications, owing to the difficulties in measuring the weight.

This does not mean that you cannot have a series of short clauses within one sentence. In the example below, readers do not have to change their perspective while moving from one clause to the next.

In Old English, the language spoken in English over 1000 years ago, a word could be placed almost anywhere in a sentence, and often with no change in meaning.

Of course, the rule not to insert parenthetical information, like every rule, should not be regarded as sacrosanct - i.e. you are at liberty to break it. If you think that the insertion makes the sentence flow better and be clearer, then ignore the rule.

2.8 Don't separate the verb from its direct object

When a verb is followed by two possible objects, place the direct object (i.e. the thing given or received) before the indirect object (the thing it is given to or received by).

This kind of construction is often found with verbs followed by 'to' and 'with': associate X with Y, apply X to Y, attribute X to Y, consign X to Y, give X to Y (or give Y X), introduce X to Y, send X to Y (or send Y X).

NO!	YES
We can *separate*, with this tool, *P and Q*.	We can *separate P and Q* with this tool.
We can *associate* with these values *a high cost*.	We can *associate a high cost* with these values.

In S1 below, the direct object is very long and consists of a series of items, so the reader has to wait a long time before discovering what all these items are associated with. The solution, S2, is to put the indirect object after the first item and then use 'along with'. S3 and S4 are other alternatives to dealing with this problem.

S1. *We can *associate* a high cost, higher overheads, a significant increase in man-hours and several other problems *with these values*.

S2. We can *associate* a high cost *with these values*, *along with* higher overheads, a significant increase in man-hours and several other problems.

S3. We can *associate several factors with these values*: a high cost, higher overheads, a significant increase in man-hours and several other problems.

S4. The *following can be associated with these values*:

- a high cost

- higher overheads

- a significant increase in man hours

2.9 Put the direct object before the indirect object

Don't put the indirect object (in *italics*) at the beginning of the sentence or main clause. This is not the usual word order in English.

NO!	YES
However, only *for some cases* this operation is defined, these cases are called...	However, this operation is only defined *for some cases*, which are called...
Although *in the above references* one can find algorithms for this kind of processing, the execution of ...	Although algorithms for this kind of processing are reported *in the above references*, the execution of...
This occurs when *in the original network* there is a dependent voltage.	This occurs when there is a dependent voltage *in the original network*.

2.10 Don't use a pronoun (*it, they*) before you introduce the noun that the pronoun refers to

It is OK to use a pronoun at the beginning of the sentence, provided that this pronoun refers back to a noun in a previous sentence (i.e. a backward reference). For example:

S1. *Beeswax* is a very important substance because... In fact, *it* is...

In S1 it is clear that *it* refers to beeswax. But in S2, below, *it* refers to a noun that comes after (i.e. a forward reference). The reader does not know what the pronoun refers to and thus has to wait to find out.

S2. *Although *it* is a very stable and chemically inert material, studies have verified that the composition of *beeswax* is ...

A better version is S3, which immediately tells the reader what the subject is.

S3. Although *beeswax* is a very stable and chemically inert material, studies have verified that *its* composition is ...

2.11 Locate negations near the beginning of the sentence

The order you put the words in your sentence should be designed to take your reader through a logical progression of thoughts. These thoughts should move forward, never backtracking, never forcing the reader to reconsider or reinterpret what they have just read in the light of what they are reading now.

In S1 and S2 readers cannot predict how the sentence might progress. They are forced to wait to the end before being able to understand what they have just read.

> S1. * Data regarding the thyroid function and the thyroid antibodies before the beginning of the therapy *were not available*.
>
> S2. * *All* of the spectra of the volatiles *did not* show absorptions in the range …

Both S1 and S2 appear to begin in a positive way and then suddenly change direction.

Instead, S3 and S4 help the reader to immediately understand the central purpose and driving force of the sentence (also known as the 'thrust of a sentence').

> S3. *No data were available* regarding thyroid function and thyroid antibodies before the beginning of the therapy. // Before the beginning of the therapy, *no data were available* regarding …
>
> S4. *None* of the spectra of the volatiles showed absorptions in the range …

Negations (*no, do not, does not, none, nothing* etc) are often a key element in the thrust of a sentence - try to locate them as close as possible to the beginning of a sentence.

Below are some more examples:

NO!	YES
The number of times this happens when the user is online is generally *very few*.	This *rarely* happens when the user is online.
Documentation on this particular matter is almost *completely lacking*.	There is *virtually no documentation* on this particular matter.
*Consequently *we found* this particular type of service *not* interesting.	Consequently *we did not find* this particular type of service interesting.

As highlighted in the first two NO! examples, English tends to express negative ideas with a negation. This helps the reader to understand immediately that something negative is being said. The last example is incorrect English because the verb and the negation (*not*) have been separated. See 15.16 in *English for Research: Grammar, Usage and Style*.

2.12 Locate negations before the main verb, but after auxiliary and modal verbs

The word *not* should be placed <u>before</u> the main verb it is associated with.

In S1 *not* is placed after the verb and is thus incorrect.

> S1. * Patients *seemed not* to be affected by intestinal disorders.
> S2. Patients *did not seem* to be affected by intestinal disorders.

When the verbs *to have* and *to be* are used in the present simple or past simple, *not* is located after the verb.

> S3. These findings *are not* significant.
> S4. Their results *had no* value. // Their results *did not have* any value.

Not is located after modal verbs and auxiliary verbs.

> S5. Such patients *should not* be treated with warfarin.
> S6. We *have not* encountered such a problem before.

2.13 State your aim before giving the reasons for it

When you explain a new game to someone, do you tell them the rules/strategies and then the objective, or vice versa? Which sounds more logical to you: S1 or S2?

> S1. You need to develop a strategy, make decisions as to whether to collaborate or not with the other players, also keep an eye on the progress of the other players, and finally make the most money *in order to win the game*.
> S2. *In order to win the game* you need to make the most money. To do this, you need to develop ...

Game players and readers have the same expectations: they want to know the aim of the game before learning how to carry it out - i) aim ii) means (i.e. how).

In S1 you are forcing the reader to wait for the key information, which only appears 38 words into the sentence. In S2 the aim is immediately established.

However, if the sentence is short, it does not make too much difference which element (aim or means) you put first. So both S3 and S4 could be used.

> S3. In order to win the game you need to make the most money.
> S4. You need to make the most money in order to win the game.

2.14 Deciding where to locate an adverb

The rules for deciding where to locate an adverb are complex. This section only gives some very basic guidelines.

If you are in doubt about where to put the adverb, the following rules apply to most adverbs including *only* and *also*. Locate the adverb:

- Immediately before the <u>main verb.</u>

  Dying neurons do not *usually* <u>exhibit</u> these biochemical changes.
  The mental functions are slowed, and patients are *also* <u>confused.</u>

- Immediately before the <u>second auxiliary</u> when there are two auxiliaries.

  Language would *never* <u>have</u> arisen as a set of bare arbitrary terms if …
  Late complications may not *always* <u>have</u> been notified.

- After the present and past tenses of 'to be'

  The answer of the machine is *thus* correct.

However other types of adverbs (e.g. certainty, manner, time) follow different rules.

For full details see Chapter 17 in *English for Research: Grammar, Usage and Style*.

2.15 Put adjectives before the noun they describe, or use a relative clause

Adjectives normally go before the noun they describe.

NO!	YES
This is a paper particularly interesting for PhD students.	This paper is particularly interesting for PhD students.
	This is a paper that is particularly interesting for PhD students.
We examined a patient, 30 years old, to investigate whether …	We examined a 30-year-old patient to investigate whether …
	We examined a patient, who was 30 years old, to investigate whether …

If you want to put the adjective after the noun, you have to use a relative clause as in the second alternatives in the Yes column above (i.e. *which, that, who* - see 6.10)

2.16 Do not put an adjective before the wrong noun or between two nouns

Never put an adjective before a noun that it does not describe.

Generally, you cannot put an adjective between two nouns.

NO!	YES
The main document *contribution*	The main *contribution* of the document
The editor *main* interface	The *main* interface of the editor
The algorithm *computational* complexity	The *computational* complexity of the algorithm

2.17 Avoid creating strings of nouns that describe other nouns

You cannot indiscriminately put nouns in front of each other in a string. For example, you cannot say *art state technology* (state-of-the-art technology) or *mass destruction weapons* (weapons of mass destruction). But you can say *a software program* or *an aluminum tube*.

Native speakers do tend to string nouns together, but they intuitively know how to do it. In fact, they are not following any written rules, but they base themselves on examples that already exist. If you are a non-native speaker I strongly recommend that you verify on Google Scholar that your proposed string of nouns already exists and has been used by native English-speaking authors.

If it does not exist, it will sound very strange to any native English-speaking referees, and more than one occurrence of such structures could cause the referee to recommend that your English be revised.

If it has not been used by native English-speaking authors, then you need to change the order of the words, which normally entails inserting some prepositions. To learn how to do this, see 12.3.

2.18 Summary

➤ Basic English word order is: (1) subject, (2) verb, (3) direct object, (4) indirect object. Keep these four elements in this order and as close to each other as possible.

➤ If you have a choice of subjects, choose the one that is the most relevant and leads to the shortest construction.

➤ Avoid delaying the subject. So don't begin a sentence with the impersonal *it*.

➤ Avoid inserting parenthetical information between the subject and the verb.

➤ Most adverbs are located just before the main verb, and before the second auxiliary verb when there are two auxiliaries.

➤ Put adjectives before the noun they describe, or use a relative clause. Do not insert an adjective between two nouns or before the wrong noun.

➤ Do not indiscriminately put nouns in a string.

Rules tend to have exceptions. The rules given in this section also have exceptions, and so you might find sentences written by native English speakers that contradict my rules.

Chapter 3

Structuring Paragraphs

Factoids

The results of two research projects – the Poynter Institute's Eyetrack survey, and an analysis by Jakob Nielsen (a Danish web usability expert) – show that only half of readers who begin an article, will actually finish it, and if the article is read online, only a fifth of readers will finish it.

*****

Nobel Prize Winner in Physics, Tony Leggett, notes that "in Japanese it seems that it is often legitimate to state a number of thoughts in such a way that the connection between them, or the meaning of any given one, only becomes clear when one has read the whole paragraph or even the whole paper." This is not the case in what is considered good written English, where the meaning should become clear very quickly.

*****

Tracy Seeley, an English professor at the University of San Francisco, noted that after a conversation with some of her students she discovered that "most can't concentrate on reading a text for more than 30 seconds or a minute at a time. We're being trained away from slow reading by new technology."

© Springer International Publishing Switzerland 2016
A. Wallwork, *English for Writing Research Papers*,
English for Academic Research, DOI 10.1007/978-3-319-26094-5_3

3.1 What's the buzz?

Try to memorize the information contained in the following texts. Why is it hard to do so?

NON-NATIVE SPEAKERSTYPICALLYSAYTHATENGLISH ISASIMPLE LANGUAGE BECAUSE IT FAVORS SHORT CLEAR SENTENCES SuCh NoN-nAtiVe spEAkeRS thEn saythattheirownlanguageisnotlikeEnglishbecauseitfavorslong complex sentences

00399340788304

different languages use punctuation in different ways before you submit your text for google translation if possible try to punctuate it in an English way keep the sentences short replace semicolons with full stops and where appropriate use commas to break up the various parts of the sentence

The texts are difficult to read because they are not in the usual or optimum form for presenting information. The same effort that it took you to read the above texts is similar to the effort that will be required by a referee or native English speaker to follow your text if it is

- poorly structured

- poorly punctuated

- written in long paragraphs and sentences

- full of ambiguity and redundancy

If you force your reader to spend a lot of energy and time on deciphering your papers, you are also stopping them from spending the same time and energy on their work.

I am sure you would agree that the information at the beginning of this page would be better presented as:

Non-native speakers typically say that English is a simple language because it favors short clear sentences. Such non-native speakers then say that their own language is not like English because it favors long complex sentences.

0039 934 0788 304

Different languages use punctuation in different ways. Before you submit your text for Google translation, if possible try to punctuate it in an English way. Keep the sentences short, replace semicolons with full stops, and where appropriate use commas to break up the various parts of the sentence.

To take the example of the telephone number: it may be quicker for you to write your phone number as one long uninterrupted sequence of numbers, but it is not quicker for your reader to dial or remember the number.

****

This chapter covers how to structure a paragraph by linking sentences together in the most logical order possible. It also suggests ways to break up a long paragraph. You will learn that good writing means always thinking from a reader-perspective:

- how can I make it easier for the reader to follow what I am saying and clearly understand the benefits of my methods and findings?

- how can I do all this while expecting the minimum possible amount of effort from my readers?

3.2   First paragraph of a new section – begin with a mini summary plus an indication of the structure

Readers do not necessarily read the paper from beginning to end. They may begin with any section in the paper.

This means you could consider starting some sections (e.g. Introduction, Discussion, Conclusions) with a one or two-sentence summary of the main aims and/or findings of the paper. This style is also typical if you are writing chapters in a book.

However, check the general style of papers in your chosen journal. If they do not begin sections in such a way, then don't do it yourself. Instead go for a more direct approach (see Sect. 4.5).

Here are some examples of mini summaries at the beginning of a section:

The X Committee has for some years encouraged collaborative clinical trials in X by reporting the results in the medical literature. In this section we describe the first of two unreported results that we believe deserve such publication and which constitute the main contribution of this paper.

As mentioned in the Introduction, a principal concern in the field of X is to understand why... This section attempts to answer the question...

Our aim is to provide a simple alternative to the complex theoretical models that attempt to explain... In this section we present a simplified model, which we believe is...

This section reviews the process of... This process provides the backbone to the system that is at the core of our research.

In addition to this mini summary, some authors also briefly outline what will be contained in the rest of the section. Here are four examples:

S1. In this section, we briefly review the broad perspectives that have shaped the direction of thinking about ...

S2. In this section, the numerous advances in cosmology are described, with emphasis on the vast new area of ...

S3. In this section, we will ask the question: 'Under what circumstances will a paper be rejected?'

S4. In this section we define our approach and show how it can be very naturally used to define distributions over functions. In the following section we show how this distribution is …

The examples highlight different styles for introducing the topic. S1 and S2 are the standard approach, using a personal style (*we* in S1) and an impersonal style (the passive form in S2). S3 represents a variation because it asks a question – this may be a good solution for creating some variety in the way you begin each section.

Note how in S4 the author also refers to future sections. Such references help the reader to see how the current section fits in with the logical progression of the rest of the paper. However, you should keep such references as short as possible as they can become quite heavy and annoying for the reader.

3.3   First paragraph of a new section – go directly to the point

Particularly in shorter papers, you may not have the space to have mini summaries at the beginning of your section or subsections (3.2). In any case, readers often don't have the time or the inclination to read them. In such cases you need a more direct approach.

Being direct does not necessarily entail telling the reader what you did, but telling them what it means. A typical sentence to open the Results section is:

S1. An analysis of the number of words used in English with respect to Italian, showed that the average sentence in English was 25 words long, whereas in Italian it was 32 words long (see Table 1). This indicates that when an Italian document is translated into English, there is …

A much more direct approach is to say:

S2. Italian tends to use more words per sentence than English, so when an Italian document is translated into English, there is …

S2 begins with the main information, and then provides the implications. You do not necessarily need to tell the reader the exact details of what you did (this would be more appropriate in Methods) but just what you found.

3.4 Choose the most relevant subject to put it at the beginning of a sentence that opens a new paragraph

Clear English requires that you put the subject at the beginning of the sentence.

Generally you will have a choice of possible subjects.

X was elicited by Y.

Y elicited X.

In the simple example above, your choice will depend on whether you want to emphasize X or Y. The one you want to emphasize should be put as the subject.

As readers, we tend to focus on the areas of a sentence that come immediately before and after a full stop. This is because there is extra white space between one sentence and another, which acts as a restful pause for the eye. Our eyes are also drawn to the capital letter that begins each sentence. These are the moments where you potentially have the reader's attention, so don't waste them.

If the first few words routinely contain no useful or new information, then it becomes very tedious.

So the best solution is to shift 'no value added' phrases to later on in the sentence and preferably reduce them to one word. Otherwise you are encouraging readers to skim i.e. to read very fast and skip words, sentences and even whole paragraphs and sections.

The sentences below contain exactly the same information, but the grammatical subjects are different:

S1. Particularly interesting for *researchers in physics* is the new feature, named X, for calculating velocity.

S2. *Physics* now has a new feature, named X, for calculating velocity.

S3. *Velocity* can now be calculated with a new feature, named X, which is particularly interesting for physicists.

S4. *X is a new feature* for calculating velocity. It is particularly interesting for physicists.

When deciding what the subject is for the first sentence in a paragraph, it is generally best to choose the most recent or newest information. S1 and S2 refer to known situations – physics, and physicists – they do not give any new information, so they are not well-constructed sentences.

S3 also begins with a known, in this case *velocity*. This is fine if velocity is the main focus. However, given that velocity is a common factor for physicists, then S4 may be the best solution as it begins with completely new information. The choice between S3 and S4 will depend on where the author wants to put the focus.

In summary, put the key element to your 'story' in the first position (also known as the 'topic position') of a new paragraph.

However, within a paragraph it may make sense to put the old information (i.e. info mentioned earlier in the paragraph) in the topic position. This enables you to link sentences together so that the reader understands that info given in a previous sentence is now being further defined in a new sentence.

3.5 Deciding where to put new and old information within a sentence

S1 and S2 begin with the same subject *English*, which is the main topic of the sentence. They then present the same two pieces of information, but in a different order.

S1. English, *which is the international language of communication*, is now studied by 1.1 billion people.

S2. *English, *which is now studied by 1.1 billion people*, is the international language of communication.

In both cases if you removed the 'which' clause (in italics) the sentence would still make sense. But if you removed the final clause it wouldn't. This would seem to indicate that the final clause is where we locate the most important information. Thus the relative position of the various parts of the phrase tells the reader the relative importance of the information contained on those parts.

In S1, the order of the information tells you that the fact that English is *the international language of communication* is old news, but that *1.1 billion people* is new information that the reader probably does not already know. Thus, the order of the information in S2 is a little strange because it puts the new information (*1.1. billion people*) before the old information (*international language*).

Readers tend to focus on the first and last words of a sentence, so avoid placing your most important information in the middle of a long sentence. Readers don't want to make an effort to identify the key points, they want to be told immediately.

Here are some more examples that show how by changing the order of information within a sentence you can achieve a different effect:

- S3. English is now studied by 1.1 billion people, though this number is expected to drop with the rise in importance of Chinese.
- S4. Although English is now studied by 1.1 billion people, this number is expected to drop with the rise in importance of Chinese.
- S5. Although the importance of Chinese is expected to lead to a drop in the numbers of people studying English, 1.1 billion people still study English.

S3–S5 all contain the same information, but the weight that this information is given varies.

In S3 the reader learns some information. This information is then qualified with *though*, which is used to introduce some new information that the author imagines that the reader does not know.

In S4 the reader is immediately alerted to the fact that the information contained at the beginning of the sentence is going to be qualified by new information in the second part. The order of the information in S4 is thus more logical than in S3.

In S5 the writer assumes that the reader already knows the importance of Chinese and instead focuses on the fact that despite the increase in the number of Chinese speakers, English is *still* studied by a lot of people. 'still' is the key word and it is located very close to the end of the sentence.

In S1–S5 there are two parts to each sentence, and the writer gives more emphasis to the second part. Sometimes, you may want to give equal weight to the two parts.

- S6. English is the international language of communication. It is now studied by 1.1 billion people.
- S7. The importance of Chinese is expected to lead to drop in the numbers of people studying English. Despite this, 1.1 billion people still study English.

In S6 and S7, the writer wants the reader to notice and absorb the two pieces of important information separately. She does this by presenting the information in two distinct sentences. This device should not be used too often because it can lead to a series of very short sentences, which after a while begin to sound like a list.

3.6 Deciding where to put new and old information within a paragraph

Known information is traditionally placed at the beginning of a sentence or paragraph. Below are the first three sentences from the abstract of a fictitious paper entitled 'Readability and Non-Native English Speakers' intended for a journal dedicated to communication in the world of business.

> VERSION 1 Readability formulas calculate how readable a text is by determining the level of difficulty of each individual word and the length of sentences. All types of writers can use these formulas in order to understand how difficult or readable their texts would be for the average reader. However, readability formulas are based purely on what is considered difficult for a native English speaker, and do not take into account problems that may be encountered by non-natives. In this paper...

The first word, *readability*, is one of the author's key words. It immediately alerts the reader to the topic of the sentence and of the abstract (and paper) as a whole. However, the information contained in it is not new – readability formulas and their indexes are well established in the literature on business communication.

The role of the first two sentences is thus to set the context and gently guide the reader into the paragraph. The third sentence then introduces the new element, i.e. the fact that readability indexes do not take into account non-native speakers. The third sentence thus highlights the problem that the paper intends to tackle.

However, the abstract could have begun like this:

> VERSION 2 Current readability formulas are based purely on what is considered difficult for a native English speaker. They fail to take into account problems that may be encountered by non-natives. One thousand five hundred PhD students from 10 countries were asked to evaluate the difficulty of five technical texts from their business discipline written by native English speakers. Three key difficulties were found: unfamiliar vocabulary (typically Anglo-Saxon words), unfamiliar cultural references, and the use of humor. The paper also proposes a new approach to assessing the level of readability of texts to account for such difficulties.

In Version 2, the author still begins with his key word, *readability*. But he precedes it with *current*, which signals to the reader that the author will then probably propose an alternative. The author also assumes that his readers will be aware of what a readability formula is, so he feels he doesn't need to mention it. Thus, in the second sentence he immediately underlines a critical problem with current formulas. In the third sentence he then tells his readers what his research was and then what was found.

Version 3, below, contains only new information.

> VERSION 3 Unfamiliar vocabulary (typically Anglo-Saxon words), unfamiliar cultural references, and the use of humor: these, according to our survey of 1500 PhD students, are the main difficulties non-native speakers have when reading a business text in English. Our results highlight the need to adjust current readability formulas in order to take non-native

speakers into account. The paper also proposes a new approach to assessing the level of readability of texts to account for such difficulties.

This version is designed to immediately attract the reader's attention. In contrast, the first 50 words of Version 1 contain no new information at all. Version 2 has 40–50% new information or more, depending on whether readers are familiar with the limitations of readability formulas with regard to non-natives.

So, which version should you use?

The best version to use depends on two factors:

1. the section of the paper
2. what you are trying to achieve

Version 1 would only be appropriate in an Abstract if the journal where it is being published does not usually deal with communication and / or readability indexes. In this case the readers need the context to be set for them. It might be more acceptable in an Introduction in a slightly more specialized journal. In an Introduction the aim is not principally to attract attention. If readers are reading your Introduction you can presume that you already have their attention.

So the information contained in Version 1 would be used in an Introduction just to remind the readers of the context. This is a very typical way to begin an Introduction – it is what readers expect and therefore it is generally a good technique.

Version 2 would be appropriate as an Abstract or Introduction in a specialized journal on business communication.

Version 3 would only be appropriate in an Abstract and exclusively in a very specialized journal. It can only be used if you have clear findings, or a clear new methodology, to report. It works very well because it does not force readers to read background information that they are probably already familiar with.

You might also choose Version 3 as an Abstract for a congress. In such cases you are competing for the attention of the referees who will use your Abstract to decide whether to include your contribution at the congress. If your Abstract is accepted, you will then be competing with other authors / presenters in motivating the audience to come and watch you rather than a parallel session.

In many languages Versions 2 and 3 would not be acceptable. In the words of one of my Greek PhD students:

> New information in Greek comes at the very end. The rule is that first the author gives extensive background information and only at the end he / she introduces the new concept. This is the generally accepted (and considered correct) way of writing.

This means that when you write in English you may be going against what is considered good style in your own language. But don't let breaking a taboo stop you from expressing yourself in the way that will best highlight your results and thus attract more readers.

3.7 Use 'generic + specific' constructions with caution

Generic statements are often redundant.

Do you notice anything missing in the following paragraph?

> S1. Devices are becoming increasingly miniaturized, powerful, cheap and have become part of our daily lives. Notable examples include smart phones and smart watches equipped with a plethora of sensors, home appliances and general purpose devices such as tablets and ultra-thin notebooks. We are surrounded by all these devices daily in a pervasive way, at home, work and also in public spaces – as anticipated in Mark Weiser's visionary observation: "The most profound technologies are those that disappear."

The original version of S1 contained the following introductory sentence:

> S2. The last decade has been characterized by advances in device manufacturing.

S2 says nothing that the reader doesn't already know, and its main point is repeated in the next sentence. Moreover, its very generic nature does not invite the reader to continue reading. It can therefore be deleted.

Using an introductory sentence at the beginning of a new section or paragraph is clearly a good idea as it acts as a topic-sentence alerting the reader about what is coming next.

However, where possible the introductory sentence should also be eye-catching.

A sentence such as *Devices are becoming increasingly miniaturized, powerful, cheap and have become part of our daily lives* does not attract attention.

Remember that your readers will not be reading every word, sentence or paragraph of your paper. Their eyes will be skimming down the page (rather than slowly reading across the page horizontally). Their eyes are waiting to rest on something that attracts their attention.

So a better start to S1 would be:

> S3. Way back in 1991 Mark Weiser observed that "The most profound technologies are those that disappear." In fact, increasingly miniaturized, powerful, and cheap devices have

become part of our daily lives, for example smart phones and smart watches, home appliances, tablets and ultra-thin notebooks. We are surrounded by all these devices: at home, work and also in public spaces.

Note how S3 attracts much more attention by

- including a date and a name at the beginning of the sentence. Numbers and names (with their initial capital letters) stand out in a text

- removing all the generic phrases that add no real value: notable examples include ... equipped with a plethora of sensors ... general purpose devices such as ... in a pervasive way

- concluding with a sentence that recalls the introductory sentence, thus giving the paragraph a sense of cohesiveness

Clearly, I have been quite extreme in the number of generic phrases I have removed, but this is to show you how often we tend to write too many phrases that give no new information and simply fill the text unnecessarily and thus make the reader waste time.

3.8   Try to be as concrete as possible as soon as possible

Compare these two texts:

S1. Smart devices may have to manage sensitive information that, often, must be protected against unauthorized diffusion or from malicious attacks. Some notable examples of sensitive information are data concerning the health conditions of a patient or data gathered from caregivers about the status of an elderly person.

S2. Smart devices may have to manage sensitive information, for example the health conditions of a patient or data gathered from caregivers on the status of an elderly person. Clearly, such data must be protected against unauthorized diffusion or from malicious attacks.

In S1, readers have to wait to understand exactly what sensitive information is and why it has to be protected.

S2 tells readers immediately what sensitive information is, and therefore enables readers to understand why it should be protected. S2 also uses fewer words.

I am not suggesting that you should always use S2 rather than S1. Just be aware that the same information can be presented in a different order. Your aim is to choose the most effective order.

3.9 Link each sentence by moving from general concepts to increasingly more specific concepts

A key issue when linking up sentences in a paragraph is to decide how to link one sentence to the previous one. The following is an extract from the beginning of a paragraph from a paper on pollution in soil. It fails to make a strong impact because of its lack of logical progression between S3 and S4.

> (S1) The *soil* is a major source of *pollution*. (S2) Millions of *chemicals* are released into the environment and end up in the soil. (S3) The impact of most of these *chemicals* on human health is still not fully known. (S4). In addition, *in the soil* there are naturally occurring amounts of potentially *toxic substances* whose fate in the terrestrial environment is still *poorly known*.

S1 puts *the soil* as the topic of the sentence. S2 is more specific and talks about the quantity of this pollution – *millions of chemicals*. S3 reports the impact of the chemicals mentioned in S2. But S4 does not continue this logical progression from general to increasingly more specific. Instead, it begins by putting *soil* in the topic position. This breaks the logical progression, because *soil* was the topic of S1.

The following sentence would be a good replacement for S4 because it continues the logical structure developed in S1–S3.

> There are also naturally occurring amounts of potentially toxic substances *in the soil* whose fate in the terrestrial environment is still poorly known.

The formula is thus:

1. S1: main topic (*soil*) introduces subtopic 1 (*pollution*)
2. S2: subtopic 1 is specified by introducing subtopic 2 (*millions of chemicals*).
3. S3: subtopic 2 is specified by introducing subtopic 3 (*impact of these chemicals*).
4. S4: a further / related aspect of subtopic 3 is introduced via subtopic 4 (*impact of toxic substances, i.e. chemicals, is poorly understood*).
5. etc.

Basically each sentence is a link in a chain. A full chain is a paragraph. And a series of linked chains makes up a section.

3.10 Don't force readers to hold a lot of preliminary information in their head before giving them the main information

S1 imposes a lot of effort on the reader.

> S1. Considering that peach skin is particularly rich in antioxidants (Figs. 1A, 1B, 2A, 2B), positively reacts to UV-B radiation at the end of postharvest by increasing antioxidant activity (Fig. 3A), and, differently from flesh, is directly exposed to UV-B radiation under natural conditions, the study of free radical generation was performed specifically on this tissue.

S2 resolves the problem by splitting the sentence into three. This means that the reader can absorb the information in manageable chunks, i.e. you feed the reader small pieces of information at a time. This enables readers to progress forwards without having to re-read anything.

> S2. Peach skin is particularly rich in antioxidants (Figs. 1A, 1B, 2A, 2B) and reacts positively to UV-B radiation at the end of postharvest by increasing antioxidant activity (Fig. 3A). Unlike the flesh, the skin is directly exposed to UV-B radiation under natural conditions. Consequently, the study of free radical generation was performed on peach skin.

For more on splitting up sentences see Chapter 4.

3.11   Present and explain ideas in the same (logical) sequence

Readability can be increased massively if you take some time to think about the best way to present information. The OV below is in perfect English, and it may seem fine until you see how the RV makes the information much easier to assimilate.

ORIGINAL VERSION (OV)	REVISED VERSION (RV)
Memory can be subdivided into various types: long-term memory, which involves retaining information for over a minute, and short-term memory, in which information is remembered for a minute or less, for example, the memory required to perform a simple calculation such as $5 \times 7 \times 3$. Another type of short-term memory is also recognized: sensory memory, for example we see a video as a continuous scene rather than a series of still images. Research shows sex differences in episodic (i.e. long term) memory: women tend to remember better verbal situations, whereas men have a better recollection of events relating to visuals and space. Long-term memory can be further subdivided into recent memory, which involves new learning, and remote memory, which involves old information.	Memory is the capacity to store and recall new information. It can be subdivided into two main types: short-term and long-term. Short-term memory involves remembering information for a minute or less, for example, the memory required to perform a simple calculation such as $5 \times 7 \times 3$. Another type of short-term memory is sensory memory, for example, we see a video as a continuous scene rather than a series of still images. Long-term memory can be further subdivided into recent memory, which involves new learning, and remote memory, which involves old information. Interestingly, research shows sex differences in remote memory: women tend to remember better verbal situations, whereas men have a better recollection of events relating to visuals and space.

In the OV, the beginning of the first sentence gives the illusion to the reader that the various types of memory will be introduced in a logical order. In reality a rather random selection of information is given, with no clear sequence. This makes it hard for the reader to follow. The RV uses shorter sentences and follows a much more logical series of steps:

- definition of memory given

- clear indication of the number of types of memories (OV *various* types, RV *two main* types)

- short-term memory mentioned first, as later in the paragraph long-term memory will be developed in more detail

- additional information about short-term memory (the discussion of short-term memory ends here)

- returns to second topic (long-term memory), which is then subdivided into *recent* and *remote*

- interesting fact about remote memory

In the RV, each sentence extends the information given in the previous sentence, and the reader can sense the logical progression. The author presents a list of topics at the beginning of a paragraph that he intends to discuss further in the later part of the paragraph. He then deals with the topics in the same order and format as he initially presented them: first short-term memory, then long-term.

3.12 Use a consistent numbering system to list phases, states, parts etc.

When you need to describe the various stages in a procedure, methodology, project and so on, it helps to use a numbering system. For example, *first(ly), second(ly), third(ly), finally*. It is also important to continue your numbering system in the same way that you started it, and not to abandon it. Compare these two versions:

ORIGINAL VERSION	REVISED VERSION
Our methodology can be divided into three main parts: first of all the characterization of demographic changes between 2000 and 2010, in order to obtain a scenario for the future with regarding to population shifts. The results from this first part were used as inputs to obtain maps for 2010 to 2015. The resulting maps and input maps regarding climatic and political characteristics were inserted into our model in order to predict future patterns.	Our methodology can be divided into three main stages. *Firstly*, we characterized demographic changes between 2000 and 2010, in order to obtain a future scenario for population shifts. *Secondly*, we used the results from the first part as inputs to obtain maps for 2010 to 2015. *Finally*, the resulting maps along with input maps regarding climatic and political characteristics were inserted into our model in order to predict future patterns.

The OV is a little misleading. The colon in the first sentence gives the reader the impression that the author is going to mention all three stages together within the same sentence. The second two stages are not clearly marked. The RV separates the OV's first sentence into two parts. In the RV, first the author announces that there are three stages. Then she talks about these three stages in three separate sentences, which begin with a number indicator. This also makes the paragraph visually easier to follow.

3.13   Break up long paragraphs

Look at the paragraph below. Does it invite you to read it?

The only advantage of a long paragraph is for the writer, not for the reader. It enables writers to save time because they avoid having to think about where they could break the paragraph up to aid reader comprehension. But breaking up long paragraphs is extremely important. Firstly, long blocks of text are visually unappealing for readers, and tiring for their eyes. They fail to meet the basic rule of readability – make things as easy as possible for your reader. Evidence of this can be found in newspapers. If you look at newspapers from 100 years ago, they were basically big blocks of text that took a great deal of effort to read. Today many online newspapers have one sentence per paragraph, with lots of white space between each paragraph. Secondly, your points and the related logical sequence of these points will be much more clearly identifiable for the reader if they are in a separate paragraph. Thirdly, you will find that you will write more clearly if you use shorter paragraphs. This is because it will force you to think about what the main point of your paragraph is and how to express this point in the simplest way. If you just have one long paragraph, the tendency is just to have one long flow of frequently disjointed thoughts. This tendency is known in English as 'rambling'. Fourthly, having shorter paragraphs enables you (and your co-authors) to quickly identify if you need to add extra information, and allows you to do this without having to extend an already long paragraph. Likewise, it enables you to identify paragraphs that could be cut if you find you are short of space. The third and fourth points are also valid reasons for using short sentences. The maximum length of a paragraph in a well-written research paper is about 15 lines. But most paragraphs should be shorter. If you have already written more than 8–12 lines or 4–6 sentences, then you may need to re-read what you have written and think about where you could start a new paragraph. When you begin to talk about something that is even only slightly distinct from what you have mentioned in the previous 4–6 sentences, then this is a good opportunity to begin a new paragraph. For example, when you have been talking about how another author has approached the problem of X, and you then want to make a comparison with your own approach. The topic (i.e. X) is the same, but the focus is different. Likewise, if you have been comparing X and Y, and you have spent a few sentences exclusively on X, then when you start on Y you can use a new paragraph. Basically, there is an opportunity to begin a new paragraph every time there is a change in a focus.

Now, read the above paragraph again and think where you could divide it up.

Finally, compare the points where you divided the paragraph with my version below. Which version (the one above or below) is easier to read and assimilate?

The only advantage of a long paragraph is for the writer, not for the reader. It enables writers to save time because they avoid having to think about where they could break the paragraph up to aid reader comprehension.

Breaking up long paragraphs is extremely important.

1. Long blocks of text are visually unappealing for readers, and tiring for their eyes. They fail to meet the basic rule of readability – make things as easy as possible for your reader. Evidence of this can be found in newspapers. If you look at newspapers from 100 years ago, they were basically big blocks of text that took a great deal of effort to read. Today many online newspapers have one sentence per paragraph, with lots of white space between each paragraph.

2. Your points and the related logical sequence of these points will be much more clearly identifiable for the reader if they are in a separate paragraph.

3. You will find that you will write more clearly if you use shorter paragraphs. This is because it will force you to think about what the main point of your paragraph is and how to express this point in the simplest way. If you just have one long paragraph, the tendency is just to have one long flow of frequently disjointed thoughts. This tendency is known in English as 'rambling'.

4. Having shorter paragraphs enables you (and your co-authors) to quickly identify if you need to add extra information, and allows you to do this without having to extend an already long paragraph. Likewise, it enables you to identify paragraphs that could be cut if you find you are short of space.

The third and fourth points are also valid reasons for using short sentences (see Chap. 5).

The maximum length of a paragraph in a well-written research paper is about 15 lines. But most paragraphs should be shorter. If you have already written more than 8–12 lines or 4–6 sentences, then you may need to re-read what you have written and think about where you could start a new paragraph.

When you begin to talk about something that is even only slightly distinct from what you have mentioned in the previous 4–6 sentences, then this is a good opportunity to begin a new paragraph. For example, when you have been talking about how another author has approached the problem of X, and you then want to make a comparison with your own approach. The topic (i.e. X) is the same, but the focus is different. Likewise, if you have been comparing X and Y, and you have spent a few sentences exclusively on X, then when you start on Y you can use a new paragraph.

Basically, there is an opportunity to begin a new paragraph every time there is a change in a focus.

For more on the importance of beginning a new paragraph see 8.3.

3.14 Look for the markers that indicate where you could begin a new sentence or new paragraph

The table below shows the typical phrases used to connect one sentence to the next in order to create a logical progression of thought. These typical phrases also act as markers to indicate that you could begin a new paragraph.

TYPICAL PHRASES	FUNCTION OF THE PHRASE
In order to do this / To this end / With this in mind	To state the purpose of something. For instance, you outline a requirement, and then you begin to say how you could meet this requirement
Then / Following this / Afterwards	To indicate a temporal relationship
For example, / An example of this is / In fact, / Unlike / Nevertheless,	To give an example or supporting/negating evidence. By 'example' I don't mean just a list of items, but a complete example or evidence that supports or negates what you have just been saying and that requires several sentences to explain
In addition / Another way to do / An additional feature of	To add additional points. For instance, if you are focusing just on one thing (e.g. X) and you talk about X's attributes
On the other hand / However / In contrast	To qualify what you have just said: i.e. to indicate an exception or the two sides of an argument
Due to / Since / Although	To give reasons for something
Thus / Therefore / Consequently / Because of this	To indicate a consequence
This means that / This highlights that / These considerations imply that / In conclusion / In sum	To announce and give a mini conclusion about what you have said in the previous sentences
Figure 1 shows / As can be seen in Table 2	To talk about figures, tables etc.
Firstly, secondly, finally	To introduce elements in a list
As far as X is concerned, / In relation to X / In the case of / With regard to / As noted earlier	To introduce a new element; to recall something mentioned earlier
It is worth noting that / Interestingly	To add some additional information or make some comment, not necessarily directly about something you have mentioned before but as an aside.

In all the examples in the table, I am talking about cases where you need at least three sentences (or two quite long ones) to achieve the function desired. For example, when you use *firstly, secondly* etc., you only need to begin a new paragraph if the sentence that begins *firstly* is then followed by another two or more sentences. If you only need one sentence for each item, then you don't need to begin a new paragraph.

There is no minimum length to a paragraph. A paragraph can occasionally be just one sentence. However, a series of paragraphs containing only one or two short sentences would be a little strange.

Where you begin a new paragraph will also depend on which section you are writing. In the review of the literature, you may want to begin a new paragraph when (i) you begin to talk about a different phase in the logical build up of research in your field, or (ii) you start talking about another author. In the Methods, it may help the reader to identify the various components or understand the various steps, if these components or steps are in separate (probably quite short) paragraphs.

3.15 Begin a new paragraph when you begin to talk about your study and your key findings

If you have phrases such as *This study shows that / Our findings highlight / These results indicate that* in the middle of a long paragraph, readers may not even notice the sentence. Thus you lose a good opportunity to get the reader to focus on your findings. So whenever you want to highlight the importance of your study or findings, begin a new paragraph (Sect. 8.2).

3.16 Concluding a paragraph: avoid redundancy

Throughout this section I have underlined the need to help the reader understand the logical progression of your ideas. But if your writing is clear, you don't need to help the reader too much. This means that the beginning of a paragraph should move on from where the previous paragraph ended. So there is no need for a summary sentence between the two paragraphs, but just a clear and logical link in terms of advancing one idea to the next.

Some authors end a section by talking about the coverage of the next section, but such information is often redundant, particularly if it is repeated again at the beginning of the next section.

3.17 How to structure a paragraph: an example

In the early 1960s, senior staff scientist at NASA, Sam Katzoff wrote a 30-page pamphlet entitled 'Clarity in Technical Reporting'. This short document was designed to help his colleagues at NASA to write clearly and to think of better ways to express themselves. His pamphlet is still being read – not just by NASA scientists – but all over the English-speaking world. It is a truly great introduction to writing skills, for native and non-native speakers alike.

I am now going to analyze how Katzoff writes the first paragraph at the beginning of a section entitled 'Organization of a Technical Report'.

Different writers have different methods of organizing their reports, and some seem to have no discernible method at all. Most of the better writers, however, appear to be in remarkably close agreement as to the general approach to organization. This approach consists of stating the problem, describing the method of attack, developing the results, discussing the results, and summarizing the conclusions. You may feel that this type of organization is obvious, logical, and natural. Nevertheless, it is not universally accepted. For example, many writers present results and conclusions near the beginning, and describe the derivation of these results in subsequent sections.

Let's begin with some statistics.

WORDS, SENTENCES, PUNCTUATION	REPETITIONS OF KEY WORDS
Total words = 101	*approach* 2
Total sentences = 6	*method* 3
Average words per sentence = 16.8	*organization* 3
Longest sentence = 22 words	*results* 4
Shortest sentence = 6 words	*writer* 3
Full stops (.) = 6	
Commas (,) = 10	
Semicolons (;) = 0	

If you analyzed a paragraph in a typical research paper, you would very likely get very different data. Try looking at some of your own work. With respect to Katzoff's paragraph, you will probably notice a big increase in the number of words, commas and semicolons per sentence. The typical sentence length will be around 30–40 words, but also up to 70–80. I imagine there will also be a considerable decrease both in the number of full stops and in repetitions of key words.

Sam Katzoff was a top scientist. His document was intended for fellow scientists, who were, like him, native English speakers. These fellow scientists were also amongst the most brilliant scientists in the world. They could potentially understand even the most complex text. Yet Dr Katzoff decided to write his document in the simplest and clearest way possible, and he encouraged his fellows to do the same. According to a fellow colleague:

> He was the kind of person who could look at a paper and tell whether it was a lot of bull. If you were writing a paper and were publishing, he would review it and that would help a lot of people in the field to come up with a better way of saying what they were trying to get across.

By *bull* the colleague was politely saying *bullshit*, i.e. words, phrases and paragraphs that clearly made no sense, but were just included for effect.

Now let's analyze the structure of Katzoff's paragraph.

> (S1) Different writers have different methods of organizing their reports, and some seem to have no discernible method at all. (S2) Most of the better writers, however, appear to be in remarkably close agreement as to the general approach to organization. (S3) This approach consists of stating the problem, describing the method of attack, developing the results, discussing the results, and summarizing the conclusions. (S4) You may feel that this type of organization is obvious, logical, and natural. (S5) Nevertheless, it is not universally accepted. (S6) For example, many writers present results and conclusions near the beginning, and describe the derivation of these results in subsequent sections.

S1 introduces the general topic and summarizes current practice with regard to report writing. S2 qualifies what was said in S1. The reader is warned of this qualification by the link word *however*.

Katzoff repeats the word *writer* from S1 to link it into S2, but precedes it with a different adjective (*different, better*) to show that he is moving from something general (all authors) to something more specific (better authors). The repetition of *approach* in S3 serves a similar linking purpose. It gives readers the feeling that they are being guided step by step along the path on which Katzoff develops his topic.

In S4 he addresses the reader directly, which is probably something that you would not do in a paper. Instead you would probably phrase such a concept in the passive: *it may be argued that*. Katzoff's idea is to anticipate possible objections to what he is about to say. S5 is only six words long. Such a short sentence is rare in academic work. Yet it is very effective in capturing reader attention. The link word, *nevertheless*, placed prominently at the beginning of the sentence, also catches the reader's eye and helps to underline the importance of what is being said.

In S6 he uses another link word, *for example*. These link words all serve to show how each sentence relates to what has been said before. Without these link words, the reader would be forced to figure out Katzoff's train of thought. However, Katzoff only uses link words when they really serve a purpose.

As can be seen in the second column of the table on page 52, one constant device Katzoff uses is to repeat words. He uses the word *writer* three times. He could easily have found synonyms, e.g. author, researcher, technician. But this might have confused readers who might think that there was a difference in meaning between these terms.

Another massive aid to helping readers understand, is to have a maximum of two ideas per sentence. S4 and S5 contain just one idea. S6 contains two ideas linked by *and*.

3.18 Summary

➤ Always think about your readers – order the information you give them in the most logical way and in the simplest form.

➤ Begin each paragraph with a topic sentence, then use the rest of the paragraph to develop this topic. If appropriate have a short concluding sentence at the end of the paragraph.

➤ Decide whether to begin a new section with a short summary, or whether to go directly to the main points.

➤ Put the topic as the subject of the paragraph or sentence, then give known information (context, background) followed by new information. Consider not giving the known information if it will be obvious for your readers.

➤ Move from the general to the increasingly specific, do not mix the two.

➤ Always progress in the most logical and consistent order, do not go backwards and forwards.

➤ Break up long paragraphs.

➤ Begin a new paragraph when i) you move on to a new topic (e.g. you move from general background info to discussing a particular case; ii) you have been talking about the literature and now you start talking about your contribution; iii) you are talking about your contribution and you want to mention a specific gap that your contribution fills; iv) you are discussing your results, and you want to highlight a key finding

➤ Avoid redundancy in the final paragraph of a section.

Chapter 4

Breaking Up Long Sentences

Factoids

A survey carried out at Stanford University revealed that 86.4% of students admitted that in order to appear more intelligent they used complex language in their essays, theses and dissertations.

*****

The average length of a sentence in English has become shorter and shorter over the centuries. In Shakespeare's time it was about 45 words, 150 years ago it was about 29 words, and today's experts recommend between 15 and 18 words.

*****

In *The Effective Communicator*, communications expert John Adair reports that approximately 90% of people understand an 8-word sentence on first reading, but only about 4% understand a 27-word sentence first time around, especially if it is poorly punctuated.

*****

You will lose more readers in the first 50 words than you will in the next 250.

*****

The Viennese art historian, Ernst Gombrich wrote many of his books in English rather than in his native German. His *Story of Art*, first published in 1950, is one of the most widely accessible art history books ever published, precisely because it is written in a clear, simple, unpretentious style.

© Springer International Publishing Switzerland 2016
A. Wallwork, *English for Writing Research Papers*,
English for Academic Research, DOI 10.1007/978-3-319-26094-5_4

4.1 What's the buzz?

(1) Read the 73-word sentence below and decide if it was written by a native or non-native English speaker.

When we reflect on the vast diversity of the plants and animals which have been cultivated, and which have varied during all ages under the most different climates and treatment, I think we are driven to conclude that this greater variability is simply due to our domestic productions having been raised under conditions of life not so uniform as, and somewhat different from, those to which the parent-species have been exposed under nature.

(2) The sentence below is from an Abstract. Is it easy to read without much mental effort?

The aim of our study was firstly to assess changes in the level of tolerance of natives of one country towards immigrants over the course of a 50-year period in order to be able to advise governmental agencies on how to develop strategies based on those countries that have been more successful in reducing racism as already investigated in previous studies, but not in such a systematic way, and secondly to establish correlations with data from the USA, which until now have been reported only sporadically.

Now look at the four short sentences below, which have been extracted from the long sentence above. Put them in the most logical order.

(a) The main aim was to be able to advise governmental agencies on how to develop strategies based on those countries that have been more successful in reducing racism.

(b) The second aim was to establish correlations with data from the USA, which until now have been reported only sporadically.

(c) This aspect has already been investigated in previous studies, but not in such a systematic way.

(d) We assessed changes in the level of tolerance of natives of one country towards immigrants over the course of a 50-year period.

Most English-speaking readers today are not prepared to read long sentences. The text in Exercise 1 comes from Darwin's *On the Origin of Species*. In 1859, when Darwin's book was published, it was quite common among native English-speaking scientists to use more than 70 words in a sentence. But the average sentence length today, outside academia, is around 20 words.

No research has ever proved that long sentences are an aid to reader comprehension.

A lot of research has, however, proved that shorter sentences make comprehension much easier for the reader.

You may think that writing in a simple way with short sentences is not elegant and is superficial.

But the point is not whether what you write is elegant or inelegant.

The question to ask is: Is this text effective or not? Will my readers be able to understand it easily?

John Kirkman is a British consultant specializing in research and training in scientific and technical communication. In his book *Good Style - Writing for Science and Technology* he says:

> To be easy to digest, sentences must be reasonably short and not too complex. The reasons for this are not grammatical: they are connected with the number of items of information the reader can absorb in a single unit or 'thought'.

In fact, whether they are Nobel Prize winners, Oxford professors, or first-year university students, all readers prefer sentences that they:

- only need to read once

- can read quickly because the sentence does not require intense concentration

- can process word by word and thus understand the build-up of the author's logic immediately, rather than only being able to reach their interpretation of the whole meaning at the end of the sentence

These goals are much easier to achieve if you write short sentences. In the world of academic writing, I think you should aim for an upper limit of around 25 words.

****

Sections 4.2–4.7 explain why and how long sentences get created, the pros AND cons of using short sentences for your readers, and the benefits of using short sentences for both your readers and co-authors.

Sections 4.8–4.16 explain how to convert a long sentence into short sentences. For more details see Chapter 15 in *English for Research: Grammar, Usage and Style*.

4.2   Analyse why and how long sentences are created

First we need to decide what constitutes a long and complex sentence.

> S1.   English owes its origins to the Angles and Saxons, two tribes from what is now northern Germany and Denmark.

S1 is nineteen words long. It is easy to read even though it has two parts (separated by the comma). S1 is neither too long nor too complex – it is a good clear sentence.

S2 is long (49 words). However, its content is simple and it would probably be understood by most readers without too much difficulty.

> S2.   Owing its origins to the Anglo Saxons (a tribe who lived in what is now Denmark and Northern Germany), English is the international language of communication, in part due to the importance of the USA, rather than the Queen of England, and is now studied by 1.1 billion people.

Long sentences become a problem when they contain difficult concepts, and when there are several of them in sequence. Although S2 does not contain difficult concepts, it is not the optimal construction. There is not a logical progression of thought. S3 is a better solution.

> S3.   English owes its origins to the Anglo Saxons, who were a tribe from what is now Denmark and Northern Germany. // It has become the international language of communication. // This is in part due to the importance of the USA, rather than the Queen of England. // English is now studied by 1.1 billion people.

S4 is 51 words long. It is still possible to understand on a first reading but it requires more effort on the part of the reader. Because it is so long, the reader cannot be sure which are the most important elements in it.

However, if we expand it too much (by using the words in italics) it becomes more difficult to read:

> S4.   *We did several surveys aimed at investigating whether stress increases in proportion to the number of children a couple has *and* each survey led to the same result, i.e. that there is no correlation, *thus confirming* the hypothesis that stress in the family is generally connected to factors other than size.

The reader could assimilate and judge the weight of the information if S4 were divided up into three parts as in S5.

> S5.   We did several surveys aimed at investigating whether stress increases in proportion to the number of children a couple has. Each survey led to the same result, i.e. that there is no correlation. This confirmed the hypothesis that stress in the family is generally connected to factors other than size.

In S5 the reader can easily and immediately understand the information because it is now presented in three shorter blocks. Basically, you should be able to read a sentence in one breath – try reading S5 aloud without stopping to breathe. It is not easy.

So a good general rule is that if the first part of a sentence is more than 12–15 words long, don't add a second part that is more than 10–12 words.

Finally, you will notice how using shorter sentences forces you to write much more clearly. It is in fact much easier to write using long sentences – that is, it is easier for you, but not for your reader!

4.3 Using short sentences will help your co-authors if they need to modify your text

Manuscripts are often written by several co-authors. Having short sentences in the initial draft means that co-authors can:

- add to them without making the resulting sentence too long

- change their order

For example S1 could easily be re-ordered (S2).

S1. English owes its origins to the Anglo Saxons, who were a tribe from what is now Denmark and Northern Germany. // It has become the international language of communication. // This is in part due to the importance of the USA, rather than the Queen of England. // English is now studied by 1.1 billion people.

S2. English is now studied by 1.1 billion people. // It owes its origins to the Anglo Saxons, who were a tribe from what is now Denmark and Northern Germany. // It has become the international language of communication. // This is in part due to the importance of the USA, rather than the Queen of England.

4.4 Using short sentence often entails repeating the key word, thus improving clarity

When you divide up a long sentence you will inevitably have to repeat some key words. You can see some examples of this in S5 in 4.1 and in S1 in 4.2, where the words *survey* and *English* are repeated in close proximity. Repeating key words is NOT bad style in technical writing (see 6.4 and 6.5). In fact repetition helps readers to follow your text, and it also helps your co-authors if they need to modify the order of the sentences in your draft.

4.5   Only use a series of short sentences to attract the reader's attention

You cannot and should not write a whole paper using short sentences.

The series of short sentences in the text below would be considered unsuitable by most journals.

> We investigated the meaning of life. We used four different methodologies. Each methodology gave contradictory results. The results confirmed previous research indicating that we understand absolutely nothing. Future research will investigate something more simple: the cerebral life of a PhD student.

The text above consists of four sentences: 6 words, 5, 5, and 11. Such a sequence of short sentences is the equivalent of traveling in a car with a learner driver over a bumpy surface – there is no flow and the result is discomfort for the passenger, i.e. irritation for the reader.

A sequence of short sentences like this would, however, be perfect for highlighting some important point in the Results or the Discussion or when expressing the key aims of your research.

4.6   Combine two short sentences into one longer sentence if this will avoid redundancy

This chapter advocates short sentences over long sentences.

However, two short sentences should be combined into a longer sentence if this will reduce the amount of redundancy and improve readability.

S1 contains two short sentences, but a lot of redundancy (in italics). S2 combines the two sentences into one much cleaner sentence.

S1.   * *On the one hand*, companies are increasingly *and significantly* making use of green claims in advertising their products (Grün and Verde, 2017). *On the other hand*, consumers often believe that these claims are not reliable *and, because of this*, they are not orienting their purchasing decisions towards greener products.

S2.   Although companies increasingly make use of green claims in advertising their products (Grün and Verde, 2017), consumers often believe that these claims are not reliable and thus do not orient their purchasing decisions towards greener products.

The rest of this chapter explains how to break up longer sentences.

4.7 When expressing your aims, consider dividing up a long sentence into shorter parts

Often you need to explain the rationale for adopting a particular procedure or line of research. To do this, writers typically use expressions such as *in order to, with the purpose of, with the aim to, in an attempt to.*

This is fine if you can express the rationale in a few words, as in this example:

> In order to test our hypothesis, we sampled a random selection of documents.

But if your rationale is longer than about 15 words, you probably need to split the sentence up, as shown below:

ORIGINAL VERSION (OV)	REVISED VERSION (RV)
Our readability index is based on a series of factors – length of sentences and paragraphs, use of headings, amount of white space, use of formatting (bold, italics, font size etc.) – in order to provide writers with some metrics for judging how much readers are likely to understand the writers' documents.	*We wanted to provide* writers with some metrics for judging how much readers are likely to understand the writers' documents. *We thus produced a readability index* based on a series of factors – length of sentences and paragraphs, use of headings, amount of white space, and use of formatting (bold, italics, font size etc.).
In order to establish a relationship between document length and level of bureaucracy and to confirm whether documents, such as reports regarding legislative and administrative issues, vary substantially in length from one language to another, *we conducted an analysis of A, B and C.*	(1) *We conducted* an analysis of A, B and C. *The aim of the analysis was to* establish.... (2) *We wanted to establish* a relationship between .. language and another. *To do this*, we conducted ...

The two techniques shown in the RV are

1. either say what you did and then why you did it
2. or give your rationale and then say what you did

The first is generally more helpful for the reader because it helps to put the rationale in context.

4.8   If possible replace *and* and *as well as* with a period (.)

In the OV below, *and* is used in two different ways:

(1)   to join two verbs (*speak and write*) and two nouns (*English and Italian*)

(2)   to add additional information (*and that this is true .. and to this end*)

In the first case there is no problem, but the second usage makes the sentence too long (65 words). The revised version rearranges the order in which the information is given, and divides the sentence into three parts.

ORIGINAL VERSION (OV)	REVISED VERSION (RV)
The aim of this paper is to confirm that how we speak *and* write generally reflects the way we think *and* that this is true not only at a personal but also at a national level, *and* to this end two European languages were analyzed, English *and* Italian, to verify whether the structure of the language is reflected in the lifestyle of the respective nations.	How we speak and write generally reflects the way we think and act. *This* paper aims to prove that this thesis is true not only at a personal but also at a national level. *Two* European languages were analyzed, English and Italian, to verify whether the structure of the language is reflected in the lifestyle of the respective nations.

The OV below contains three ideas that are linked together using *and*, thus creating one long sentence.

ORIGINAL VERSION (OV)	REVISED VERSION (RV)
The treatments are very often expensive and technically difficult, *and* their effectiveness very much depends on the chemical and physical characteristics of the substances used for impregnation, *and* on their ability to ...	The treatments are very often expensive and technically difficult. *Their* effectiveness very much depends on the chemical and physical characteristics of the substances used for impregnation. *Also important* is their ability to ...

The RV replaces the first *and* with a full stop – which is generally the simplest way to reduce the length of a sentence. The second occurrence of *and* cannot simply be replaced by a full stop. Instead, the writer uses *also* to alert the reader of additional details and then uses *important* to recall the concept of effectiveness.

Sentences containing multiple uses of *and* are often found in the materials and methods sections of a paper. It is much easier for readers to understand what materials you used and what procedures you followed if you divide your descriptions into short sentences. Each sentence should only cover one or two items or steps – however see Sect. 15.4 for cases where this is not applicable.

S1.   *All samples were collected at the same time (9 AM) every day to prevent any effects of possible circadian variation *and* then stored after treatment at 4°C until assay.

S2.   All samples were collected at the same time (9 AM) every day to prevent any effects of possible circadian variation. *They* were then stored after treatment at 4°C until assay.

In S1 readers initially think that the *and* clause is going to introduce a second prevention. Readers then have to revise their perception when they realize that *and* actually introduces the next step. S2 resolves this initial ambiguity by beginning a new sentence to highlight that the author is now talking about a different step. Here are two more examples that illustrate the same point.

ORIGINAL VERSION (OV)	REVISED VERSION (RV)
Seeds, sterilized for 3 min in NaOCl (1% available chlorine) *and* rinsed with distilled water, were germinated on moist filter paper (Whatman No. 2) in Petri dishes *and* grown in the dark at 23°C.	The seeds were sterilized for 3 min in NaOCl (1% available *chlorine), and* rinsed with distilled water. *They* were then germinated on moist filter paper (Whatman No. 2) in Petri dishes and grown in the dark at 23°C.
At the beginning we performed 2D and 3D forward modeling of a medium where only the lithological discontinuities were taken into account *and* compared the apparent synthetic resistivity *and* phase curves with our experimental data.	At the beginning we performed 2D and 3D forward modeling of a medium where only the lithological discontinuities were taken into account. *We* then compared the apparent synthetic resistivity and phase curves with our experimental data.

as well as is used similarly to *and* to add some additional information. It is often used as an alternative to *and* when the sentence might otherwise contain too many *ands* and would thus confuse the reader. If using *as well as* will create a very long sentence, it is best to break the sentence. However you cannot begin the new sentence with *as well as*. Instead you have to repeat some part of the previous sentence, as in the two RVs below:

ORIGINAL VERSION (OV)	REVISED VERSION (RV)
This finding could be explained by the specific properties of gold, silver and platinum *as well as* by the conditions in which these metals were found, for example silver was found in ...	(1) This finding could be *explained* by the specific properties of gold, silver and platinum. *Another explanation could be* the conditions ... (2) ... silver and platinum. *The conditions* in which these metals were found could *also* be an *explanation*. For example, ...

The techniques used for dealing with *and* can also be used for sentences containing words and phrases that have a similar meaning to *and*, such as *in addition, furthermore*, and *moreover*.

ORIGINAL VERSION (OV)	REVISED VERSION (RV)
The treatments are very often expensive and technically difficult, moreover their effectiveness very much depends on ...	The treatments are very often expensive and technically difficult. Moreover, their effectiveness very much depends on ...

4.9   Be careful how you use link words

WHEREAS, ON THE OTHER HAND, ALTHOUGH, HOWEVER

You cannot always break up a long sentence that contains a link by beginning a new sentence using that link word. This is because not all link words can be used at the beginning of a sentence. For example, when *whereas* is used to compare two findings in one long sentence, it should be replaced with *on the other hand* when the sentence is split into two.

ORIGINAL VERSION (OV)	REVISED VERSION (RV)
The levels of cadmium in Site C were comparable to the levels found in Sites A and B in the previous years, *whereas / on the other hand* the levels for copper were much lower in Site C with respect to the values found in the previous sampling campaigns in 2008 and 2010.	The levels of cadmium in Site C were comparable to the levels found in Sites A and B in the previous years. *On the other hand*, the levels for copper were much lower in Site C with respect to the values found in the previous sampling campaigns in 2008 and 2010.

The use of *although* and *however* is the same as with *whereas* and *on the other hand*, respectively.

ORIGINAL VERSION (OV)	REVISED VERSION (RV)
The levels of cadmium in Site C were comparable to the levels found in Sites A and B in the previous years, *although /however* this was not the case for the levels found in the south-east part of Site C.	The levels of cadmium in Site C were comparable to the levels found in Sites A and B in the previous years. *However,* this was not the case for the levels found in the south-east part of Site C.

Although can only be used in a two-part sentence, where one part depends on the other. For example:

Although this book was written for non-native speakers, *it can also* be used by native speakers.

In the RV above, *although* would not be possible because there is no dependent clause.

Some link words are used to give explanations in the middle of a sentence such as *because, since, as*. If you split the sentence, you cannot begin immediately with the same link word.

BECAUSE, SINCE, AS, IN FACT

Words such as *since* and *although* are often used in a subordinate clause at the beginning of a sentence, as in S1 below.

S1.   **Since* English is now spoken by 1.1 billion people around the world and is used as a lingua franca in many international business and tourism scenarios between people of different languages and between native English speakers and non-native speakers, *the learning of foreign languages in the United Kingdom has suffered a huge decline.*

The problem with S1 is that readers are forced to carry an idea in their head before they understand how this idea relates to the idea in the main clause (in italics). It would be much easier for readers to understand if S1 was split into two parts and rewritten as in S2.

S1.   English is now spoken by 1.1 billion people around the world and is used as a lingua franca in many international business and tourism scenarios between people of different languages and between native English speakers and non-native speakers. The consequence is that the learning of foreign languages in the United Kingdom has suffered a huge decline.

Like *although* (see Sect. 3.8) the link words *since* and *as* require a dependent clause. For example:

> *Since / As you are* a PhD student, *you* probably have to write a lot of papers in English.

This means that *since* and *as* could not be used in the RV below.

ORIGINAL	REVISED
The chemical characterization of organic paint materials in works of art is of great interest in terms of conservation, *because / since / as* the organic components of the paint layer are particularly subject to degradation.	The chemical characterization of organic paint materials in works of art is of great interest in terms of conservation. *This is because / In fact* the organic components of the paint layer are …

OWING TO, DUE TO, AS A RESULT OF, CONSEQUENTLY, THUS ETC.

These link words are used to explain the reasons for 'something' that has just been mentioned (S1) or is about to be mentioned (S2). The 'something' to be done in the examples below is to simplify a procedure.

S1.   *It was found necessary to make some simplifications to our procedures (essentially we did A, B and C), due to the difficulties in measuring the weight of the various compounds, particularly with regard to the weights of X, Y and Z.

S2.   *Owing to the difficulties in measuring the weight of the various compounds, particularly with regard to the weights of X, Y and Z, it was found necessary to make some simplifications to our procedures, essentially by doing A, B and C.

In such cases, it might be clearer for the reader if you split the sentence into three (S3).

S3.   We encountered difficulties in measuring the weight of the various compounds, particularly the weights of X, Y and Z. We thus decided to make some simplifications to our procedures. This entailed doing A, B and C.

For more information on link words see Chapter 13 in *English for Research: Grammar, Usage and Style*.

4.10 Avoid *which* and relative clauses when these create long sentences

which is used to add information. For example:

S1. English is now the world's international language, *which* is why it is used in scientific papers.

S2. English, *which* has now become the world's international language, is studied by more than a billion people.

S3. English, *[which is] now spoken* by more than a billion people, is the world's international language.

In S1 *which* is used to introduce an additional piece of information (in this case an explanation). In S2 *which* gives some extra information about the subject of the sentence (the English language). In S3, *which* serves the same purpose as in S2, it is in brackets because it could be cut.

In all three cases, the meaning is quick and easy to understand because the sentences are quite short.

Problems arise when sentences are longer, as highlighted in the OV below.

ORIGINAL VERSION (OV)	REVISED VERSION (RV)
English is now the world's international language and is studied by more than a billion people in various parts of the world thus giving rise to an industry of English language textbooks and teachers, *which* explains why in so many schools and universities in countries where English is not the mother tongue it is taught as the first foreign language in preference to, *for example*, Spanish or Chinese, *which* are two languages that have more native speakers than English.	English is now the world's international language and is studied by more than a billion people in various parts of the world thus giving rise to an industry of English language textbooks and teachers. *This* explains why in so many schools and universities in countries where English is not the mother tongue it is taught as the first foreign language. *For example*, English is taught in preference to Spanish or Chinese, *which* are two languages that have more native speakers than English.

In the OV the introduction of two new pieces of information using *which* makes the sentence unnecessarily long (79 words). In the RV, the first occurrence of *which* is replaced by *this*, which stands for *this fact*. Using *this* either alone or associated with a noun (e.g. *this fact, this decision, this method*) is a very common and useful way to reduce the length of a sentence.

The OV below contains an example of the use of *which* as in S2.

ORIGINAL VERSION (OV)	REVISED VERSION (RV)
English, *which* has now become the world's international language and is studied by more than a billion people in various parts of the world thus giving rise to an industry of English language textbooks and teachers, is generally used in scientific papers.	(1) English is generally used in scientific papers. In fact, English has now become the world's international language and is studied by more than a billion people in various parts of the world. This has given rise to an industry of English language textbooks and teachers. (2) English has now become the world's international language and is studied by more than a billion people in various parts of the world. This has given rise to an industry of English language textbooks and teachers. Today, English is generally used in scientific papers.

In the OV, the subject (*English*) and the main verb (*is*) are separated by 35 words. This means that by the time readers reach the main verb, they may have forgotten what the subject is.

There are two ways to resolve this problem. In the first RV, the author has decided to make scientific papers the key topic, so now this appears at the beginning of the sentence rather than at the end. In the second RV, the author first gives some information about English and then talks about scientific papers. The choice of using the first or the second technique, will depend on the emphasis you want to give to each piece of information.

The OV below contains an example of the usage given in S3. Even in short sentences, this kind of usage is dangerous as you may not know whether you can or cannot omit *which*.

ORIGINAL VERSION (OV)	REVISED VERSION (RV)
English, [which is] *now spoken* by more than a billion people from all over the world, the biggest populations being those in China and India, and more recently in some ex British colonies in Africa, is the world's international language.	English is the world's international language. It is *now spoken* by more than a billion people from all over the world. The biggest populations are those in China and India, and more recently in some ex British colonies in Africa.

The OVs below show two other examples where *which* has been omitted. Note how the words *area* and *distinction* are repeated. This repetition is not considered bad style in English scientific writing.

ORIGINAL VERSION (OV)	REVISED VERSION (RV)
Using the method described by Peters et al. (2010), we assessed the state of pollution of three sites in a coastal area [which was] *characterized* by high levels of agricultural, industrial and tourist activity, as well as occasional volcanic activity (the last major eruption was in 1997).	Using the method described by Peters et al. (2010), we assessed the state of pollution of three sites in a coastal *area. This area is characterized* by high levels of agricultural, industrial and tourist activity, as well as occasional volcanic activity (the last major eruption was in 1997).
Using the approach described by Smith and Jones (2011), a *distinction*, [which was] *useful* for analysis purposes, particularly in the final stages of the project, was made between the three types of pollution: agriculture, industry and tourism.	Using the approach described by Smith and Jones (2011), a *distinction*, was made between the three types of pollution: agriculture, industry and tourism. *This distinction* was useful for analysis purposes, particularly in the final stages of the project.

4.11 Avoid the – *ing* form to link phrases together

Another way writers typically link phrases together is to use the – *ing* form of a verb. If using the – *ing* form will significantly add to the length of a sentence, you can use another form of the verb and begin a new sentence.

ORIGINAL VERSION (OV)	REVISED VERSION (RV)
Using automatic translation software (e.g. Google Translate, Babelfish, and Systran) can considerably ease the work of researchers when they need to translate documents *thus saving* them money (for example the fee they might have otherwise had to pay to a professional translator) and *increasing* the amount of time they have to spend in the laboratory rather than at the PC.	Using automatic translation software (e.g. Google Translate, Babelfish, and Systran) can considerably ease the work of researchers when they need to translate documents. *Such software saves* them money, for example the fee they might have otherwise had to pay to a professional translator. It *also increases* the amount of time they have to spend in the laboratory rather than at the PC.

The RV above shows two ways to deal with the – *ing* form. First, you can repeat the subject (*software*) and then change the -ing form into the present tense (*saves, increases* rather than *saving, increasing*), or whatever tense is appropriate.

In the OV below, the – *ing* form is used instead of a relative clause: the author could have written *which indicates*. In such cases, you can break the sentence immediately before the – *ing* form and then start a new sentence with *This*.

ORIGINAL VERSION (OV)	REVISED VERSION (RV)
As can be seen from Table 1, the concentrations were far higher than expected especially in the first set of samples, *indicating* that one cause of pollution was ...	As can be seen from Table 1, the concentrations were far higher than expected especially in the first set of samples. *This indicates* that one cause of pollution was ...

4.12 Limit the number of commas in the same sentence

When commas are used in lists, they are fine:

Many European countries are now part of the European union, these include France, Germany, Italy, Portugal, Spain, ...

However, when commas are used to separate various clauses within a sentence, readers have to constantly adjust their thinking. Also, the more commas there are in a sentence, the longer the sentence is likely to be.

ORIGINAL VERSION (OV)	REVISED VERSION (RV)
As a preliminary study, in an attempt to establish a relationship between document length and level of bureaucracy, we analyzed the length of 50 European Union documents, written in seven of the official languages of the EU, to confirm whether documents, such as reports regarding legislative and administrative issues, vary substantially in length from one language to another, and whether this could be related, in some way, to the length of time typically needed to carry out daily administrative tasks in those countries (e.g. withdrawing money from a bank account, setting up bill payments with utility providers, understanding the clauses of an insurance contract). The results showed that ...	Our aim was to see if there is a direct relationship between the length of documents produced in a country, and the length of time it takes to do simple bureaucratic tasks in that country. Our hypothesis was: the longer the document, the greater the level of bureaucracy.
	In our preliminary study we analyzed translations from English into seven of the official languages of the European Union. We chose 50 documents, mostly regarding legislative and administrative issues. We then looked at the length of time typically needed to carry out daily administrative tasks in those countries. The tasks we selected were withdrawing money from a bank account, setting up bill payments with utility providers, and understanding the clauses of an insurance contract.
	The results showed that ...

The OV demonstrates that the excessive use of commas is a sign of lazy writing. The writer simply begins a sentence and keeps adding details to it, without thinking about how the reader will assimilate all these details. It also indicates that the writer is probably not clear in his / her own mind about what he / she wants to say.

Note that the RV:

- uses more words in total, but is considerably easier to follow

- rearranges the various subordinate clauses and puts them into a more logical order and in separate sentences

- divides up the information into paragraphs – the first explains the rationale, the second shows how the investigation was carried out. This makes the connection between ideas much clearer

Commas can also be dangerous if you use them to build up a series of phrases each of which describes the previous one, as in S1.

S1. In particular, the base peak is characteristic of the fragmentation of dehydroabietic acid, the main degradation marker formed by aromatization of abietadienic acids, the major constituents of pine resins.

Initially when reading S1 it seems that the *peak* is a *characteristic* of a series of items separated by commas. Then as we read further we understand that *the main degradation marker* is not in fact a second element in a series of items. Given that *the main degradation marker* comes immediately after *dehydroabietic acid* we assume that this acid must be a *marker*. We then realize that in fact it refers back to *fragmentation*. S1 thus requires much interpretative effort by the reader and is better rewritten as in S2:

S2. The base peak is characteristic of the fragmentation of dehydroabietic acid. *This fragmentation* is the main degradation marker formed by aromatization of abietadienic acids, *which are* the major constituents of pine resins.

S2 divides S1 into two separate sentences and also clarifies the relationships between the various elements.

4.13 Consider not using semicolons

Semicolons (;) are not commonly used in modern English. If you tend to use a semicolon before introducing an additional idea or additional information, think about using a period (.) instead.

> By 1066 English, or Old English as it is known, was firmly *established; it* was a logical language and was also reasonably phonetic. This situation changed dramatically when England was invaded by the Normans in *1066; in* fact, for the next 250 years French became the official language, and when English did come to be written again it was a terrible concoction of Anglo-Saxon, Latin and French.

The author of the above extract used semicolons to show that the two parts of the sentence to some extent depend on each other. Although this usage could be considered correct, today it is considered as unnecessary. Thus the two semicolons could easily be replaced by full stops, with no change of meaning for the reader.

When we read we automatically pause for an instant when we reach a full stop. This is our mental equivalent to pausing and inhaling air when we are speaking. Semicolons don't allow for such a pause and thus make the reading process slightly more tiring. Semicolons also make the sentence look longer, which makes them more tiring on our eyes.

Some writers also use a colon (:) in the same way as a semicolon. Again, if your sentence is going to be very long as a result of using a colon, it is better to replace the colon with a full stop and begin a new sentence.

S1. Old English had two distinct advantages over Modern English: it had a regular spelling system and was phonetic.

S2. Old English, which was the language spoken in most parts of England over 1,000 years ago, was a relatively pure language (the influence of Latin had not been particularly strong at this point, and the French influence as a result of the Norman Conquest was yet to be felt) and had two distinct advantages over Modern English: it had a regular spelling system and the majority of words were completely phonetic.

S3. Old English was the language spoken in most parts of England over 1,000 years ago. It was a relatively pure language since the influence of Latin had not been particularly strong at this point, and the French influence as a result of the Norman Conquest was yet to be felt. It had two distinct advantages over Modern English: it had a regular spelling system and the majority of words were completely phonetic.

In S1 the use of the colon (:) is fine, because the whole length of the resulting sentence is less than 20 words. But S2 is already too long even without the subsidiary clause introduced by the colon. S2 would in fact be better divided up into three parts as in S3.

4.14 Only use semicolons in lists

The only time you really need to use semicolons is to divide up short lists to show how each element in the list relates to each other. Note how S2 is clearer than S1 through the helpful use of semicolons.

S1.   *The partners in the various projects are A, B and C, P and Q, X and Y and Z.

S2.   The partners in the various projects are A, B and C; P and Q; X; and Y and Z.

S2 shows more clearly that there are four groups of partners: (1) A, B, C; (2) P, Q; (3) X; (4) Y, Z.

But if your list is long, as in the OV below, it is better to divide it up into shorter sentences.

ORIGINAL VERSION (OV)	REVISED VERSION (RV)
Our system is based on four components: it has many data files (the weather, people, places, etc.); it has procedures which it tries to use to combine these files by working out how to respond to certain types or patterns of questions (this entails the user knowing what types of questions it can answer); it has a form to understand the questions posed in a natural language (so the user may need to know English) which it then translates into one of the types of questions it knows how to answer; finally, it has a very powerful display module, which it uses to show the answers, using graphs, maps, histograms etc.	Our system is based on four components. Firstly, it has many data files, for example the weather, people, and places. Secondly, it has procedures which it tries to use to combine these files by working out how to respond to certain types or patterns of questions and this entails the user knowing what types of questions it can answer. Thirdly, it has a form to understand the questions posed in a natural language, which means the user needs to know English. It then translates the natural language into one of the types of questions it knows how to answer. Finally, it has a very powerful display module, which it uses to show the answers. These answers are shown using graphs, maps, histograms etc.

The RV is longer than the OV but it is much clearer for the reader because it:

- uses six short sentences rather than one long one. The semicolons have been replaced by full stops.

- clearly distinguishes the four components by using *firstly, secondly* etc.

- removes the brackets

4.15 Restrict use of parentheses to giving examples

Phrases in parentheses can considerably increase the length of a sentence. Parentheses are best used just to give short lists that act as examples. For example:

> Several members of the European Union (e.g. Spain, France, and Germany) have successfully managed to reduce their top tax threshold from 42 to 38%.

In the example above the information in parentheses does not interrupt the logical flow of the sentence and it does not occupy much space.

Parentheses should be avoided when giving explanations or examples that are not lists. For example:

ORIGINAL VERSION (OV)	REVISED VERSION (RV)
Using automatic translation software *(e.g. Google Translate, Babelfish, and Systran)* can considerably ease the work of researchers when they need to translate documents thus saving them money *(for example the fee they might have otherwise had to pay to a professional translator)* and increasing the amount of time they have to spend in the laboratory rather than at the PC.	Using automatic translation software *(e.g. Google Translate, Babelfish, and Systran)* can considerably ease the work of researchers when they need to translate documents. Such software saves them money, *for example the fee they might have otherwise had to pay to a professional translator.* It also increases the amount of time they have to spend in the laboratory rather than at the PC.

In the OV the first use of parentheses is fine, but the second interrupts the flow of the sentence and considerably adds to its length.

4.16   Final guidelines

Write your first draft without thinking too much about the length of the sentences. Then

1. look for long sentences
2. read them aloud

If you have to inhale, you need to divide up the sentence.

Here are some general rules:

- Do NOT write a long series of sentences of only 5–15 words.

- Occasionally use short sentences to attract attention (particularly in the Abstract and Discussion).

- Generally speaking, avoid sentences of more than 35 words.

- Clarity and readability are independent of sentence length.

Your main aim is to maintain readers' interest so that they continue reading.

If your sentence contains one or more of the following, you probably need to divide it up:

- *which + which*

- *and + and + and*

- *, + , + , + , +ˌ*

- *also + in addition / furthermore*

- *;*

Read S1 and S2. Can you understand them immediately?

S1*.   Using four different methodologies previously used in the literature in separate contexts each of which gave contradictory results in this study the meaning of life as seen through the perspective of a typical inhabitant of western Europe was investigated confirming previous research indicating that as a general rule we understand absolutely nothing. (63 words)

S2.   Using four different methodologies each of which gave contradictory results, we investigated the meaning of life confirming previous research indicating that we understand absolutely nothing. (25 words)

If you can make sense of the sentence without punctuation then it is probably OK.

S1 would certainly be more difficult for your readers than S2.

Moral of the story: Make it easy for them!

4.17 Summary

You don't lose any of the complexity of your thoughts by dividing up a long sentence into shorter ones. The information contained is exactly the same. All you have done is to present that information in a way that is easy for the reader to absorb at a first reading. But do not exclusively use short sentences.

To increase readability:

➤ don't separate the subject from its verb using more than 8–10 words

➤ avoid adding extra information to the end of the main clause, if the main clause is already about 15–20 words long

➤ check to make sure that a sentence has a maximum of 30 words, and don't use more than three or four 30-word sentences in the whole paper

➤ consider beginning a new sentence if the original sentence is long and contains one or more of the following (or equivalents): *and, which,* a link word, the *-ing* form, *in order to*

➤ maximize the use of periods (.). Use the minimum number of commas (,), avoid semicolons (;) and parentheses

➤ don't worry about repeating key words. If dividing up a long sentence into shorter sentences means that you have to repeat key words, this is not a problem. In fact this repetition will increase the clarity of your writing

Note: using *and, which* and the *-ing* form often leads to ambiguity (Sects. 6.1–6.5).

Chapter 5

Being Concise and Removing Redundancy

Factoids

The English language has evolved by eliminating unnecessary elements: gender (Old English had masculine, feminine and neuter), case (no nominative, accusative etc), verb endings (only the -s of the third person remains), and all the different forms of *you* (the current day *you* was originally the second person plural, and not the second person singular as is commonly thought – i.e. it is the equivalent of the French *vous* rather than *tu*).

*****

The language with the least number of words is Toki Pona. With its 123 word vocabulary its inventor, Sonja Lang, claims that you can say anything with no ambiguity. It takes 30 hours to master the language.

*****

Many journals, particularly widely-read ones such as *Science* and *Nature*, have restrictions on the number of words per article. On its website, *Nature* states: Our experience has shown that a paper's impact is maximized if it is as short as is consistent with providing a focused message, with a few crucial figures or tables.

*****

A study conducted by Jakob Nielsen in 2006 tracked the movements of readers' eyes as they read webpages. He found that as the number of words on a page increased, the time spent by readers on reading a whole page only increased slightly. He told his clients, i.e. webpage producers for companies, that when 'verbiage' (extra unnecessary words) is added to a page, only 18% of such verbiage will actually be read.

*****

Researchers at University College London revealed that readers typically stop reading an online article or a book after only two pages. The study concluded that readers today read in a new way, which the researchers named 'power browsing'.

© Springer International Publishing Switzerland 2016
A. Wallwork, *English for Writing Research Papers*,
English for Academic Research, DOI 10.1007/978-3-319-26094-5_5

5.1   What's the buzz

1) Look at the three quotations below. How do they relate to writing a research paper?

Read over your compositions, and wherever you meet with a passage which you think is particularly fine, strike it out.

Samuel Johnson (1709–1784), English writer

A good scientific theory should be explicit to a barmaid.

Ernest Rutherford (1871–1937), British / New Zealand chemist and physicist

The ability to simplify means to eliminate the unnecessary so that the necessary can speak.

Hans Hoffman (1880–1966), German-born American abstract expressionist painter

I don't want to bother readers unless I think it is important.

Barbara Kingsolver (b. 1955), American novelist

Human beings are not logical mechanisms into which information can be fed.

Bruce Cooper, author of Writing Technical Reports

2) How much of what you write in a paper, email, letter etc do you think is redundant or could at least be expressed more concisely?

3) Think of at least three advantages of writing clearly and with the fewest words possible.

****

The underlying message of this chapter is:

- Don't think that using complex terms will make you sound more intelligent.

- Write using the simplest most direct terminology.

- Cut everything that is not essential – this will let your key ideas stand out (be seen) more easily.

Your aim is NOT to receive a referee's report like this one (the italics are mine; MS stands for *manuscript*):

> *It is the duty of the authors to present their MS in a way that it is readable and to the point. Only then can a reviewer critically evaluate the most essential data on which the conclusions are built.* When a MS is written in a highly redundant way it takes *too much time and effort* to judge whether or not all the analyses have been done correctly.

> The MS is far too detailed making it *unreadable*. There is *a lot of redundancy* in the text, some parts are written as if this is a chapter in a text book. There are 144 references!!! And 12 pages of discussion!!

> *The result is that the actual findings that could be interesting are completely lost. There is no focus on what the authors really want to tell to the readers.*

> My suggestion to the editor is to reject this MS and give the authors the opportunity to *resubmit a much more focused and condensed MS.*

This chapter begins by giving you good reasons to avoid redundancy, and then shows you how to be concise.

However, being concise does not always mean using the least number of words.

It means using the least number of words that make the meaning 100% clear.

5.2 Write less and you will make fewer mistakes in English, and your key points will be clearer

The less you write, the fewer opportunities you will have to make mistakes in your English!

Imagine you are not sure in S1 if *aimed* should be followed by *at* or *to*, or in S2 whether *choice* or *choose* is the correct spelling of the noun.

S1. The activity aimed *at* / *to* the extrapolation of the curve is not trivial.
S2. We did the calculation manually. This *choice* / *choose* meant that ...

If you make the sentences more concise by removing the redundancy you will avoid the problem and thus avoid risking making a mistake when using them!

So S1 and S2 could be rewritten as S3 and S4.

S3. The extrapolation of the curve is not trivial.
S4. We did the calculation manually. This meant that ...

By the way, *aimed at* and *choice* would be the correct versions in S1 and S2.

Note how S3 and S4 are much more effective than S1 and S2 in highlighting the key information for the reader. There is no distracting information hiding such information. This is particularly important in the Abstract (Chapter 13) and Discussion (Chapter 18).

5.3   Cut individual redundant words

The words in square brackets below could simply be removed without having to make further changes to the sentence.

It was small [in size], round [in shape], yellow [in color] and heavy [in weight].

This will be done in [the month of] December for [a period of] six days.

Our research [activity] initially focused [attention] on [the process of] designing the architecture.

The [task of] analysis is not [a] straightforward [operation] and there is a [serious] danger that [the presence of] errors in the text ...

The analyses [performed in this context] highlighted [among other things] the [fundamental and critical] importance of using the correct methodology in a consistent [and coherent] manner [of conduction].

This was covered in the Materials and Methods [section].

Note how the words that have been cut are more generic than the words that have been left (e.g. *color* rather than *yellow*). Wherever possible use the most concrete word available (see next subsection).

Avoid using strings of words with little or no difference in meaning. In the sentences below, just one of the words in italics would be sufficient.

So far, researchers have failed to solve this equation due to various *issues, problems* and *difficulties*.

This point is *critical* and *fundamental* for our research purposes.

Your language may have adopted English words, and when you use them in your own language such words may require an additional associated word. So whereas in your language, you might have to say *make a skype call* or *an email message*, in English it is enough to say *to skype* and *an email*.

5.4 Consider cutting abstract words

Words such as *activity* and *task* (see 5.1) add no value to what you are saying. They are very abstract and not memorable words for the reader. If you find that your paper is full of the words listed below, first decide if you could cut them, if not try to find a more concise and concrete alternative.

> activity, case, character, characteristics, choice, circumstances, condition, consideration, criteria, eventuality, facilities, factor, instance, intervention, nature, observation, operation, phase, phenomenon, problem, procedure, process, purpose, realization, remark, situation, step, task, tendency, undertaking

For example what value does *the process of* add in the follow sentence?

> The process of registration can take up to ten minutes.

Ask yourself: What is important about my work? What is new about it? What real contribution am I making?

You can only write in a concrete way if you know the answers to those questions. And then you can use specific examples to explain the importance.

Not all abstract nouns should be cut. Abstract words that express a clear concept should be retained, e.g. *freedom, love, fear*.

5.5 Avoid *generic* + *specific* constructions

What could you cut in the sentences below?

> *Meetings will be held twice a year in June and December.*

> *We investigated two countries (i.e. Italy and France), both of which …*

If you can, immediately give your readers specific information without preceding such information with a generic statement. In the sentences above, *twice a year* and *two countries* add no value for the reader.

5.6   When drawing the reader's attention to something use the least number of words possible

Occasionally, you may want to draw the reader's attention to an important point. You will do this more effectively if you use two words rather than ten. This will produce a short sentence. Short sentences tend to stand out from the rest of the text, and thus get noted more.

All the phrases below could be replaced by *Note that* ...

> It must be emphasized / stressed / noted / remarked / underlined ...

> It is interesting to observe that ...

> It is worthwhile bearing in mind / noting / mentioning that ...

> It is important to recall that ...

> As the reader will no doubt be aware ...

> We have to point out that ...

5.7   Reduce the number of link words

While watching a film we unconsciously make hundreds of logical connections that enable us to follow the story line easily. We certainly don't think about the hours of film that have been cut out. Readers too make connections as they move from sentence to sentence, paragraph to paragraph. When papers reflect a clear, logical progression of ideas, the reader follows the argument without excessive promptings such as:

> *It is worthwhile noting that ...,*

> *As a matter of fact ...,*

> *Experience teaches us that ...*

The following link words could all be replaced by *since*:

> *considering that, given that, due to the fact that, on the basis of the fact that, notwithstanding the fact that, in view of the fact that, in consequence of the fact that*

Now compare the two versions below. Note how some of the link words from the OV have been removed in the RV, some have remained, and others have been added.

ORIGINAL VERSION (OV)	REVISED VERSION (RV)
Our data highlighted a significant toxic effect. (1) *In fact*, cell survival in cultures inoculated with elutriates was about 75% of the control, respectively. (2) *Considering that* several heavy metals (HMs) are known to be carcinogenic compounds, the metal contamination may explain some of the toxicity. (3) *Moreover*, in complex mixtures, HMs may also act as co-mutagens, (4) increasing the toxic activity of other compounds (Brogdon, 2011). (5) *In particular*, cadmium could be responsible for the mutagenic effects. (6) *In addition*, the high concentrations of chromium may be responsible for the toxic effects, (7) *given that* chromium is a potent mutagenic compound (Ray, 1990) and it is also …	Our data highlighted a significant toxic effect. (1) *In fact*, cell survival in cultures inoculated with elutriates was about 75% of the control, respectively. (2) Several heavy metals (HMs) are known to be carcinogenic compounds, *thus* the metal contamination may explain some of the toxic results. (3) In complex mixtures, HMs may also act as co-mutagens, (4) *thus* increasing the toxic activity of other compounds (Brogdon, 2011). (5) Cadmium could be responsible for the mutagenic effects. (6) *In addition*, the high concentrations of chromium may be responsible for the toxic effects. (7) Chromium is *in fact* a potent mutagenic compound (Ray, 1990) and it is also …

Below is an analysis of the seven points indicated in the OV.

1. *In fact* is needed because it gives evidence of what was said in the previous sentence.
2. *considering that* forces the reader to wait until the second half of the sentence before understanding the meaning of the phrase. In the RV *considering that* has been replaced, later in the sentence, by *thus*. The resulting structure is: tell readers something then tell them the consequence.
3. *Moreover* is unnecessary as the sentence also contains the word *also* which has the same function as *moreover*.
4. In the RV *thus* has been added before *increasing*. This is necessary as the reader could interpret the sentence in a completely different way, i.e. that the way heavy metals act as co-mutagens is <u>by</u> increasing the toxic activity. For more on the difference between *thus* and *by* before an *-ing* form see Sect. 6.10.
5. In the OV, this is the fourth consecutive sentence that begins with a link word. Such a style of writing soon becomes repetitive and also delays the subject of the sentence. The expression *in particular* is rarely useful. In the RV it has been removed.
6. *In addition* is useful here as it alerts the reader that more is going to be said about the findings mentioned in the previous sentence, rather than this sentence moving on to a new topic.
7. In the RV, the original sentence is terminated after *effects* and a new sentence is begun. In order to avoid the tedium of having link words always at the beginning of the sentence, *in fact* has been placed after the subject.

5.8 When connecting sentences, use the shortest form possible

When drawing consequences or introducing the next point that follows on from information given in the previous sentences, avoid redundancy (italics in S1 and S2), instead simply insert *thus* (as in S3 and S4):

S1*. *From the previous list of properties, it emerges that* cooperation with devices is a complex task.

S2*. *Under this respect*, the design of a suitable gateway is necessary in order to guarantee the interoperability between the gateway and other communication protocols.

S3. Cooperation with devices is *thus* a complex task.

S4. The design of a suitable gateway is *thus* necessary in order to guarantee the interoperability between the gateway and other communication protocols.

5.9 Choose the shortest expressions

Try to use the expression that requires the least characters.

X is large in comparison with Y. (26 characters)

X is larger than Y. (15 characters)

Instead of using an adjective + a generic noun (*way, mode, fashion*), use the adverb form of the adjective.

ORIGINAL VERSION (OV)	REVISED VERSION (RV)
To do this, the application searches for solutions *in an automatic way / fashion / mode*.	To do this, the application searches for solutions *automatically*.
This should be avoided since *it is generally the case that* it will fail.	This should be avoided since it *generally* fails.
From a financial standpoint, it makes more sense to …	*Financially*, it makes more sense to …

Other examples:

in the normal course of events (normally), on many occasions (often), a good number of times (many times, frequently), from time to time (occasionally), in a rapid manner (rapidly), in a manual mode (manually), in an easy fashion (easily), from a conceptual point of view (conceptually).

5.10 Cut redundant adjectives

Whenever you use an adjective decide if it really is necessary.

an *acute* dilemma, a *real* challenge, a *complete* victory, a *novel* solution, an *interesting* result, an *appropriate* method

Only use an adjective and adverb if it adds precision to your sentence. If you really think that such adjectives are necessary you should explain why something is *novel, interesting, appropriate.*

Don't use pairs of adjectives or nouns that essentially mean the same thing. What contribution, if any, do the words in square brackets below add to the reader's understanding of the sentence?

This is [absolutely] necessary as the reader could interpret the sentence in a [completely] different way.

This has made it possible to review the analysis of important [fundamental and practical] problems [and phenomena] of engineering.

Numerical methods have increasingly become quick [and expedient] means of treating such problems.

Equation 1 is [readily] amenable to numerical treatment.

The method lends itself [most amiably] to being solved by ...

5.11 Cut pointless introductory phrases

Often you can avoid an introductory phrase when it is preceded by a heading. For example, immediately after a heading entitled Results, the following phrases would be completely redundant.

The salient results are summarized in the following.

The results of this work may be synthesized as follows.

Let us recapitulate some of the results obtained in this study.

Likewise, under a heading entitled Conclusions don't begin by saying:

In conclusion, we can say that ...

5.12 Replace impersonal expressions beginning *it is* …

Expressions that begin a sentence with *it is* … tend to delay the subject. You can replace impersonal expressions by:

(a) using modal verbs (*can, must* etc.).

ORIGINAL VERSION (OV)	REVISED VERSION (RV)
It is necessary / mandatory to use X.	X *must* be used.
	X is necessary / mandatory.
It is advisable to clean the recipients.	The recipients *should* be cleaned.
It is possible that inflation will rise.	Inflation *may* rise.

(b) using adverbs (*surprisingly, likely* etc.). For the position of adverbs in a sentence, see Sect. 2.14.

ORIGINAL VERSION (OV)	REVISED VERSION (RV)
It is surprising that no research has been carried out in this area before.	*Surprisingly*, no research has been carried out in this area before.
It is regretted that no funds will be available for the next academic year.	*Unfortunately*, no funds will be available for the next academic year.
It is clear / evident / probable that inflation will rise.	Inflation will *clearly / probably* rise.

(c) rearranging the sentence

ORIGINAL VERSION (OV)	REVISED VERSION (RV)
It is possible to demonstrate [Kim 1992] that …	Kim [1992] *demonstrated* that …
It is anticipated / believed that there will be a rise in stock prices.	We *expect* a rise in stock prices.
	We *believe* there will be a rise in stock prices.
	A rise in stock prices *is expected*.
It may be noticed that … *It is possible to observe* that …	*Note* that …

However, impersonal phrases may be useful when you want to hedge your claims (Chap. 10).

5.13   Prefer verbs to nouns

English tends to use more verbs than nouns. This reduces the number of words needed, makes sentences flow better, and provides variety. Too many nouns make a sentence heavy to read.

ORIGINAL VERSION (OV)	REVISED VERSION (RV)
X was used in the *calculation* of Y.	X was used to *calculate* Y.
Symbols will be defined in the text at their first occurrence.	Symbols will be defined *when they first occur* in the text.
Lipid *identification* in paint samples is based on the *evaluation* of characteristic ratio values of fatty acid amounts and *comparison* with reference samples.	Lipids are generally *identified* in paint samples by *evaluating* the characteristic ratio values of fatty acid amounts and *comparing* them with reference samples.

5.14   Use one verb (e.g. *analyze*) instead of a verb+noun (e.g. *make an analysis*)

If you use a verb + noun construction, you have to choose a 'helper' verb to associate with the noun. For example, should you say *do* or *make* a *comparison* of x and y? If you simply say *to compare x and y*, you avoid choosing the wrong helper verb.

ORIGINAL VERSION (OV)	REVISED VERSION (RV)
X *showed* a better *performance* than Y.	X *performed* better than Y.
Heating of the probe can be *obtained* in two different ways:	*The probe can be* heated *in two different ways*:
The *installation* of the system is *done* automatically.	The system is *installed* automatically.
The *evaluation* of this index *has been carried out* by *means* of the correlation function.	This index was *evaluated using* the correlation function.
The *monitoring* of the kinetics was possible by irradiation.	The kinetics *were monitored* by irradiation.

Other examples:

> *achieve* an improvement (improve), *carry out* a test (test), *cause* a cessation (stop), *conduct* a survey (survey), *effect* a reduction (reduce), *execute* a search (search), *exert* an influence (influence), *exhibit* a performance (perform), *experience* a change (change), *give* an explanation (explain), *implement* a change (change), *make* a prediction (predict), *obtain* an increase (increase), *reach* a conclusion (conclude), *show* an improvement (improve), *subject to* examination (examine).

The above verbs in italics add no value for the reader. The OV below highlights the redundancy that such verb + noun constructions cause, for example the author uses verbs *(rises rapidly)*, rather than a verb + noun construction *(undergoes a rapid rise)*.

ORIGINAL VERSION (OV)	REVISED VERSION (RV)
In Figure 2 the curve *exhibits a downward trend* (portion A–B); then it *undergoes a rapid rise* (part B–C), it then *assumes a leveled state* (zone C–D). It *possesses a peak* at point E before displaying a slow decline … On the other hand, the curve in Fig 3 *is characterized by a different behavior.*	In Figure 2 the curve initially *falls* (segment A–B) and then *rises rapidly* (B–C). It then *levels off* (C–D). Finally it *peaks* at point E before falling slowly … On the other hand, the curve in Fig 3 *behaves* differently.

However, sometimes using the noun is inevitable:

> *Detection* was carried out at 520 nm, using a Waters 2487 dual λ UV-visible detector.

> *Chromatogram analysis was* performed using Millennium 32 (Waters).

Note that many nouns in English have a verb equivalent, including new coinages. So you can, for example, avoid saying *to send an email* or *to do a search on Google*, and simply say *to email* and *to google*.

5.15 Reduce your authorial voice

Readers will not appreciate being continually given a commentary on what you are doing in your paper, as in the first five examples in the OV below. Also, avoid *we* to refer to you and your readers, as in the last example.

ORIGINAL VERSION (OV)	REVISED VERSION (RV)
As in the previous case we observe that there are three distributions of this measure:	There are three distributions of this measure:
We can identify two categories of users..	There are two categories of users..
It is now time to turn our attention, in the rest of the paper, to the question of..	The rest of the paper focuses on the question of ...
We find it interesting to note that x = y.	Interestingly, x = y.
As we can see in Fig. 1, for each network we have a series of different relationships.	Figure 1 highlights that there is a series of different relationships for each network.

For more on this topic see 7.6, 7.7 and 7.8.

5.16 Be concise when referring to figures and tables

The RVs below highlight how it is not difficult to be concise when referring to figures and tables.

ORIGINAL VERSION (OV)	REVISED VERSION (RV)
Figure 1 shows schematically / gives a graphical representation of / diagrammatically presents / pictorially gives a comparison of two components	Figure 1 shows a comparison of two components.
From the graphic / picture / diagram / drawing / chart / illustration / sketch / plot / scheme that is depicted / displayed / detailed / represented / sketched in Figure 3, we can say that ...	Figure 3 shows / highlights / reports that ...
The mass spectrum, reproduced in the drawing in Figure 14, proved that ...	The mass spectrum (Fig. 14) proved that ...
We can observe / As can be seen from Table 3 that ...	Table 3 highlights that ...
From an analysis / inspection of Table 3 it emerges that ...	

If you refer your readers to a figure, you don't need to describe the figure using words like *graphically* or *schematically*. You don't need to use many different synonyms either to describe what kind of figure it is or to say what it shows. If possible use active verbs – *this figures shows x*, rather than *x is shown in this figure*.

In your text, avoid duplicating information that can be easily found in tables and figures. Just give the highlights.

5.17 Use the infinitive when expressing an aim

You can often save space by expressing your purposes and objectives in the shortest form possible.

ORIGINAL VERSION (OV)	REVISED VERSION (RV)
We use X *for the purposes of showing* the suitability of Y for the description of Z.	We use X *to show* how Y is suitable for describing Z.
In order to maximize channel utilization …	*To maximize* channel utilization …
The design of software is aimed at supporting *multimedia services*.	The software is designed *to support* multimedia services.
	The software *supports* multimedia services.

5.18 Remove unnecessary commonly-known or obvious information

Don't include extended amounts of information that even non-expert readers will be familiar with. The problem of including such information is that readers will feel that they are not learning anything new, and thus will likely skip the paragraph. If they start skipping paragraphs, then the risk is that they will skip both irrelevant AND relevant paragraphs.

Only feed your readers with relevant information thereby reducing the readers' tendency to skim your text rather than read it in detail.

In the text below, the redundant information is highlighted in italics.

Devices in a smart environment (SE) can be deployed as stationary or mobile devices. Stationary devices are installed permanently in specific locations *and they are supposed not to change their location*; for example a smart plug and some kinds of environmental sensors or appliances *do not move from their initial deployment*. On the other hand, mobile devices *can change their position over time*; for example a smart phone, a smart watch or a wristband *are not deployed in SE hot spots*, *but* are worn by people within the SE and their mobility is tightly linked with the mobility of the person carrying them. *The numbers of mobile devices are increasing in our daily lives and thus they are even more present in the SE in which we spend most of the time. We observe that* the mobility of a device affects the way and the quality of the services that are provided by devices.

5.19   Be concise even if you are writing for an online journal

You may think that because you are writing for an electronic journal there are no issues about the length. This is not the case. If you want people to read what you have written and cite your work, then the importance of your work must be clear. It won't be clear if it is hidden in a mass of redundancy.

5.20   Consider reducing the length of your paper

My wife and I run an editing agency. When we receive a paper of over 20 pages, our hearts often sink. This is not because we are not passionate about our work, but simply because often the longer the paper, the less likely it is that the author will be focused and the more difficult it is for us to make sense of the paper.

Bear in mind what Mark Twain, the American author and humorist, once wrote: *I didn't have time to write a short letter, so I wrote a long one instead.*

Ask yourself:

- is my paper 40 pages long, simply because it was easier to report everything rather than taking the time to really consider what was the most important information? Or does it contain 40 pages of meaty essential information?

- how are my editor and reviewers likely to react to my massively long paper?

- when my 40-page paper is published, will readers naturally want to read it rather than a 10–20 page paper on a similar topic?

Having said that, there is no evidence to prove that a shorter paper is likely to be cited more than a longer paper. In fact, research on medical papers has found that longer papers with multiple authors tend to be cited more (see References for a link). However, to be cited your paper:

- has to have been published – excessive length is likely to be an issue for reviewers

- has to contain useful data written in a clear, understandable way

In themselves, shortness and length are not key indicators of a paper's worth.

If a paper is long, but with no redundancy, it will certainly stand a better chance of being published and consequently cited, than a long paper full of redundancy. So get cutting!

5.21 Summary

You can be more concise by:

➢ deleting any words that are not 100% necessary

➢ finding ways of expressing the same concept with fewer words

➢ using verbs rather than nouns

➢ choosing the shortest words and expressions

➢ avoiding impersonal phrases that begin *it is* ...

A frequent result of reducing the overall number of words is that the subject of the sentence tends to be shifted closer to the beginning of the sentence. This means that the reader gets a much quicker picture of the topic of the sentence. Also, if you use the minimum number of words, the importance of what you are saying will stand out more clearly for the reader.

These rules in this chapter are designed to help you write in a more concise way. However it is also important to vary the way you write. It is perfectly acceptable to write a long phrase or sentence, or a complicated construction, provided that you only do this occasionally.

Finally, note that on some occasions, conciseness can produce unintelligible phrases. It is always better to put clarity first, even if it means having to use more words.

Chapter 6

Avoiding Ambiguity, Repetition, and Vague Language

Factoids

In 1905 a treaty between Russia and Japan nearly fell apart due to ambiguity in language. The draft of the treaty was written in English and French, and *control* and *contrôler* were both attributed the same meaning, whereas the English word meant 'dominate' and the French word 'inspect'.

*****

A United Nations Security Council resolution in November 1967 called for the withdrawal of Israel from territories occupied in the Six Day War. The English version was: *Withdrawal of Israeli armed forces from territories occupied in the recent conflict.* The French version (another official language of the UN) contained the definite article before *territories*, thus implying all the territories, whereas the English version could be interpreted as some territories but not necessarily all.

*****

Legal battles have been fought over the usage of *and*. Suppose a research institute promises to 'pay you €10,000 and give you a full contract if you finish the research within 18 months'. What happens if you don't finish within 18 months? Do you still get the €10,000? Well you would only get the money if there was a comma before the *and*. The comma would indicate that the €10,000 and the finishing of the research are two different issues.

© Springer International Publishing Switzerland 2016
A. Wallwork, *English for Writing Research Papers*,
English for Academic Research, DOI 10.1007/978-3-319-26094-5_6

6.1 What's the buzz?

1) The following are newspaper headlines – they are all real! In which cases is there ambiguity (i.e. more than one possible interpretation), and it which cases is there only one interpretation?

  1. Panda mating fails; vet takes over
  2. Miners refuse to work after death
  3. Juvenile court to try shooting defendant
  4. Killer sentenced to death for second time in 10 years
  5. Red tape holds up new bridge
  6. Astronaut takes blame for gas in spacecraft
  7. Plane too close to the ground, crash probe told
  8. Kids make nutritious snacks
  9. Local high school dropouts cut in half
  10. Sex education delayed, teachers request training

2) The author resources section of Nature highlights the importance of writing in a 'simple and accessible style':

Many papers submitted for publication in a Nature journal contain unnecessary technical terminology, unreadable descriptions of the work that has been done, and convoluted figure legends. Our journal subeditors and copyeditors edit the manuscript so that it is grammatically correct, logical, clear and concise, uses consistent search terms, and so that the terminology is consistent with that used in previous papers published in the journal. Of course, this process is assisted greatly if the authors have written the manuscript in a simple and accessible style, as the author is the best person to convey the message of the paper and to persuade readers that it is important enough to spend time on.

****

Subsections 6.2 to 6.9 give some general ideas on how to avoid ambiguity and unnecessary repetition. The other subsections highlight particular grammar and vocabulary misusages that can lead to ambiguity. If you read nothing else in this chapter, ensure that you read 6.3 to 6.5 on the dangers of pronouns and synonyms.

6.2 Place words in an unambiguous order

A sentence or phrase is ambiguous or vague when it has more than one interpretation or its interpretation is not obvious. If referees are not clear about what you are saying in a particular sentence, this may affect their overall understanding of the contribution of the paper. They may thus feel that they are not in a position to judge the merits of your paper. Just two or three ambiguous sentences are enough for referees to recommend delaying publication until 'the English has been revised by a native-speaking expert'.

Ambiguity arises when a phrase can be interpreted in more than one way, as highlighted by S1 and S2.

S1. *Professors like annoying students.

S2. *I spoke to the professor with a microphone.

In S1 it is not clear if 'annoying' describes the students, or it refers to what professors enjoy doing. Depending on the meaning, S1 could be disambiguated as in S3 or S4:

S3. Professors like to annoy their students.

S4. Professors like students who are annoying.

In S2 – did I use the microphone or was the professor holding it? Depending on the meaning, S2 could be disambiguated as in S5 or S6:

S5. Using a microphone, I spoke to the professor.

S6. I spoke to the professor who was holding a microphone.

S7 is another example where poor word order can create confusion:

S7. To obtain red colors, insects and plant roots were used by indigenous people.

In S7 readers may initially think that *red colors* and *insects* are part of the same list. Readers will only understand that *insects and plant roots* is the subject of the verb when they get to the end of the sentence. To avoid this problem there are two possible solutions. S8 puts *insects and plant roots* as the main subject and S9 *primitive people*. The choices of S8 or S9 will probably depend on whether the primitive people have already been mentioned or not.

S8. Insect and plant roots were used to obtain red colors.

S9. To obtain red colors, primitive people used insects and plant roots.

We tend to read words in small groups. Often we think that if two or three words immediately follow each other they must be related in some way. S10 is initially confusing.

S10. The European Union (EU) adopted various measures to combat these phenomena. This resulted in smog and pollution levels reduction.

When we read *resulted in smog and pollution*, our initial interpretation is that the smog and pollution are the result of the EU's measures. Then when we move on and read *levels* we have to reprocess the information. This is not important if readers have to change their interpretation only once or twice in a paper. But if they have to do it many times, the cumulative effort required becomes too much. Some readers will stop trying to guess the meaning and stop reading. In your case, it may mean that your paper could be initially rejected. S11 is a much clearer version of S10.

S11. The European Union adopted various measures to combat these phenomena. This resulted in a reduction in smog and pollution [levels].

6.3   Beware of pronouns: possibly the greatest source of ambiguity

Some sentences that would not be ambiguous in your language may become ambiguous in English. For example:

S1. *I put the book in the car and then I left *it* there all day.

In English we do not know whether *it* refers to the *book* or the *car*. Some languages have a case system or a gender for nouns. Thus if your word for *book* is – for instance – masculine, and your word for *car* is feminine, you will use a different form of *it* to indicate whether the noun *it* refers to is masculine or feminine, and this will make it clear for your reader. In English *it* can refer to all nouns (apart from those that refer to human beings).

In any case, if you use *it* in one sentence to refer to a noun you have mentioned in a previous sentence, you may be forcing the reader to re-read the previous sentence to remember what *it* refers to. So if you think that there could be possible ambiguity or that the reader may have forgotten the subject, then simply repeat the key word:

S2. I put the book in the car and then I left the book there all day.

You may think this is not very elegant, but it is much clearer for your reader and is not considered bad style in technical English.

In S3 does *they* refer to all three locations, to Canada and the Netherlands, or just to the Netherlands?

> S3. *We could go to Australia, Canada or the Netherlands, *but they* are a long way from here.

To avoid misunderstandings, be more specific:

> S4. ... Australia, Canada or the Netherlands, all of which are a long way from here.
>
> S5. ... Australia, Canada or the Netherlands. But Canada and the Netherlands are a long way from here.
>
> S6. ... Australia, Canada or the Netherlands. But the Netherlands are a long way from here.

In S7 what do *one / this / these* refer to? (a) user names (b) passwords?

> S7. * No user names or passwords are required, unless the system administrator decides that one is necessary. ... decides that this is necessary. ... decides that these are necessary.

Interpretations (a) and (b) are much clearer rewritten as in S8 and S9, respectively.

> S8. ... unless the system administrator decides that a user name is necessary.
>
> S9. ... unless the system administrator decides that a password is necessary.

In S10 and S11 what do *this* and *them* refer to?

> S10. *There are two ways to learn a language: take private lessons or learn it in the country where the language is spoken but this entails spending a lot of money.
>
> S11. *We cut the trees into sectors, then separated the logs from the branches, and then burnt them.

Does *this* in S10 refer to the cost of private lessons, the cost of living in the country where the language is spoken, or both? Does *them* in S11 refer to just the branches or the logs as well? To clarify, you just need to repeat the key concept.

> S12. There are two ways to learn a language: take private lessons or learn it in the country where the language is spoken. However living in a foreign country entails spending a lot of money.
>
> S13. There are two ways to learn a language: take private lessons or learn it in the country where the language is spoken. However both these solutions entail spending a lot of money.

In S12 it is now clear the cost only refers to living in a foreign country, and S13 clarifies that lessons plus living in a foreign country have a high cost. In S13, *solutions* has been used to replace *ways* in the first part of the sentence – using synonyms for non-key words is fine.

To clarify S11, you just need to replace *them* with *branches* (if it is just the branches that were burnt), or with *both of them* (if both branches and logs were burnt).

In my experience as an editor, pronouns cause more ambiguity than all the other sources of ambiguity combined. This is also due to the way we read. You as the author expect your readers to read every word, sentence and paragraph. However few readers will have the time or energy to do this. Thus if you refer to something, let's call it X, that you mentioned a few sentences before, or in the paragraph before, and you refer to X using *this, these, it, them, which, the former etc*, then you risk losing your reader who simply may not have read the original instance of X.

It makes life much simpler for everyone if, where ambiguity could arise, you replace pronouns with the noun that they refer to.

6.4 Avoid replacing key words with synonyms and clarify ambiguity introduced by generic words

When you were at school learning your own language, your teachers probably encouraged you not to use the same word in the same sentence more than once, and maybe not even in the same paragraph. Finding synonyms was good. Consequently, like many researchers you probably now suffer from monologophobia – the fear of using the same word twice!

Monologophobia can cause ambiguity or confusion for the reader. For example, do the three words in bold in S1 have a different meaning?

S1. **Companies* have to pay many taxes. In fact, occasionally *enterprises* fail because of over-taxation. Some *firms* resolve this problem by moving their headquarters to countries where the tax rate is lower.

For the author, they probably have the same meaning, but not necessarily for the reader. The reader cannot be sure and may try to work out what the difference between the three terms is. The author is thus forcing the reader to make an unnecessary mental effort.

If you decide to use words that have similar – but slightly different – meanings, then you should define these differences for the reader. In S1 you would need to define the difference between a company, an enterprise and a firm.

A very important rule in scientific English is: never find synonyms for key words – avoid synonymomania!

S1 could thus be rewritten as S2.

> S2. *Companies* have to pay many taxes and occasionally may fail because of over-taxation. Some *[companies]* resolve this problem by moving their headquarters to countries where the tax rate is lower.

This problem is accentuated when authors use different words to express the same concept over several paragraphs. For instance, in paragraph 1 the author uses the word *test*, in paragraph 2 *experiment*, and in paragraph 3 *trial*. The reader cannot be sure if *test*, *experiment* and *trial* all refer to the same scientific procedure or to two/three different procedures.

Authors come up with ingenious solutions for not repeating the same word. One device is to replace the key word with a generic description of it.

> S3. *Our findings demonstrate that treatment with *chitosan* resulted in the significant protection of Arabidopsis leaves against the necrotrophic fungus Botrytis cinerea. This is closely related to the fact that this *compound* is perceived by the plant as a powerful elicitor.

> S4. *The maximum solubility of *mercury* occurs in an oxygenated environment, which is the typical condition found in soil. The principle forms that are found in soil are $Hg(OH)_2$ and $HgCl_2$. With these ions, this *metal* can form soluble complexes that are …

Readers will probably understand that in S3 *compound* refers to *chitosan*, and in S4 that *metal* refers to *mercury*. But it will help readers if you repeat the word for them (*to the fact that chitosan is perceived, … these ions, mercury can form*), so that they don't have to read backwards to check. This is particularly important when the generic word (*compound, metal*) appears several lines later than the original concrete word (*chitosan, mercury*).

So, be careful when you use words such as *process, parameter, element, feature, function* to refer to a key word – can you be sure that your readers will associate these generic words with the key word?

Sometimes it is not clear at all what the generic phrase refers to, as in this example:

> S5. *Moreover, it is strongly discouraged to restrain horses while monitoring their cardiac activity, because *this unnatural condition* leads to stressing stimuli.

It seems like *this unnatural condition* refers to *restraining* horses, whereas in fact the author was referring to *monitoring* the cardiac activity as being unnatural. The simple solution, as always, is to repeat the key word (i.e. *monitoring*).

> S6. Moreover, it is strongly discouraged to restrain horses while monitoring their cardiac activity, because such monitoring leads to stressing stimuli.

Another typical device to avoid repetition is to use *one* or *that* as in S5 and S6.

S7. *This can be done by using either a *chromatographic pump or a peristaltic one.*

S8. *With regard to the *TTC* output the *arbitrariness* of a g_{pk} parameter can be exploited by starting from *that* of g_{pa}.

To a native English speaker S4 and S5 sound quite strange and could easily be rewritten as:

S9. This can be done by using either a *chromatographic or peristaltic pump.*

S10. With regard to the *TTC* output the arbitrariness of a g_{pk} parameter can be exploited by starting from the *arbitrariness* of g_{pa}.

6.5   Restrict the use of synonyms to non-key words

Synonyms are helpful for replacing repetitive usage of adjectives and verbs. Examples:

We would like to *stress / underline / emphasize / highlight* that x = y.

We *performed / carried out / did* several experiments.

This is a *critical / very important / fundamental* issue.

Another typical case where synonyms are useful is to avoid repetition of the same generic word (or derivatives). For example:

The identification is *mainly* based on three *main* strategies.

This function has three main *aims* all *aimed* at reducing stress.

The *use* of synonyms is *useful* to replace *overuse* of the same adjective.

Such unnecessary repetition may irritate some readers, so you could replace *mainly* with *generally*, or alternatively *main* with *principal*, and *aims* with *objectives* or *aimed* with *targeted*. In the last case (*use ... useful ... overuse*) you can simply delete *the use of* and replace *useful* with *helpful*.

Note how in the sentence immediately preceding this one I have specified what *the last case* refers to by putting the example words in brackets. Otherwise you might have initially thought that *the last case* referred to the previously mentioned case (i.e. *aimed with targeted*). Putting an explanation in brackets or using *i.e.* is a great way of clarifying what you mean, particularly when you are forced to use a generic phrase that could be open to ambiguity.

Avoid repeating the same link words when they are close to each other either in the same sentence or a series of sentences. Again, some readers will find such repetition irritating. For example:

> The lack of *tolerance* towards the plight of others generally showed by rich people is likely *due to* their *family* background. In fact such *intolerance* can either be due to the fact that their *family* has always had *money*, therefore they are almost immune to the rest of the world and live literally on their own planet. Alternatively it may be *due to* the fact that their *family* actually had very little *money*, and in this case *due to* the allure of money, and *due to* the fact that the person feels justified in accumulating *money* (they never want to feel *poor* again) the *poor* people that surround them seem to vanish into the background.

In the above extract several words are repeated. *Tolerance, family,* and *money* are key words and there is no need to replace them. The repetition of *poor* is acceptable – it is highlighting an important point. However, the repetition of *due to* is unnecessary as there are many alternative forms: *caused by, as a result of, because of* etc.

Finally, don't be worried if a sentence contains two instances or more of the same preposition (typically *of*). Most prepositions don't have exact synonyms, so don't be creative in trying to find them! This is particularly true when deciding on the title for your paper (see 12.3).

However, do check that you have used the preposition correctly, for example we say 'an increase *of* 10%' but 'an increase *in* inflation' (*of* plus a percentage, *in* plus a noun – see 14.11 in *English for Research: Grammar, Usage and Style*).

Synonyms are also essential when you need to paraphrase the work of others or your own work (see 11.5–11.9).

6.6 Don't use technical / sector vocabulary that your readers may not be familiar with

The author of S1 is a computer scientist. She uses a word that a social scientist or psychologist might be familiar with, but not a fellow computer scientist. Can you spot the word?

S1 * People in smart environments do not move randomly – their mobility is affected by (i) the kinds of social-relationships they are involved in, and (ii) their personal activities. Concerning the first aspect, the homophily among humans introduces additional features in the way people (and hence devices) in a mobile social network move and behave.

If your language does not derive from Greek or Latin, then you are unlikely to be familiar with the term *homophily*. Homophily indicates the tendency to bond with people who are similar to us. The author has probably used it as the concept it refers to is the kinds of social-relationships people are involved in, which she has already mentioned in the previous sentence. But if the reader doesn't know the meaning of *homophily* then he/she will not understand that the author is merely using a synonym. The best solution is to replace the 'technical' word with an explanation.

S2 ... and (ii) their personal activities. The tendency of individuals to associate and bond with similar people (i) introduces additional features in the way people ...

Using the technique in S2 also means that you may be able to avoid generic phrases such as *concerning the first aspect*.

6.7 Be as precise as possible

If possible, aim at precision. Instead of saying something happened *in a number of cases*, be more exact: *this happened in 11 cases*. If you think that stating the exact number is not important or you do not have the exact number available, then try to use a concise expression.

SHORT	LONG
about	of the order of
few	few in number
many	a high percentage of
many	a large proportion of
most	vast majority of
never	never at any time
several	a good number of
some / -	a number of

A common mistake by authors is in making assumptions about what the reader will understand. This is because you as the author know your topic extremely well, in fact you may have been working on it for several months, even years. This means that you may use words and expressions which to you are clear, but to the reader may not be. Below are a few examples of words and expressions that could be interpreted in many different ways. In all cases you need to be more specific:

in the short term, in the near future

a relatively short / long duration

[quite a] high / low number of

recently, recent – bear in mind that the reader may be reading your paper several years after its publication

Referees often criticize authors for sentences such as:

- S1. *Usually* the samples were cooled to room temperature.
- S2. It was necessary to study the problem with *attention*.
- S3. In the late 1990s *nearly all newspapers* created a companion website.
- S4. Subjects performed *fairly* well and their results were *substantially* better than their counterparts.

S1: If you use adverbs such as *usually* and *normally* when referring to experiments or results then the reader might want to know what happens or happened in other cases.

S2: What exactly does *attention* mean? It may be useful to provide details regarding the level of attention and what it entailed.

S3: This was the first sentence in an abstract analyzing online newspapers in Italy. It is not clear whether this is a general statement about newspapers in all the world, or just in Italy. This is a classic case of when the author knows what he / she is referring to, but the reader is left in doubt.

S4: Adverbs such as *fairly* and *substantially* mean different things to different people. Other examples of potentially ambiguous adjectives and adverbs are: *adequate, appreciable, appropriate, comparatively, considerable, practically, quite, rather, real, relatively, several, somewhat, suitable, tentative,* and *very*. These adjectives and adverbs do not have a single unequivocal meaning. They can be open to interpretation by the reader. Often they are redundant or need to be made more precise.

6.8 Choose the least generic word

Another way to be more precise is to choose the least abstract / generic word. In S1 and S2 a generic word is followed by specific definition – this type of construction is often an unnecessary repetition.

S1. *This kind of investigation, i.e. the analysis of the AS profiles*, also aims to find sets of nodes which behave similarly and ...

S2. *Climatic conditions (i.e. temperature, rainfall)* were also checked.

Decide whether you can delete the preceding phrase and just use the definition. S3 and S4 are more concise, more precise, and save the reader from reading redundant abstractions.

S3. By analyzing AS profiles we can also find sets of nodes that behave similarly and ...

S4. Temperature and rainfall were also checked.

Obviously, there are occasions where you may want to be deliberately vague (see Sect. 10.5). But if you can, use the most specific word possible so that readers will be able to follow you much better.

6.9   Use punctuation to show how words and concepts are related to each other

Punctuation in English is used exclusively to show how words and concepts are related to each other. This is not true of all languages.

Most languages have a rule that a comma cannot be used before *and*. This was once a rule in English too, before people started to question its utility and simply asked why not?

Here is an example from an email:

S1.   *I will be free the whole of Monday *and* Tuesday *and* Thursday morning unless one of the professors decides to arrange an extra class.

Does this mean that she will be free (a) all Monday and Tuesday, or (b) all Monday and also Tuesday and Thursday mornings? If it is case (a), then the sentence would be better rewritten as S2, and case (b) as S3:

S2.   I will be free the whole of Monday and Tuesday, and (also) Thursday morning.

S3.   I will be free the whole of Monday, and (also) Tuesday and Thursday morning.

If you have lists of items, you need to show how the various items relate to each other.

In some cases semicolons can be useful, as in S4.

S4.   The languages were grouped as follows: Spanish, Italian and Romanian; German and Dutch; and Swedish and Norwegian.

However, S4 would be better written as S5.

S5.   The languages were allocated to three groups: (1) Spanish, Italian and Romanian; (2) German and Dutch; and (3) Swedish and Norwegian.

Hyphens are used in English to show the relationship between words in a sequence, which without a hyphen would be ambiguous. For example, what does S6 mean?

S6.   We have a little used car in the garage.

Does it mean that we don't use the car very often (S7) or that we bought the car second-hand (S8)? Hyphens can be used to make this differentiation clear.

S7.   We have a *little-used* car in the garage.

S8.   We have a little *used-car* in the garage.

6.10   Defining vs non-defining clauses: *that* vs *which / who*

Look at the two sentences below – in which case do I have more than one sister?

S1.   My sister, *who* lives in Paris, is a researcher.

S2.   My sister *that* lives in Paris is a researcher.

In S1 the information contained between the two commas is not essential. S1 tells the reader that I have only one sister and she is a researcher – the fact that she lives in Paris is just additional information. I could simply say: *My sister is a researcher.*

But in S2 I am giving very different information. I am telling you that I have more than one sister, and that the sister that lives in Paris is a researcher. Perhaps my other sister is a doctor and I am using Paris to distinguish between my two sisters.

This difference between *who* and *that* is the same as the difference between *which* and *that*.

In scientific English, *which* and *that* have distinct uses. For example, imagine you are instructed to do the following:

S3.   *Correct the sentences below which contain grammatical mistakes.

Does S3 mean (i) that all the sentences contain grammatical mistakes, or (ii) that you should correct only those sentences that contain mistakes? If all the sentences contain mistakes, S3 should be rewritten as S4. If only some sentences contain mistakes, S3 should be rewritten as S5.

S4.   Correct the sentences *below, which* contain grammatical mistakes.

S5.   Correct the sentences *below that* contain grammatical mistakes.

The rule is that if you are simply adding extra information (S4) then use *which* (things) or *who* (people) preceded by a comma (,). If you are defining the previous noun then use *that*.

Given that not many people are aware of this distinction, it is probably better to rewrite the sentences more explicitly. Thus S4 and S5, become S6 and S7, respectively.

S6.   Correct the sentences *below, all of which* contain grammatical mistakes.

S7.   Correct *only those sentences below that* contain grammatical mistakes.

S1 and S4 are grammatically known as non-defining clauses. In a non-defining relative clause you add extra information. You could remove the clause and the resulting sentence would still make sense. In non-defining clauses *which* (for things) and *who* (for people) are used.

S2 and S5 are examples of defining clauses, also known as restrictive clauses. They give essential information without which the sentence would make no sense. In defining clauses, only *that* can be used.

Here is another ambiguous example:

> S8.   *The table below gives details of the parameters which are not self-explanatory.

The reader does not know if the writer

- has forgotten to put a comma after *parameters* and thus means that none of the parameters are self explanatory

- should have put *that* instead of *which* and thus means that the table only gives details of those parameters that need to be explained

A similar problem arises when the author does not use either *which* or *that*, as in S9. S9 would not be considered correct English by most language experts.

> S9.   *This is followed by a characterization of the states *poorly represented* at atmospheric pressure.

S9 can be disambiguated as in S10 (non-defining) and S11 (defining).

> S10.   This is followed by a characterization of the states, which are poorly represented at atmospheric pressure.
> S11.   This is followed by a characterization of all those states that are poorly represented at atmospheric pressure.

Note: In spoken English, people do not usually make such a distinction and may simply use *which* for things, and *who* for people, irrespective of whether they are using defining or non-defining clauses.

6.11 Clarifying which noun you are referring to: *which, that* and *who*

Which, that and *who* should only refer to the noun that immediately precedes them.

S1. *A group of patients was compiled using this procedure, as proposed by Smith and Jones [2010], *who* had died under surgery.

An initial reading of S1 gives the impression that Smith and Jones died under surgery! This ambiguity arises because the subject (*patients*) has been separated from its verb (*had died*) by a subordinate clause (*as proposed* ...). The solution is to keep the subject and verb as close as possible to each other.

S2. A group of patients *who* had died under surgery was compiled using this procedure, as proposed by Smith and Jones [2010].

Here is a similar example (S3), which is less dramatic and less open to ambiguity but could be rewritten more clearly (S4):

S3. Each scheduling service is characterized by a mandatory set of QoS parameters, as reported in Table 1, *which* describes the guarantees of the applications.

S4. Each scheduling service is characterized by a mandatory *set* of QoS parameters, as reported in *Table 1*. *This set* describes the guarantees of the applications.

In this case, the solution (S4) is to split the sentence in two and repeat the key word (*set*).

6.12 *-ing* form vs *that*

Authors sometimes use the *-ing* form in what is effectively a relative clause (i.e. a clause that begins with *that, which* or *who* – see Sect. 6.10). This usage is acceptable in phrases such as:

S1. Those students *wishing* to participate in the call for papers should contact ...

S2. The professor *giving* the keynote speech at the conference is from Togo.

S1 could be rewritten as *students that / who wish*, and S2 the professor *that / who is giving*. However, there is no possible ambiguity because the *-ing* form comes immediately after the noun it refers to.

However, in S3 it is not clear who has the good level of English: the students or Prof. Rossi.

S3.   *Professor Rossi teaches the students *having* a good level of English.

S4 clarifies that it is the students that have good English. In S5 Prof. Rossi is the subject of both verbs (*teach, have*), so in this case we need to change the structure of the sentence and use *since, because* or something similar (S6).

S4.   Professor Rossi teaches the students *that have* a good level of English.
S5.   Professor Rossi teaches the students *since he has* a good level of English.
S6.   Professor Rossi, *who has* a good level of English, teaches the students.

6.13   - *ing* form vs. subject + verb

In clear unambiguous writing, verbs should be immediately preceded by their subject.

S1.   *If you take your young daughter in the car, don't let her put her head out of the window *while driving*.
S2.   *After consuming* twenty bottles of wine, the conference chair presented the awards to the fifty best PhD students.

In S1 it initially seems that *driving* refers to the young daughter. This is because the person located in the phrase nearest to the word *driving* is the girl not *you*. In S2 it seems that the conference chairperson consumed 20 bottles of wine, whereas presumably it was the students who did the drinking. The sentences should thus be rewritten:

S3.   If you take your young daughter in the car, don't let her put her head out of the window *while you are driving*.
S4.   After the fifty best PhD *students had consumed* twenty bottles of wine, the conference chair presented them with the awards.

In S3 and S4 the -*ing* form has been replaced with an active form of the verb (*are driving, had consumed*) preceded by the subject (*you, students*). If you use an active form you will be forced to use a subject and this will make your writing clearer.

In S5 below, there is an initial ambiguity as the order of words makes it seem that psocoptera read books! (*Psocoptera* are an order of wingless insects that attack paper).

S5.   *We cannot understand how psocoptera survive by reading books alone. Instead we need to …

If we rephrase the sentence by putting the *-ing* form at the beginning, the true meaning is a little clearer:

S6. By reading books alone, we cannot understand how psocoptera survive. Instead we need to ...

However the clearest way is to avoid the *-ing* form completely and replace it with a subject + verb construction:

S7. If we only read books, we cannot understand how psocoptera survive. Instead we need to ...

So, beginning a sentence with the *-ing* form can be dangerous, because the reader doesn't know who or what is carrying out the activity introduced by the *-ing* form.

S8. *By sitting and watching too much television, our muscles become weaker.

In S8, it initially seems that the muscles are watching television, though this is clearly absurd. The solution is to put a subject (*we*) in front of the verb, as in S9.

S9. When we sit and watch too much television, our muscles become weaker.

6.14   Avoiding ambiguity with the – *ing form*: use *by* and *thus*

S1 is ambiguous – why?

S1. *This will improve performance *keeping* clients satisfied.

Does S1 mean: (a) the way to improve performance is if clients are kept satisfied? or (b) as a consequence of improving performance clients will be satisfied?

We can show the true meaning if, before the *–ing* form, we insert *thus* or *by*:

S2. This will improve performance *thus keeping* clients satisfied.
S3. This will improve performance *by keeping* clients satisfied.

S2 means that if performance improves, clients will be satisfied – *thus* means *as a consequence*. In S3 the way to improve performance is through client satisfaction – *by* indicates how something is done.

Often it is a good idea simply to break up the sentence or use *and*. An alternative to S3:

> S4.   This will improve performance *and* clients will (*thus*) be satisfied.

S5 is another ambiguous sentence. It can be disambiguated as in S6 and S7, both of which have the same meaning.

> S5.   *The Euro indirectly raised prices, *causing* inflation.
> S6.   … raised prices. This *consequently / subsequently caused* inflation.
> S7.   … raised prices *and so / thus caused* inflation.

It is best to replace the *–ing* form with *and* when you are simply giving additional information. Thus S9 is clearer than S8.

> S8.   * This section focuses on the reasons for selecting these parameters, trying to explain the background to these choices.
> S9.   This document focuses on the reasons for selecting these parameters, and tries to explain the background to these choices.

Finally, note the difference between these three sentences.

> S10.   To burn CDs you just need some software.
> S11.   Burning CDs now takes only a few seconds.
> S12.   By burning CDs we deprive artists of royalties.

The infinitive (S10) means *If you want to / If your aim is to …*

The *-ing* form with no preceding preposition (S11) refers to the activity of burning CDs, it acts as the subject of the sentence. S12 means *If we burn CDs we will deprive artists of royalties.*

6.15   Uncountable nouns

A countable noun is something you can count – *one apple, two apples*. An uncountable noun is something that, at least in English, you cannot count. You cannot say *an information, these informations* etc. *Information* is considered a mass, and for English speakers it is not easily split into different parts.

Spinach leaves can be clearly separated and counted, but when cooked they become one big mass. You cannot clearly and easily identify cooked spinach as separate parts – so you cannot say *these spinaches taste very good*, but only *this spinach tastes very good*. Similarly, you can count *cars* but not *traffic*, *steps forward* but not *progress*, *comments* but not *feedback*.

These kinds of subtleties do not normally cause problems. But when an uncountable noun is referred to in a later phrase with a plural pronoun (*they, these, those*) or adjective (*many, few*) it can create confusion for readers.

> S1. *Such *feedbacks* are* vital when analyzing the queries. At subsequent stages in the procedure, for instance after steps 3 and 4, *they* are also useful for assessing ...
> S2. *Such *feedbacks* are* vital when analyzing the queries. At subsequent stages in the procedure, for instance after steps 3 and 4, *many of them* are also useful for assessing ...

Note: *feedback* is uncountable, so it has no plural form. S1 and S2 are thus not correct English.

In S1, a native speaker would think that *they* must refer to *queries*, since *queries* is plural. In S2, the reader would be totally confused and would probably be unable to understand what *many of them* refers to. Possible revised versions of S1 and S2 are:

> S3. Such feedback is vital when ... At subsequent stages ... it is also useful for ...
> S4. Such feedback is vital when ... At subsequent stages ... much of it is also useful for ...

Pronouns are in any case a constant source of ambiguity in English, so the best solution is to repeat the noun that the pronoun refers to.

> S5. Such feedback is vital when ... At subsequent stages ... (a lot of) this feedback is also ...

6.16 Definite and indefinite articles

The usage of articles is very complex in English – for full details see Chapters 1–5 in *English for Research: Grammar, Usage and Style*.

In brief, here are the differences in meaning.

S1. *A researcher* spends many days in the lab.
S2. *One researcher* spends many days in the lab.
S3. *Researchers* spend many days in the lab.
S4. *The researcher* spends many days in the lab.
S5. *The researchers* spend many days in the lab.

S1 – a generic researcher, who we have not mentioned before.

S2 – we have already mentioned a group of researchers, now we are focusing on one individual who spends many days in the lab, unlike the others in her group who are rarely in the lab.

S3 – researchers in general, i.e. 'all researchers', so the non use of *the* is correct.

S4 – the researcher has already been mentioned before so that the reader knows which researcher we are talking about.

S5 – same as S4, though this time we are talking about more than one researcher.

If S4 or S5 appeared at the beginning of a new section in a paper, the reader might be confused and would be forced to look back to earlier sections to see if he / she could find a previous reference to the researcher/s. In fact, if you use *the* with a countable noun it implies that you have already mentioned this noun before.

Here is an example of the *a* versus *one* rule:

S6. We made one experiment before the equipment exploded.
S7. We made an experiment before the equipment exploded.

In S6 we imply that we had planned a series of experiments (at least two), but that these were interrupted by the explosion. In S7 no such series is implied. The two sentences thus have very different meanings.

So where is the possible ambiguity?

If you have done some tests and you want to say what these tests have shown then you should not say:

S8.   Tests have shown that cell phones can cause cancer.

S8 indicates that some tests, not carried out by the author, have shown that cell phones can cause cancer. It would be better to write 'the tests', thus referring the reader back to the tests described earlier in the paragraph / section. Even better would be 'our tests'.

Similarly, if you only carried out one test for your research, you should not write:

S9.   One test revealed that cell phones can cause cancer.

S9 implies that you carried out several tests, and the reader would probably understand that one test revealed cancer but another one (or two or three etc) did not.

6.17   Referring backwards: the dangers of *the former, the latter*

When you refer back to something you mentioned before, it is often not immediately clear what *the former* and *the latter* refer to.

S1.   *Africa has a greater population than the combined populations of Russia, Canada and the United States. In *the latter*, the population is only ...

In S1 does *the latter* refer just to the US alone, or to the US and Canada? The simplest and clearest solution is to replace *the latter* with the exact word or words it refers to. This gives:

S2.   Africa has a greater population than the combined populations of Russia, Canada and the United States. In the USA the population is only ...

S3.   Africa has a greater population than the combined populations of Russia, Canada and the United States. In Canada and the USA, the population is only ...

It is not a problem to repeat words if the result is that the reader will be clear about what you want to say. This is particularly true if the word that *the former / the latter* refers to is some distance away. For example:

S4.   *Smith was the first to introduce the concept of readability in websites. In his seminal paper, written in 1991, he realized that the way we read pages on the web is totally different from the way we read a printed document. Five years later, Jones studied the differences between the way that people of different languages, whose scripts are written left right (e.g. English), right left (e.g. Arabic) and top down (e.g. Japanese), read texts on the web. The former author then wrote another paper ...

By saying *the former author* you are forcing the reader to go back four or five lines in order to remember which author you are talking about. By simply saying *Smith then wrote* you save the reader time and frustration.

Clearly there are some occasions when using *the former* and *the latter* is not ambiguous:

> S5. Water organisms can be contaminated directly or indirectly. The former occurs by contact or ingestion of the substance dissolved in water, whereas the latter happens when the contaminant is accumulated in the food chain.

In S5 there is no ambiguity. But S5 would be better written as S6 and would have more impact:

> S6. Water organisms can be contaminated directly or indirectly. Direct contamination occurs by contact or ingestion of the substance dissolved in water, whereas indirect contamination happens when the contaminant is accumulated in the food chain.

Specific words (*contamination*) are more readily absorbed and memorable than generic words (*the former*).

The problem with ambiguity in back-referencing is not just with *the former* and *the latter*. What does *Concerning this last topic* refer to in S7?

> S7. *In recent years, these skills have been applied to the study of heavy metal accumulation and toxicity in mammalian cells and the modulation of neurotransmitter-gated ion channels by metal ions in primary neuronal cultures and in recombinant receptors expressed in heterologous systems. Concerning this last topic, there has been much interest in ...

The problem is that the use of *and* three times makes it initially hard for the reader to divide up the sentence into different topics. Maybe *this last topic refers* exclusively to *recombinant receptors*. However, it might refer to *modulation of neurotransmitter-gated ion channels* and *recombinant receptors*. By simply repeating the topic, as in S8, the reader can immediately understand what the writer is referring to.

> S8. ... and in recombinant receptors expressed in heterologous systems. With regard to such recombinant receptors, there has been much interest in ...

6.18 Referring backwards and forwards: the dangers of *above, below, previously, earlier, later*

When making reference to things that are mentioned earlier or later in your documents do not give readers generic locations.

> S1. * As mentioned *above / before / earlier / previously*, these values are important when …
>
> S2. * These points are dealt with in detail *below / later* …

If readers are interested in these things, then they need an exact location, for example: *see Sect. 1.1 / see the above paragraph / see points 4–5 below.*

The term *previously* is often ambiguous because the reader may be not sure if you mean:

- at some point earlier in this paper

- in another of your papers

- in someone else's paper

It is acceptable to say *as mentioned above* or *as mentioned before* when you don't want the reader to go back to what you said before, but simply to reassure them that you are aware that you are saying the same thing again. However, ask yourself if the reader really does need such reassurance.

6.19 Use of *respectively* to disambiguate

Respectively is a very useful word for clarifying how items are related to each other. In S1, a basic knowledge of geography makes it clear that London is associated with England, and Paris with France.

> S1. London and Paris are the capitals of England and France.

But such connections are not always so obvious, as in S2:

> S2. *… where X is the function for Y, and f1 and f2 are the constant functions for P and Q.

Are f1 and f2 constant functions for both P and Q? If so:

> S3. … and f1 and f2 are the constant functions for *both* P and Q.

Or is f1 for P and f2 for Q? If so, use *respectively*:

> S4. … and f1 and f2 are the constant functions for P and Q, *respectively*.

Most style books recommend placing *respectively* at the end of the phrase. It is best to put a comma before *respectively*.

6.20 Distinguishing between *both … and,* and *either … or*

Both … and is inclusive. *either … or* is exclusive.

> S1. We studied both English and Spanish.
> S2. You can study either English or Spanish.

S1 means that we studied English and we studied Spanish.

S2 means that you can only study one language. You cannot study English and Spanish. You can study English or you can study Spanish.

> S3. You cannot study both Russian and Korean.
> S4. You cannot study either Russian or Korean.

S3 means that you have to choose between Russian and Korean. You can only study one of the two languages.

S4 means that these two languages are not offered. Neither of them can be studied.

The position of *both* can change the meaning. Note the difference between these two sentences:

> S5. This is true both for the students and the professors.
> S6. This is true for both the students and the professors.

In S5 there are several students (and professors) involved, in S6 there are only two students and an undefined number of professors.

In S7 just two parks are being referred to, whereas in S8 there is an unknown number of parks.

> S7. We had fun in both the parks we visited and also the museums.
> S8. We had fun both in the parks and the museums.

6.21 Talking about similarities: *as, like, unlike*

Be careful when you are comparing your methods and results with those of another author. In S1 below it is not 100% clear whether you are or are not in agreement with Walker's suggestion.

S1. We also demonstrated that x does not equal y as suggested by Walker (2016).

Does S1 mean that Walker suggested that x is equal to y and is thus in contrast to what you are saying? If so, S1 should be written as S2 or S3.

S2. Unlike what was suggested by Walker (2016), we demonstrated that x does not equal y.

S3. Our findings do not concur with Walker (2016). In fact, we have clearly demonstrated that x does not equal y.

Or does S1 mean that he, like you, found that x does not equal y (if so rewrite as S4).

S4. In agreement with Walker (2016), we demonstrated that x does not equal y.

Ambiguity affects readability. If you force your reader to constantly interpret what you are writing, the reader will soon want to stop reading.

6.22 Differentiating between *from* and *by*

These two words have different meanings: *from* (origin) and *by* (agent).

S1. This paper was drafted *by* several different authors *from* three different universities.

S2. We received an email *from* Professor Southern written *by* her secretary.

In S1 and S2 if you used by instead of from, or vice versa, this would not lead to ambiguity.

However in S3 the use of *from* or *by* helps us to understand what *smartcon* is. In this case *created from* would mean that *smartcon* is a material, *created by* that *smartcon* is the creator – these are two very different meanings.

S3. This product was created *from / by* smartcon.

6.23   Be careful with Latin words

The problem with many Latin expressions is that you may know what they mean, but your reader may not. In the examples below *i.e.* (used for defining) and *e.g.* (for giving examples) are not interchangeable.

S1.   Great Britain, *i.e.* England, Scotland and Wales, is the ninth biggest island in the world and the third most populated.

S2.   Some EU members, *e.g.* Spain, Italy and France, are not in agreement with this policy.

In S1 *i.e.* is used to define Great Britain, which contains <u>only</u> those three countries.

In S2 *e.g.* means that Spain, Italy and France are just some examples of countries in European Union that do not agree with the policy – but the implication is that there are other countries involved as well.

If you are not short of space then it is generally better to use alternative versions. Another way to say *i.e.* is *that is to say*. Other ways to say *e.g.* are: *for example, such as*, and *for instance*.

Unless they are commonly used in your chosen journal, try to avoid other Latin expressions such as *a priori, a posteriori, ex ante, in itinere, ex-post, ceteris paribus* and others. Some readers, including native English speakers, may not know what they mean. Thus S3 would be better rewritten as S4:

S3.   This argument holds, a fortiori, in mergers, where the reduction of the number of firms in the market is an explicit objective.

S4.   This argument holds for similar but even more convincing reasons in mergers, where the reduction of the number of firms in the market is an explicit objective.

If you use Latin expressions, check with your journal whether they should be in italics or not.

6.24 False friends

False friends are words from two different languages that look very similar but have different meanings. If you speak a European language, then there is a good chance that there are several false friends between your language and English. The most common of these is *actually*, which in English means *in reality*, but its false friend in other languages means *currently / at the moment*.

Another false friend, which frequently appears in research, is to *control* which does <u>not</u> mean *verify*. Here is the difference:

S1. A thermostat is used to *control* the temperature. [i.e. adjust, act on]

S2. We *checked* the patient's temperature with a thermometer. [i.e. verify without any intervention]

In scientific papers, only a limited number of false friends tend to cause problems:

actual (real) vs *effective* (successful in producing desired effect); *alternately* (first one, then the other) vs *alternatively* (another option); *coherent* (intelligible) *consistent* (not contradictory, always acting in same way over a period of time); *comprehensive* (including everything) vs *understanding* (sympathetic awareness); *eventually* (at the end of a series of difficulties) vs *if necessary / if any*; *occur* (happen) vs *need*; *sensible* (reasonable) vs *sensitive* (quick to respond to slight changes)

6.25 Be careful of typos

What impression would a referee have if he/she read the following?

S1. There are three solutions to *asses*.

S2. A solution of lead was added to the mixture. Note: this *addiction* is likely to cause health problems.

S3. Acknowledgements: We would like to offer our *tanks* to the following people:

The author meant to write *assess* (asses = donkeys), *addition* (addiction = pathological dependence), and *thanks* (tanks = armored vehicles).

No spell checking system currently available is likely to spot such mistakes.

See 28.4 in *English for Research: Grammar, Usage and Style* for a list of typical typos of this kind.

6.26   Summary

Your writing will be much clearer if you take into account the following:

➤ *which* is used for adding information about the preceding noun, *that* defines the preceding noun

➤ *which, that* and *who* should only refer to the noun immediately preceding them

➤ Make sure it is clear what the subject of the *–ing* form is.

➤ clarify whether something is a consequence of doing something or a means to do something by using *thus* (consequence) and *by* (means) before the – *ing* form

➤ use the definite article (*the*) before a noun only if you refer to a specific example of that noun. If you are giving a generic idea, do not use the article

➤ learn the most frequent uncountable nouns and false friends in your field

➤ be very careful when you use pronouns (*this, that, them, it* etc.) – make sure it is clear what they refer to and don't be afraid of repeating the same word many times (if this will improve clarity)

➤ avoid using *the former … the latter*, simply repeat the related noun

➤ if necessary, specify exact locations when using *above* and *below*

➤ use *respectively* when it is not 100% clear how items are related to each other

➤ be careful of punctuation with *which* and *and* – punctuation must help the reader understand the relationships between the various parts of the sentence

➤ don't confuse *both … and* (inclusive) with *either … or* (exclusive); *i.e.* (definitions) and *e.g.* (examples), by (agent) and *from* (origin), and be careful when you use *as* to mean 'in a similar way'

➤ never use synonyms for key words, only for generic verbs and adjectives

➤ use the most precise word possible

There are other serious cases of ambiguity. These are dealt with in separate chapters of this book.

1. strings of nouns and adjectives (Sect. 2.15)
2. misusage of tenses – using the present instead of the past, and vice versa, can create considerable confusion, particularly in the Introduction and Discussion sections
3. poor or incorrect word order (Sect. 2.16).
4. when it is not clear if you are referring to your own work or other people's work (Sects. 7.3, 7.4, 7.7, and 7.8)

Chapter 7

Clarifying Who Did What

Factoids

❖ Cocktails: Not the Americans – their first cocktail, the *Sazerac*, was invented by a Frenchman in New Orleans in 1838. The British were the first to mix drinks – in India in around 1750.

❖ Electricity: Not Thomas Edison. The type of electricity we use today was proposed by Tesla, though Edison was the first to produce a long-lasting electric lightbulb.

❖ Guillotine: Proposed (but not invented) by Joseph-Ignace Guillotin as a less painful method of execution, but a similar apparatus had been around since the 14th century.

❖ Planes and helicopters: not the Wright brothers, but Leonardo Da Vinci.

❖ Printing: Not Johannes Gutenberg – the ancient Chinese were the first to print on block.

❖ Radio: Not Guglielmo Marconi. Tesla discovered a number of years before Marconi that radio signals could be transmitted, but never filed the patent on his discovery (Marconi patented his 'wireless telegraph').

❖ Sparkling wine: not Dom Pérignon (1638-1715), but fellow Benedictine monks in the Abbey of Saint-Hilaire, near Carcassonne, in 1531.

❖ The unconscious mind: Not Sigmund Freud (1836-1939), though he was responsible for making it popular. It was 'invented' by early psychology experimenters and thinkers, including the American, Charles Sanders Peirce (1839-1914).

© Springer International Publishing Switzerland 2016
A. Wallwork, *English for Writing Research Papers*,
English for Academic Research, DOI 10.1007/978-3-319-26094-5_7

7.1   What's the buzz?

Look at this extract from a fictitious paper entitled: *Do we talk more to people who are far from us than to those people who are next to us? How mobile phones have changed the way we communicate*, written by Joe Bloggs.

Imagine that your eye fell on this paragraph from the Results section and that this was the first paragraph in the paper that you had read so far.

> Subjects sitting in train compartments on a 60-minute journey were found to spend an average of 55 minutes either talking on their cell phone or sending messages, watching videos etc. Only 2% of passengers talked to other people, in such cases merely to say 'sorry' or 'is this seat taken'? This contrasts with research conducted in 1989 on the same train journey. Mobile phones were very rare at the time, and the study found that around 58% of passengers spoke to each other in a meaningful way for 10 minutes or more, with the prevalence being woman to woman, or man to woman. Conversations between two men were also found to be rare on the line between Copenhagen and Malmö.

Answer these questions:

1. Who found the data regarding the 55 minutes talking? a) Bloggs b) someone else
2. Who conducted the 1989 research? a) Bloggs b) someone else
3. Who conducted the Copenhagen / Malmö study? a) Bloggs b) the same author who conducted the 1989 research, in fact it was part of the same study c) another author

How sure are you of your answers?

How could the paragraph be rewritten so that the reader could answer three questions with 100% confidence?

****

In various sections of your paper, you need to compare your methodology or results with what has already been established in the literature. You must make it 100% clear to the reader whose methodology or results you are talking about.

If you don't, you will make it difficult for the referee to:

- identify your contribution

- decide how useful the contribution is

- make a decision as to whether this contribution is worth recommending for publication

For example, if you say *It was found that X = 1*, the referee needs to know whether you found that X = 1, or whether another author made this finding.

This chapter shows you how to make such distinctions.

7.2 Check your journal's style – first person or passive

Check your journal's 'guidelines to authors' to see whether you are permitted to use *we*. If you can use 'we' then it is relatively easy for you to distinguish between your work and others. Some journals, particularly those regarding Physics, tend to opt for an impersonal form in the belief that science is independent of the person writing about it. This entails adopting a lower profile and using the passive form.

If your journal insists on the passive form, you need to be extremely careful.

The most important point to remember is that YOU know which is your work and which is someone else's. But the readers do not! You must make it clear for THEM.

7.3 How to form the passive and when to use it

Active: We *performed* two tests. Blake et al. *carried out* one replication.

Passive (*is / was / will be* etc. + past participle): Two tests *were performed* (by us). One replication *was carried* out by Blake.

The passive is particularly useful when you describe a process, for example in the Methods (16.3). This is because it puts the equipment, chemicals, procedures etc. that you used in the first position in the phrase. In review papers, and in other sections of research papers, for example the Introduction and the Discussion, you may want to use the passive to describe what other authors have done, or what is already established knowledge in your domain. In such cases you can say:

S1. Bilingual children *have been demonstrated / are believed* to adapt better to new situations than monolingual children.

S2. *It has been demonstrated / It is believed* that bilingual children adapt...

The advantage of S1 over S2 is that the subject of the sentence (*bilingual children*) is at the head of the phrase, whereas it is delayed in S2.

Note that in formal English writing you cannot use *someone, one* or *people* to refer either to a particular person or a generic person. This means that you cannot replace S1 and S2 with S3 or S4:

S3 *Someone/One has demonstrated that...

S4 *People believe that...

7.4 Use the active form when the passive might be ambiguous

No research has shown that using the passive form leads to clearer sentences for the reader. Despite this, some conservative editors insist that an impersonal form is inherently more scientific and logical – such editors claim that the facts should be able to speak for themselves. Yet no studies, as far as I know, have proved that an impersonal form aids reader comprehension, and in any case the facts will "speak" and the results will be valid (or invalid) whether in an active or passive form. Other editors claim that the passive encourages precision, though I don't believe this has ever been scientifically demonstrated. Others again say it encourages probity, i.e. the quality of having strong moral principles; honesty and decency – but how can this possibly be proved?

However, lot of research has shown that the passive form is heavier than the active (see reference to John Kirkman in 4.1), and most importantly can lead to ambiguity,.

Look at S1 and S2 below, is it clear who is the subject of the verbs in italics?

S1. [In the Conclusions of a paper] This is a limitation of our data assimilation system, which *should be changed* in the near future.

S2. The same lack of regard for others was present amongst subjects who used their mobile phone while driving their car, in agreement with the higher values of selfish behavior *observed* in cigarette smokers [17].

In S1 is the author suggesting that other researchers in the community should make these changes, or is the author going to do it herself?

In S2 who made the observation, the author of the paper or the author of reference 17?

If the author is the subject of the verbs, then S1 and S2 could be rewritten, using the active form, as follows:

S3. This is a limitation of our data assimilation system, which *we plan* to change in the near future.

S4. The same lack of regard for others was present amongst subjects who used their mobile phone while driving their car, in agreement with the higher values of selfish behavior that *we observed* in cigarette smokers and which has also been found by other authors [17].

If the author is <u>not</u> the subject of the verbs, then S1 and S2 could be rewritten as follows:

S5. This is a limitation of our data assimilation system, and *we invite others in the community to suggest possible remedies.*

S6. The same lack of regard for others was present amongst subjects who used their mobile phone while driving their car, in agreement with the higher values of selfish behavior that *have been found by other authors* [17].

Often a passive form can be disambiguated by using an adverb of frequency.

In S7 it is not clear who has made the 'consideration'. S8 resolves this problem by adding an adverb. S9 deletes 'considered' and leaves 'is', thus indicating that this is general practice and not something discovered or proposed by the author.

S7. Using the x methodology *is considered* the same as using the y methodology.

S8. Using the x methodology is *generally / usually / often* considered the same as using the y methodology.

S9. Using the x methodology *is* the same as using the y methodology.

The following verbs when used in the passive are often ambiguous: *acknowledge, conceive, consider, describe, design, develop, find, observe, propose, suggest.*

Obviously, there are occasions when the passive form contains no ambiguity and is perfectly acceptable. For example:

S10. It is well known that smoking causes cancer.

S11. Mobile phone usage during meetings is often criticized.

In S10, this fact is known by everyone. In S11, it is clear that the criticism comes from other attendees at the meeting.

For more on this critical point see 18.2 and 18.6 in this book, and 10.3 and 10.4 in *English for Research: Grammar, Usage and Style.*

7.5 Consider starting a new paragraph to distinguish between your work and the literature

Throughout the Discussion, and sometimes during your Introduction, you will need to switch from talking about your work to discussing other authors' work. Each time you begin a new area of comparison, begin a new paragraph. This makes it much easier for the reader to follow.

Also consider using one paragraph to describe other authors' work and a new paragraph to describe your own. Constantly switching within the same paragraph from your work to other authors' can be quite hard for readers to follow.

The switch from one topic (your work) to another topic (the literature) is much clearer if it is also visual, i.e. if there is a paragraph break.

7.6 Ensure you use the right tenses to differentiate your work from others, particularly when your journal prohibits the use of *we*

For some good examples of how to effectively differentiate your work from others, see 18.6. This section outlines the dangers of not making a clear differentiation.

The following extract is the first paragraph of a Discussion (though something very similar might also be found in an Introduction). It is poorly written because often it is difficult to understand if the verb refers to something Wordsworth (a fictitious author) did or found, or to something another author did or found.

ORIGINAL VERSION: Bilingual children *(1) were found* to show a greater adaptability to new situations (e.g. change of school, change of diet) and demonstrated a greater ease in communicating confidently with adults [Blake, 1995]. As a result of an extensive search for bilingual children in ten European countries, 149 children *(2) were identified* (Table 1). One hundred and twenty two children with parents of different nationalities *(3) were assigned* to a group (hereafter Group A). It *(4) has been found* that those children with parents of the same nationality but who live in a foreign country (for example, a child with English parents living in Italy) *(5) have* a greater level of adaptability than those children with parents of different nationalities living in the native country of one of the parents. Similar adaptability levels *(6) have been found* in trilingual children of parents of different nationalities living in a third country [Coleridge, 2011], for example the child of a Dutch/Russian couple living in France. However, in many such cases *(7) it was found* that one of the three languages was not as strong as the other two (Table 2).

Here is an analysis of my thoughts as I read the above extract.

1. The use of the past tense (*were found*) seems to indicate that this is Wordsworth's finding. But when I get to the end of the sentence I see the reference, so I now realize that this is Blake's finding.

2. Reading the first part of this sentence I am not sure if Wordsworth is adding more information about Blake's findings or if he is now going to talk about his own results. When I reach the end I see a reference to a Table, so I now assume that Wordsworth made the identification.

3. There does not seem to be any ambiguity here. Wordsworth is talking about what he did.

4+5. The change in tense from the past simple (*were assigned* in 3) to the present perfect (*has been found* in 4) followed by the present tense (*have* in 5) suggests that I am reading about another author's findings. But in reality, I suspect that these are Wordsworth's findings.

- Because Wordsworth has misused the present perfect in 4, I think that he may have misused it again in 6, so my initial thought is that Wordsworth is talking about his own findings. But when I reach the end of the sentence I have to revise my thoughts because I now realize that these are Coleridge's findings.

- I am now completely confused. Initially, I have no idea if *it was found* refers to Wordsworth or to Coleridge. When I see the reference to Table 2, I assume that these are Wordsworth's findings, though it might be possible that Table 2 refers to Coleridge's findings.

Below is a clearer version. The changes from the OV are underlined.

REVISED VERSION: Bilingual children *show* (*1*) a greater adaptability to new situations (e.g. change of school, change of diet) and *demonstrate* a greater ease in communicating confidently with adults [Blake, 1995]. *Blake investigated children from the US and Canada. As mentioned previously, the focus of our study was Europe and* a result of an extensive search for bilingual children in ten European countries, 149 children *were identified (2)* (Table 1). One hundred and twenty two children with parents of different nationalities *were assigned (3)* to a group (hereafter Group A). It *was found (4)* that those children with parents of the same nationality but who lived in a foreign country (for example, a child with English parents living in Italy) *had (5)* a greater level of adaptability than those children with parents of different nationalities living in the native country of one of the parents. Similar adaptability levels *have been found (6)* in trilingual children of parents of different nationalities living in a third country [Coleridge, 2011], for example the child of a Dutch/Russian couple living in France. However, in many such cases *our findings revealed (7)* that one of the three languages was not as strong as the other two (Table 2).

The main difference with the original version, is that now the reader knows immediately from the beginning of the sentence whether these are Wordsworth's or another author's findings. In the original version, the reader is forced to wait till the end of the sentence before discovering whose findings are being discussed. Also, in the original version readers constantly have to make readjustments in their understanding as they move from sentence to sentence.

Now, let's analyze in detail the differences between the two versions.

- The use of the present tense (*show*) indicates to the reader that this is general knowledge, i.e. this is Blake's finding and not Wordsworth's. An alternative here would be to write *Blake [1995] showed that...* However, this is an extract from a beginning of a section and it would be unusual to begin with an author rather than the main topic of the section (bilingualism). To make doubly clear that this is not his own finding, Wordsworth could have begun: *It is well known that bilingual children.* However this would delay the key word (*bilingual*).

- One problem in the OV was that there was no real connection between the first and second sentences, and this added to the confusion about whose work was being discussed. In the revised version a new sentence has been added to explain the connection and to introduce Wordsworth's work. Some information here was also contained in Wordsworth's Methods section (i.e.

that the focus is on Europe not North America), but readers do not necessarily read all parts of the paper. If the main contribution of the paper is in the findings rather than how the tests were set up, then the readers might well skip the Methodology and go straight to the Results and Discussion. By adding a few extra sentences to the Discussion, you can help readers orient themselves better.

(2+3) Because of the addition of the extra sentence, it is clear that *were identified* and *were assigned* are Wordsworth's findings.

(4) In the previous two sentences, Wordsworth has been talking about what he did, so the reader can assume that *It was found* refers to Wordsworth's work.

(5) The use of the PAST SIMPLE (*had*) rather than the PRESENT SIMPLE (*have*) makes it clearer for the reader that these are Wordsworth's findings. The general convention (but not rule) of tense usage in Results and Discussions sections is that you use the PRESENT SIMPLE, PRESENT PERFECT OR PAST SIMPLE to refer to other authors but only the PAST SIMPLE to refer to your work. The PRESENT PERFECT should not be used to refer to work that you have carried out.

(6) The PRESENT PERFECT is fine here because Wordsworth is referring to Coleridge's work. Wordsworth could also have used the PAST SIMPLE (*were found*).

(7) By using *our*, Wordsworth makes it clear that he has returned to talking about his own findings.

The OV highlights that:

- using figures, tables and references does not necessarily help the reader to understand whose work you are talking about. The reader still has to make an effort

- mistakes and inconsistency in tense usage can completely confuse the reader. If such mistakes are made frequently it could become quite irritating for the referee or reader

The RV demonstrates that

- you can still keep your journal happy by not using *we* – for some reason they raise less objections if you use *our*!

- each sentence should be a logical progression from the previous one. If you mention someone else's work and then your work in consecutive sentences, the connection between the two must be clear to the reader. It is not enough just to use two different tenses

7.7 For journals that allow personal forms, use *we* to distinguish yourself from other authors

The simplest way to make a distinction between your results and other authors' is to use *we* – provided that your journal allows you to do this. Using *we* would make Wordsworth's Discussion (see 7.6) much clearer for the reader.

> Blake investigated children from the US and Canada, *whereas we studied* children in Europe. *We conducted* an extensive search for bilingual children in ten European countries and identified 149 children (Table 1). One hundred and twenty two children with parents of different nationalities *were assigned* to a group (hereafter Group A). *We found* that those children with parents of the same...

The above revision highlights how making contrasts between what you did and what others did is much simpler when you use *we*. However, you don't want to begin each sentence with *we*, as this would be monotonous for your readers. So you can use a mixture of active (*we found*) and passive (*it was found*).

Only use the passive to describe your work if you have clearly established that now you are talking about your work. You can do this by using *we* or *in our study* at the beginning of a paragraph – this alerts the reader that you are going to discuss your work, so even if you then use the passive the reader still knows that it is your work. If you then introduce someone else's work, make sure that the next time you talk about your own work again you begin the sentence with *we* or *in our study*.

7.8 When *we* is acceptable, even when you are not distinguishing yourself from other authors

When you describe your methodology or a procedure that you have followed, it is perfectly acceptable to use *we* or the passive, or a mixture of the two. This is illustrated in the example below.

> We selected the candidates on the basis of an initial test in which they were asked to do a short simultaneous translation. The candidates were then divided into two groups: bilinguals and trilinguals. Candidates then underwent a second test ... We then used the results of these tests to further divide the candidates into four subgroups.

The extract above could be rewritten all in the passive. However, the advantage of beginning the description of the procedure using *we* is that it makes it clear to the reader that unless stated, otherwise the rest of the paragraph refers to what you did rather than another author.

The extract highlights that using a mixture of *we* and passive enables you to choose the focus of your phrase. *The candidates were divided* puts the focus on the candidates, whereas *We then used the results* focuses on what we did (i.e. our role is being emphasized). Mixing *we* and the passive also creates variety for the reader. Note also that the active is also sometimes used (*Candidates then underwent a second test*), thus highlighting that in some cases it is still possible to write in an impersonal way using active forms.

7.9   Make good use of references

The following extract is another example from Wordsworth's paper (see 7.6) where the reader has little or no idea which author made which finding. The principal problem in the OV is not connected with problems of tense usage, but of lack of references to the literature and the failure to use *we / our*.

ORIGINAL VERSION (OV)

Measurements (1) *were made* of the speed with which bilingual adults performed simultaneous translations of politicians' speeches because politicians tend to use formal language [Anderson and Wordsworth, 2008]. (2) *Similar tests* with Nobel prize winners' acceptance speeches gave similar values of speed. This finding strongly suggests that formal language represents an easier element for translation than informal language. The performance of teenagers (3) *in analogous situations* also confirms the above finding. Considering that informal language, in particular slang, (4) *intensifies* the stress levels of subjects undertaking simultaneous translation (5) *the lack of changes in stress levels* of the bilingual adults with respect to bilingual teenagers when simultaneously translating extracts from a teenage soap opera, would seem to indicate that experience plays an important role. Consequently, stress levels in bilingual subjects *tend* (6) to decrease with age.

REVISED VERSION (RV)

In a previous paper [Anderson and Wordsworth, 2008] we made measurements of the speed with which bilingual adults performed simultaneous translations of politicians' speeches. We chose politicians because *it is well known that* they tend to use formal language. *In the same study [Anderson and Wordsworth, 2008] we* conducted similar tests with Nobel prize winners' acceptance speeches, which gave similar values of speed. *These two findings* strongly suggest that formal language represents an easier element for translation than informal language. The performance of teenagers in analogous situations also confirms the above finding [*Williams*, 2009]. *Williams* found that informal language, in particular slang, intensifies the stress levels of subjects undertaking simultaneous translation.

Therefore the lack of changes *that we found in our present research* in the stress levels of bilingual adults with respect to bilingual teenagers when simultaneously translating extracts from a teenage soap opera, would seem to indicate that experience plays an important role. *As a consequence of our latest findings, we conclude* that stress levels in bilingual subjects tend to decrease with age.

The OV is extremely confusing, even though the use of the English language is perfect.

(1) *were made* indicates that this is Wordsworth's work, but when the reader reaches the end of the sentence he/she sees a reference to another paper. Does this reference just refer to the second part of the sentence (beginning *because politicians*) or does it refer to the *measurements*, or both? The reader cannot be sure. Moreover, authors who quote from their own previous work, as Wordsworth does here, should alert the reader that it is their work and not someone else's. The problem is that readers may not remember the name of the author of the paper they are reading, so even if they see Wordsworth in the reference they may not realize that he is the author of the current paper.

(2) *similar tests* by who? (Wordsworth or someone else?) and when? (in Wordsworth's 2008 paper or his current paper?)

(3–5) Again, the reader has no idea who conducted the tests and when, or whether they refer to the current research or Wordsworth's previous research.

(6) Who is making this conclusion? Is it Wordsworth based on his research in this paper? Or is it a general conclusion made by other authors and already reported in the literature?

As usual, the problem is due to the fact that Wordsworth knows who did what, and he assumes that the reader also knows this vital information.

The RV clarifies *who* did *what* and *when*. It also divides the OV into two paragraphs: one describing previous work, and the other describing the current work. The reader is carefully guided through various studies before reaching Wordsworth's conclusions for his present paper.

This results in an increase in the number of words you will need to use – but clarity is more important than conciseness.

I cannot overstress how important it is for you to make such differentiations between your work and that of others. Lack of such a differentiation is one of the most common and serious mistakes made in research papers. It is imperative that you check through every sentence in which you report a finding, and make it 100% clear to the reader who is responsible for the finding.

7.10 Ensure that readers understand what you mean when you write *the authors*

Another problem arises when in consecutive sentences you describe your results in relation to the results of two or more authors. In S1, it is not clear who *these authors* refers to.

S1. *Our results agree with those on bilingual teenagers in Scandinavian countries by Magnusson et al. (2011), and those from the Middle East by Hussein et al. (2009), who used middle school and high school pupils; *these authors* ruled out the existence of...

These authors could refer to both Magnusson's group and Hussein's group, or just one or the other. If there is a possibility of ambiguity it is always best to specify the author again. In any case, S1 is very long and would be better written as S2.

S2. Our results agree with those obtained on bilingual children in Scandinavian countries by Magnusson et al. (2011). They also agree with studies in the Middle East by Hussein et al. (2009), who used middle school and high school pupils. Hussein et al. ruled out the existence of...

7.11 What to do if your paper is subject to a 'blind' review

Before you submit your paper, find out if the paper will be subjected to a blind review or not. A blind review is when the referees do not know the author of the paper that they are reading. This means that the editor will delete your names and institutes from the top of the manuscript. The idea is to enable referees to be totally subjective in their recommendations.

Consequently, you should avoid giving any clues as to who you are.

So if your name is John Doe, in your draft version you should <u>not</u> write a sentence such as:

S1. In a previous paper (Doe et al, 2017) we demonstrated that ...

S1 would make it clear to the referees that you are John Doe and thus defeat the objective of a blind review. Instead you could write:

S2. Doe et al (2017) demonstrated that ...

However, when the paper has been accepted for publication, you should change all such sentences to the personal form (S1) so that you enable the reader to understand that when you write *Doe et al* you are in fact referring to your own work.

7.12 Summary

➢ Follow the journal's instructions regarding whether you can use *we / I* or if you have to use the passive at all times.

➢ You may have the impression that the passive form is considered to be more elegant in scientific papers. Whether this impression is true or not, be aware that the passive inevitably creates problems for your readers because it may be difficult for them to know immediately and with certainty whether you or another author made a particular finding.

➢ Do not rely on a reference to a figure or a table, or a reference to the bibliography to distinguish your new data from those in the literature. Make sure the reference clearly indicates whether it is another author's work and not a previous paper by you.

➢ Be aware that if you make mistakes in the usage of tenses when you are comparing your work with other authors' work, you could really confuse your readers. Make sure you consistently use the correct tenses and remember that in English there is a real difference between the simple past (finished actions with time indication) and the present perfect (past to present actions, finished actions with no time indication)

➢ Avoid using *we* when it is not really necessary, i.e. to explain your train of thought.

➢ Help readers to distinguish between your work and others by using a series of short paragraphs, rather than one long paragraph.

➢ If you mention another author's paper, make sure that the reader understands why you are mentioning that paper and how it relates to your own work.

➢ Check in advance whether your paper will be subject to a 'blind review'.

Chapter 8

Highlighting Your Findings

Factoids

❖ Amp – André Marie Ampère: French mathematician and physicist. Demonstrated for the first time that a magnetic field is created when two parallel wires are charged with electricity.

❖ Braille – Louis Braille: Born in France, devised system of raised type when he was a teacher of the blind. At 20, he published his first book in Braille. He died aged 43.

❖ Diesel engine – Rudolf Diesel. This French-born German engineer is credited with inventing the diesel engine, which he described in a treatise in 1886.

❖ Galvanize – Luigi Galvani: Italian philosopher and physicist who, according to the legend, inadvertently electrocuted a dead frog and saw its muscles twitch. *Galvanize* originally meant to cause something to jolt into action, as if shocked by electricity.

❖ Jacuzzi – The seven Jacuzzi brothers founded Jacuzzi in 1915. Motivated by a family member's pain from arthritis, they invented a hydrotherapy pump for the bath. The pump was then manufactured, and sold to hospitals and schools.

❖ Morse code – Samuel Morse: American artist, developed code for use on the new electric telegraph in 1838.

❖ Petri dish – Julius Richard Petri: German bacteriologist, who in 1878 invented a transparent dish used for the culture of microorganisms – the Petri dish.

❖ Pilates – Joseph Pilates: German-born physical fitness specialist. In around 1920, he developed a system of exercises using a special apparatus after studying both Eastern and Western forms of exercise.

© Springer International Publishing Switzerland 2016
A. Wallwork, *English for Writing Research Papers*,
English for Academic Research, DOI 10.1007/978-3-319-26094-5_8

8.1 What's the buzz?

1) Are you guilty of the faults identified by these two referees?

Given that the focus of this paper is on an 'innovative methodology', the author needs to make more effort to clarify what makes his / her approach special. I truly believe that the author is making a useful contribution but I reached that conclusion only by reading between the lines.

I have the strong feeling that the authors have overstated the achievements and the significance of their project, and thus may be guilty of bias. I recommend that they check all their data again to ensure that their conclusions are valid for all the results they obtained, rather than just a subset of them.

2) What ways can you think of to highlight your findings?

****

Your findings may be extremely valid and important. However, if the referees are not able to see or understand your findings because you have neither highlighted nor described them clearly enough, then your paper may not be published. Your contribution to the community may thus vanish into oblivion.

In the words of English botanist, Sir Francis Darwin: *In science the credit goes to the man who convinces the world, not to the man to whom the idea first occurred.*

Sections 8.3 to 8.9 outline how to use visual techniques (i.e. layout and sentence / paragraph length, bullets, headings, sentence length) to make readers notice your key findings. Sections 8.10 to 8.17 discuss the importance of the use of language to attract reader's attention.

8.2 Show your paper to a non-expert and get him / her to underline your key findings

A great way of discovering how explicit you have been in presenting your key findings is to show a non-expert your paper. Ask them to underline where they think you have introduced / discussed your key findings. This task should be possible even for someone who knows very little about your topic. If they fail to underline your key findings, then you know that you need to highlight your key findings even more.

If you want to be more thorough, you could get the same person also to find places where you discuss the implications and limitations of your research – along with your findings these two are key elements that should stand out clearly for the reader.

8.3 Avoid long blocks of text to ensure that referees (and readers) can find and understand the importance of your contribution

To be able to read your key findings and to understand the contribution of your paper, readers need to be able to easily find these key findings on the page.

If your key findings are buried in the middle of a paragraph, there is less chance that readers will see them and read them. Readers tend to concentrate at the beginning and ending of paragraphs, rather than the middle.

The examples below are designed to show you the difference in terms of impact on the eye of one long block of text, and the same text divided into shorter paragraphs. You don't need to read the texts, but simply recognize the negative effect that a long paragraph has, and thus avoid such blocks of text in your own writing.

ONE LONG PARAGRAPH

This is one ridiculously long paragraph containing all kinds of information about everything that you can possibly imagine and conceive. This is one ridiculously long paragraph containing all kinds of information about everything that you can possibly imagine and conceive. This is one ridiculously long paragraph containing all kinds of information about everything that you can possibly imagine and conceive. This is one ridiculously long paragraph containing all kinds of information about everything that you can possibly imagine and conceive. Here are my findings you will be lucky if you can see them here buried in the midst of this ridiculously long paragraph containing all kinds of information about everything that you can possibly imagine and conceive. And now I will continue with this ridiculously long paragraph containing all kinds of information about everything that you can possibly imagine and conceive. So here we go again with this ridiculously long paragraph containing all kinds of information about everything that you can possibly imagine and conceive. This is one ridiculously long paragraph containing all kinds of information about everything that you can possibly imagine and conceive.

THREE SHORTER PARAGRAPHS

This is now a much shorter paragraph. This is now a much shorter paragraph. This is now a much shorter paragraph. This is now a much shorter paragraph. This is now a much shorter paragraph. This is now a much shorter paragraph. This is now a much shorter paragraph. This is now a much shorter paragraph. This is now a much shorter paragraph.

Here are my findings, which you can now see quite clearly. Note how this paragraph is also quite short. In fact, it is shorter than the previous and following paragraphs.

This is now a much shorter paragraph. This is now a much shorter paragraph. This is now a much shorter paragraph. This is now a much shorter paragraph. This is now a much shorter paragraph..

So when you have something important to say, begin a new paragraph.

Compare these two versions of the same text. This time read the texts.

READERS MAY OR MAY NOT NOTICE YOUR FINDINGS

The results showed that tourists in front of important monuments who take selfies using selfie sticks and those who drop litter have an equivalent negative empathy value suggesting that such people should be considered under the category of 'majorly selfish'. Additional observations support our view: i) subjects of the selfie group had a mean lag time of 30.3 seconds between arriving at the monument and the onset of the need to take a photograph of themselves. ii) The mean time of the litter group between arrival and dropping cans and food packages was aligned with the expected response from the selfie group to being given a warning by the monument guards. iii) The MEMEME ego ratio in the selfie group was compatible with a destructive form of graffiti writing, and not significantly different from that found in the can't-see-the-writing-on-the-wall group. iv) No significant differences in the recurrence rate of Kudnt Givadam Syndrome (KS) were observed between the groups.

READERS WILL NOTICE YOUR FINDINGS

The results showed that tourists in front of important monuments who take selfies using selfie sticks and those who drop litter have an equivalent negative empathy value, thus suggesting that such people should be considered under the category of 'majorly selfish'.

Four additional observations support our view.

Firstly, subjects in the selfie group had a mean lag time of 30.3 seconds between arriving at the monument and the onset of the need to take a photograph of themselves. Secondly, the mean time of the litter group between arrival and dropping cans and food packages was aligned with the expected response from the selfie group to being given a warning by the monument guards.

Thirdly, the MEMEME ego ratio in the selfie group was compatible with a destructive form of graffiti writing, and not significantly different from that found in the can't-see-the-writing-on-the-wall group.

Fourthly, no significant differences in the recurrence rate of Kudnt Givadam Syndrome (KGS) were observed between the groups.

The version on the right clearly takes up more space, but readers are far more likely to notice it and consequently read it than the version on the left.

8.4 Construct your sentences to help the reader's eye automatically fall on the key information

On what part of S1 does your eye fall?

> S1. The goal of the service discovery is twofold: (i) allow devices to advertise the services they provide. and (ii) allow the clients to find the services they need.

Your eye probably falls on this part: *twofold: (i) allow*

This is because our eye falls on those parts of a sentence that are different from others:

- punctuation marks – particularly brackets, colons, exclamation marks and question marks given that these are less frequently used than commas

- white spaces, for example after a full stop (period) or between paragraphs

- numbers

- capital letters

Does *twofold: (i) allow* contain any interesting information? No. So S1 wastes an opportunity to get the reader's attention. A better solution is:

> S2. The goal of the service discovery is to allow: (i) devices to advertise the services they provide, and (ii) clients to find the services they need.

In S2 the reader's eye will fall on *devices* and *clients*, exactly the two things the author wants the readers to focus on!

How is this achieved?

- *is twofold* has been removed (totally redundant as it is immediately followed by two numbers)

- *allow* has been relocated to before the colon, so that after the colon the reader immediately sees the key words (*devices* and *clients*)

The German-born American abstract expressionist painter, Hans Hoffman, once remarked: "The ability to simplify means to eliminate the unnecessary so that the necessary can speak". In fact S2 would be better rewritten as:

> S3. Service discovery enables: (i) devices to advertise the services they provide, and (ii) clients to find the services they need.

S3 is more effective because it puts the topic (*service discovery*) in first position in the sentence. Nothing in S3 is redundant, and it is around 30% shorter than S1.

However, if you are talking about goals that have still to become reality then S2 would be more appropriate – so only eliminate when doing so does not change the meaning you intended.

8.5   Consider using bullets and headings

We tend to notice bullets (bulleted or numbered) more than blocks of text. So if your journal's style guide allows, occasionally use bullets to summarize important points.

You need to follow certain conventions when using bullets. The most important is that each bullet begins with the same grammatical part. The OV below uses two different grammatical constructions, whereas in the RV the infinitive is used in both bullets. This is a stylistic rule, but it also aids reader comprehension by presenting the various elements of information in the same way.

ORIGINAL VERSION (OV)	REVISED VERSION (RV)
Equation 2 is the main result of our study. It can be used:	Equation 2 is the main result of our study. It can be used to:
• in numerical codes to evaluate the impact of the presence of anomalies in the various samples taken	• evaluate in numerical codes the impact of the presence of anomalies in the various samples taken
• for simple estimates when designing experiments	• make simple estimates for designing experiments

Your decision about whether to use standard bullets or numbered bullets will depend on whether you will refer to the elements in the bullets in the following text. If you have a list of three or more bullets, and you need to refer to them, then it is easier to number them.

For more on the use of bullets, see 25.12 and 25.13 in *English for Research: Grammar, Usage, and Style*.

If your journal allows, use subheadings to direct your readers' attention to important aspects of your work.

8.6 In review papers and book chapters, use lots of headings

Review papers and book chapters are not divided into the traditional sections (Abstract, Introduction, Methods etc). Authors thus tend to write one long paper with very few breaks in the text. These is easy for the authors, but soul-destroying (i.e. very hard work) for the reader.

You should try to have five or six main headings (depending on the length of the review or chapter), possibly in bold. Then for each main heading, a series of sub-headings, possibly in italics or bold italics – see what others have done in your chosen journal or in the other chapters of the book you are contributing to.

These headings will then help readers navigate your text. Imagine that you were reading a text for the second time, and wanted to find a particular section that you found very interesting. How could you find the section if there are no headings?

The visual aspect of writing a text is often underestimated. However it can have a massive impact on a reader's decision to continue reading or to stop due to the excessive mental effort required.

8.7 Use tables and figures to attract attention

Some readers will begin your paper by looking at the figures and tables plus their legends. Thus both the figures/tables and the legends must be immediately understandable. Otherwise, your reader may stop reading and move on to another paper.

Placing tables and figures strategically throughout the paper is also another visual way of attracting attention. The readers' eyes will inevitably be attracted to any non-textual information, such as graphs and tables. The next thing their eyes will focus on will probably be the legend to the figures, and then the paragraph immediately following the legend. So use this paragraph to make an important point.

Of course tables are also the perfect way to summarize key findings. Check the maximum number of figures and tables that your journal allows, and keep them as relevant and concise as possible.

8.8 When you have something really important to say, make your sentences shorter than normal

Readers' eyes tend to be attracted most to the white space between sentences and to the capital letter that begins each sentence (try testing this out for yourself). This means that shorter sentences are noticed more, and of course they are generally easier to follow and understand.

This visual factor is critical to the impact of your paper. It is very similar to a good oral presentation. When presenters have something important to say, they slow down the speed of their voice, speak a little louder or more emphatically, use much shorter sentences, and use particular adverbs (e.g. *importantly, interestingly, remarkably*) to attract attention. Presenters do this to (i) attract the audience's attention, (ii) to underline the importance of what they are saying, (iii) to help the audience understand what is being said.

Here is an example from a Discussion. The OV is one long sentence. The italics in the RV highlight where each new sentence begins.

ORIGINAL VERSION (OV)	REVISED VERSION (RV)
The method developed in this work relies on a sample pre-treatment that allows a low final dilution, *guaranteeing, on the other hand*, a negligible shift of pH with regard to different specimens to be tested (±0.15 units from 23 samples tested); *however, the slight shifts* of pH do not alter the response of the test, *as shown* by the overlapping of standard curves obtained by spiking buffers at different pH with IGF-1.	Our method relies on a sample pre-treatment that only requires a minimal level of dilution. *In addition, it guarantees* a negligible shift in pH with regard to the different specimens to be tested (±0.15 units from 23 samples tested). *Importantly,* the slight shifts in pH do not alter the response of the test. *This is revealed* by the overlapping of standard curves obtained by spiking buffers at different pH with IGF-1.

In the RV it is much easier for readers to quickly identify where the innovation in the author's method lies, what the results are, and how these results reveal themselves. Note the replacement of *however* with *importantly*. The link word *however* seems to suggest that something negative will follow, whereas the use of *importantly* shows that in fact it is something very positive.

To learn how to break up long sentences, see Chapter 4.

8.9 Present your key findings in a very short sentence and list the implications

It is crucial that the referee (and readers) are clearly alerted to your key findings, and that they clearly see (literally on the page) the uses and implications. In S1, the key finding (i.e. Eq. 2) is part of a 39-word sentence. It does not stand out on the page.

> S1. *Equation 2 is the main result of our study and it can be used both in numerical codes to evaluate the impact of the presence of anomalies in the various samples taken, or for simple estimates for designing experiments.

There are several ways to improve S1. The first is to use numbers.

> S2. Equation 2 is the main result of our study. It can be used: (i) to evaluate in numerical codes the impact of the presence of anomalies in the various samples taken; or (ii) to make simple estimates for designing experiments.

In S2, Eq. 2 is now in a sentence of only nine words. A very short initial sentence when introducing a key finding encourages the reader to pay more attention. Note also that in S2, the two phrases regarding the uses of Eq. 2 now have the same type of grammatical construction (infinitive form of verbs – *to evaluate* the impact, *to make* simple estimates). In the OV there was no such parallelism in construction.

If you don't want to use numbers, an alternative way to rewrite S1 is S3:

> S3. Equation 2 is the main result of our study. It can be used for two purposes. Firstly, to evaluate in numerical codes the impact of the presence of anomalies in the various samples taken. Secondly to make simple estimates for designing experiments.

A third alternative is bullets, see 8.5.

8.10   Remove redundancy

One of the most effective ways to gain your reader's attention is to remove words that serve no purpose.

Compare S1 and S2, which are the first sentence in an Introduction:

S1. *The pollution from* hexavalent chromium affects both groundwater and soils *at many contaminated sites,* as a result *of diverse industrial activities in which the metal is used,* such as metal finishing and electroplating, production of pigments in dyes, inks, and plastics, and tannery leather factories. [45 words]

S2. Hexavalent chromium pollutes both groundwater and soils as a result, for example, of metal finishing and electroplating, the production of pigments in dyes, inks, and plastics, and emissions from tanneries. [30 words]

In S1 the phrases in italics add no value for the reader. The real meat is highlighted in S2, which uses 33% fewer words to express exactly the same concept.

To learn how to remove redundancy see Chapter 5.

8.11   Think about the types of words that attract attention

There are various types of nouns, which vary greatly in impact.

Nouns and abbreviations like *ANOVA, spectrometry, equation,* i.e. words specific to particular disciplines, are key words and will always attract the reader's attention.

Nouns like *process, characterization, phase* are commonly used in science but do not attract attention and can often be deleted (5.4).

Nouns like *speed, brightness* and *lightness* are concrete words, but are often less effective than their adjectival equivalents, as demonstrated by S2:

S1. Oriental lacquers have been used since ancient times in East Asia as coatings for every kind of surfaces, because of their *brightness, toughness and durability.*

S2. Oriental lacquers are *bright, tough and durable.* They have thus been used since ancient times in East Asia as coatings for all kinds of surfaces.

S2 also highlights how changing the structure of a sentence can lead to a more dramatic impact.

Readers are more interested in reading specifics than general concepts (5.5). Particularly when you give your key findings, you need to use the most concrete and specific words and phrases possible. If you don't, you are in danger of losing the attention of the reader.

8.12 Signal to the reader that you are about to say something important by using more dynamic language

You can attract readers' attention not only through visual techniques, but also by the words you use.

The following adverbs, used at the beginning of a sentence, are effective in signaling to readers that you are now going to tell them something important:

> *importantly, intriguingly, interestingly, surprisingly, incredibly, remarkably, significantly, unfortunately*

You can also use adjectives that add a positive feeling to what you are saying, for example: *advanced, attractive, convincing, cutting-edge, effective, favorable, important, novel, productive, profitable, successful, superior, undeniable, valuable.* You can make them even stronger by adding *extremely* or *very* in front of them, but you may find that they have just as much or more impact without these extra words.

In any case, you should only use these adverbs and adjectives once or twice in the entire paper, otherwise they lose their impact or you may be considered as being arrogant (Chapter 10). If you have something less important to say, you could probably just use a link word such as:

• *in addition* – to add an additional comment, benefit or feature

• *however* – to signal that you now have something to say that qualifies what you have just said

• *in contrast* – to highlight that what you are going to say next goes against what you have just said

8.13 When discussing key findings avoid flat phrases

The way you write a phrase should reflect the importance of what you are saying. S1 reports one of the key findings of a paper.

> S1. *A comparison of X and Y revealed the presence of two Zs, one located in Region 1 as previously identified in the Z subgroup (Marchesi *et al.*, 2009), and the other in Region 2 (Figure 6). This finding suggests the presence of another transcriptor factor that ...

There is nothing in S1 that says to the reader 'Hey, this is really important. It is a key finding that I really want to draw your attention to – please take note of this'.

In reality the authors of S1 were talking about an amazing genetic discovery. Until they wrote their paper only one Z had ever been found. It had been found by

Marchesi and colleagues. The fact that the authors had found another Z in a different location was the fundamental finding of their whole paper. But they presented this information in the same way as they reported the general state of the art in their introduction. After their paper had been initially rejected, they rewrote the sentence as in S2.

> S2. Since Z has only ever been found in Region 1 (Marchesi *et al.*, 2009), we were surprised to identify Z in Region 2 as well. Our discovery suggests the presence of an unidentified transcriptor factor that ...

S2 focuses on the key finding (i.e. Z). Z is now placed at the beginning of the sentence. How they made this finding has already been described in the Results (i.e. through *a comparison of X and Y*), so they don't really need to mention X and Y here too. They use much more emotive language – *surprised, discovery, unidentified* – which is designed to draw the reader's attention to the importance and contribution of their work.

Here is an example from the Abstract of a paper on cow's milk.

> S3. *In this study, we set up a system to quantify the level of X in milk, relying on a particular kind of pre-treatment allowing a low dilution of the sample.
> S4. In this study, we set up a system to quantify the level of X in milk. Our method is highly effective and less expensive than other options currently available. In fact, it uses a special pre-treatment, which means that the sample only requires a minimal level of dilution.

S4 is much more effective in conveying the validity and utility of the author's system. It does this by:

- splitting the long sentence of S3 into two shorter sentences

- making a comparison with previous methods

- using clearer language to highlight the implications of the pre-treatment

8.14 Consider avoiding the use of phrases containing *note* and *noting*

A typical device authors use in the hope of attracting attention, is to use phrases such as *It is interesting to note, it is worth noting, it should be noted that* etc.

Such phrases are generally located at the beginning of a phrase and tend to do the exact opposite of what the author intended. What they say next will in fact lose its impact.

The beginning of the sentence should be reserved for important, or at least concrete, information (3.4). If you frequently begin sentences or paragraphs with such phrases you will annoy your readers, especially if they don't actually find what you have written to be *interesting*.

If you insist on using such phrases, then limit them to once in the entire paper and make sure that i) what you say is interesting, ii) you explain *why* it is interesting. Consider simply saying *Note that* ...

8.15 Be explicit about your findings, so that even a non-expert can understand them

Your paper may not only be read by people working in exactly the same field as you. In order to acquire funding to continue working in research, some researchers have to change from their field into a more financially retributive field. This means that some people who are not completely familiar with your field may need to read your paper.

S1 is the last sentence of an abstract dealing with the effect of Panama disease on bananas.

> S1. Results obtained have management implications and suggest that there is a high degree of improbability that sound fruit will be subject to an infection process by Panama disease and wounds have an inherent tendency towards a phenomenon of infection susceptibility with regard to bananas, therefore, necessary steps should be taken to set in place various guarantees so that bananas are handled in an adequately careful manner in order to undertake a strategy of lesion prevention.

The findings have huge implications with anyone involved in banana production and sales, yet their importance is difficult to decipher from S1.

S2 is much more concise (41 words rather than 75) and clear:

> S2. Our results highlight firstly that Panama disease is unlikely to infect sound fruit, and that secondly wounds make fruit susceptible to infection. It is thus critical to handle bananas carefully so as to prevent wounds that are conducive to this disease.

In S2 it is clear that the findings are those of the author (*our results*). The long sentence has been divided into two shorter sentences. Much of the redundancy has been removed along with abstract nouns that add no value (*tendency, process, phenomenon, strategy etc.*). Readers can now understand that there are two key findings (*firstly, secondly*). The same key terms have been used, i.e. just *wound*, rather than *wound* and *lesion* (which both have the same meaning, but readers may think they are used to mean different things).

However, the findings and implications could be made even more explicit:

> S3. Our results highlight that Panama disease is unlikely to infect sound fruit, but rather it is wounds that make fruit susceptible to infection. Thus the best way to avoid infection is by ensuring that the fruit is handled carefully and not wounded. This is clearly critical for those involved in picking, packing, transporting and displaying bananas.

S3 can be much more easily understood by non-experts, for example by those who have just begun to do research in this area, and those who are not researchers but can benefit from the research (e.g. banana producers, handlers, retailers). The relationship between the effect of the disease on sound fruit versus wounded fruit is now even clearer through the use of *but rather*. The third sentence in S3 contains information that was not given in S2, but makes the *management implications* mentioned in S1 explicit i.e. careful handling during *picking* etc.

In fact, the term *management implications* has little meaning for the readers, even though it may be obvious for the author. This is a very common problem: the author has an idea, and he / she expresses it in a very generic way and expects the readers to understand how this generic way might be specific in this particular context. It is much better to be explicit and to give examples of what you mean.

Finally, S3 is written in uncomplicated English that anyone can understand. I am not suggesting that this user-friendly style should be adopted in every sentence of the paper. In fact, you might be criticized for being 'too informal' or not sufficiently 'scientific' if you used this style throughout your paper. However, when you are saying something of critical importance, then it helps to use such a direct style. This will make your message 100% clear to everyone – to the referee, to the expert reader, and to the inexpert reader.

8.16 Convince readers to believe your interpretation of your data

Data can often be interpreted in more than one way. One reason for a paper being initially rejected is that the referee may interpret your data in a different way from how you have interpreted your data. The referee may then request that you to do further experiments / research just to check whose interpretation is correct. In some cases, such extra experiments may be useful, but they will delay your paper being published.

One way to avoid the referee making such requests is to predict what these requests are likely to be. Then you deal with them already in your initial manuscript in a way that your referees will be willing to digest (Sects. 9.11, 9.12, and 17.8).

So, let's imagine that you have made a calculation of one plus one and found that the result is three, contrary to the normal result of two. You have your own explanation for this strange result. You know that there are two other possible hypotheses for interpreting your data – H1 and H2 – but in any case you want your own hypothesis, H3, to be seen as the only possible interpretation. The secret is not to ignore H1 and H2, but to deal with them explicitly. You do this by investigating them (either fully or partially) and by proving that they are not possible explanations. The key is to do so in such a convincing way, that the referee then does not feel the need to request you to investigate H1 and H2.

Below is a fictitious example of how to convince the referee to accept your hypothesis (H3) rather than H1 or H2.

> We believe that there are three possible ways of interpreting our findings. The first, H1, is that the result of three, contrary to the normal result of two, can be explained by ... However, if this were the case, then the result should have been four. In fact, H1 is probably due to the rather low computational power, which the authors [Bing et al 2006] who originally proposed H1 later admitted ... Moreover, Bing's methodology may have suffered from ...

> The second interpretation, H2, proposes that ..... H2 has found some agreement in the literature [Chan 2009, Marx 2011], however as highlighted by [Uswe 2011], H2 is the result of a discrepancy in the X values due to ...

> We thus believe that it is reasonable to discount H1 and H2, and that H3 provides the most reliable explanation for this apparently strange result. In addition, our finding is consistent with ...

> Further evidence for H3 is that ...

The trick is to be completely open about the evidence against you and to deal with it step by step in a logical manner. In the example above, this logic is highlighted by having separate paragraphs for each element of the author's argumentation.

Link words (e.g. *thus, in fact*) are also very helpful in constructing this logic. Note how when describing the evidence against H1 and H2, the author uses *however* and *moreover. However* is often used to diminish the importance or to question the implications of what has been said before, and is thus perfect in this situation. There is a difference between *moreover* (used at the end of the first paragraph) and *in addition* (end of third paragraph). Both are used to add additional information in support of what has been previously said, but *moreover* is sometimes used to add a further negative factor, whereas *in addition* tends to be used to add a further positive factor.

Here is another example to highlight the difference between *moreover* and *in addition*:

> This paper is written badly, moreover much of the data is inaccurate.

> This paper is extremely well written. In addition, the method is very innovative.

8.17 Beware of overstating your project's achievements and significance

This chapter has been all about highlighting your findings so that readers can both physically see them on the page and also appreciate their significance. But no research, study or project is perfect. You need to be explicit not just about the strengths of your work, but also the weaknesses and potential for bias (e.g. in your selection and sampling procedures).

Particularly in the Discussion you should purposively offer alternative explanations that take into account any potential for bias or limitations in your methodology and in the interpretation of your results. Such insights into these areas will be seen by the referee and readers as a sign of the quality of your research.

On the other hand, if it seems you are overstating the meaning of what you have found, the referee may suspect you of research bias. This may mean that your paper will be initially rejected.

8.18 Summary

➢ Be aware of how the layout of your paper can affect where readers focus their eyes – break up long blocks of text using shorter paragraphs, headings, bullets, and figures / tables etc

➢ Begin a new paragraph when highlighting something important

➢ Use shorter sentences and paragraphs to make your key points

➢ Start a new paragraph when you give your conclusion / interpretation on what you have said in the preceding sentences

➢ Use headings for subsections within the results section to partition off the various results. This will enable you to give clear conclusions on each specific result

➢ Use more dynamic language to talk about your key finding(s) – make sure the reader understands immediately that you are about to say something important

➢ Don't just tell the readers that something is important – show them

➢ Tell your readers the implications of your findings

Chapter 9

Discussing Your Limitations

Factoids

❖ Cars: *That the automobile has practically reached the limit of its development is suggested by the fact that during the past year no improvements of a radical nature have been introduced.* Scientific American, January 1909

❖ Computers: *Where a calculator on the ENIAC is equipped with 19,000 vacuum tubes and weighs 30 tons, computers in the future may have only 1,000 vacuum tubes and perhaps only weigh 1.5 tons.* Popular Mechanics, March 1949.

❖ Electric light: *When the Paris exhibition closes, electric light will close with it and no more will be heard of it.* Erasmus Wilson, English surgeon and dermatologist, 1878

❖ Female scientists: *Three things happen when they are in the lab: You fall in love with them, they fall in love with you, and when you criticize them they cry.* Nobel prize winner, professor Tim Hunt, 2015

❖ Intelligence: *The most important fact about intelligence is that we can measure it.* Arthur Jensen, US psychology professor, 1969

❖ Inventions: *Everything that can be invented has been invented.* Charles H. Duell, Commissioner of the US Patent Office, 1899

❖ Nicotine: *It is my conviction that nicotine is a very remarkable, beneficient drug that both helps the body to resist external stress and also can as a result show a pronounced tranquilising effect.* Charles Ellis, Senior Scientist, British American Tobacco company, 1962

❖ Nuclear Energy: *There is not the slightest indication that [nuclear energy] will ever be obtainable. It would mean that the atom would have to be shattered at will.* Albert Einstein, 1932.

❖ Planes: *Heavier-than-air flying machines are impossible.* William Thomson (Lord Kelvin), British mathematician, physicist and engineer, 1895

❖ Surgery: *The abolishment of pain in surgery is a chimera. It is absurd to go on seeking it. . . . Knife and pain are two words in surgery that must forever be associated in the consciousness of the patient.* Dr. Alfred Velpeau, French surgeon, 1839

© Springer International Publishing Switzerland 2016
A. Wallwork, *English for Writing Research Papers*,
English for Academic Research, DOI 10.1007/978-3-319-26094-5_9

9.1 What's the buzz?

(1) What can you deduce from the following facts, figures and quotes?

1. *Even the most impressive minds are not flawless, they merely pave the way for the next level of understanding.* Mario Livio (author of *Brilliant Blunders* on scientists' breakthrough mistakes).

2. *Once we accept our limits, we go beyond them.* Albert Einstein

3. Post-it notes were created by Spencer Silver, a researcher in 3M Laboratories, while trying to make a strong adhesive. He actually inadvertently created something that was weaker than the adhesives available at the time. Ink-jet printers were invented by an engineer at Canon who mistakenly put a hot iron on a pen, and notices that ink was injected from the pen a few moments later. Alexander Fleming noticed that mold on a contaminated Petri was dissolving all the bacteria around it. He then grew the mold by itself and discovered penicillin.

4. The inventors of the following products initially had their ideas rejected by potential manufacturers: Barbie doll, the hovercraft, the board games Monopoly and Trivial Pursuit, the safety razor, the vacuum cleaner.

5. Even octogenarians can produce quality work. At the age of 87, Francis Rous was awarded the Nobel Prize for Medicine, and at 88, Michelangelo was still painting.

6. Marie Curie (researcher into radiation, winner of two Nobel Prizes), Thomas Midgley (chemist who studied leaded gasoline), and Henry Smolinski (engineer who invented a flying car) all died as a direct result of what they were studying / inventing.

(2) Describe one limitation of your research, and counter any objections to this limitation.

****

This chapter highlights the importance to the scientific community of discussing the possible limitations in your research and explains how to present your negative results.

Of course, you may have got negative results for other reasons:

- your hypothesis was incorrect and needs to be reformulated

- you had a bad experimental design and / or low statistical power

However, this chapter is based on the assumption that both your hypothesis and experimental design were reasonably sound.

9.2   Recognize the importance of 'bad data'

Every good book on scientific writing highlights the importance of admitting your limitations. Mario Livio, an astrophysicist at the Space Telescope Science Institute in Baltimore (USA), has even written a whole book – *Brilliant Blunders* – on this topic. His reason for doing so was:

> … to correct the impression that scientific breakthroughs are purely success stories. . . . The road to triumph [is] paved with blunders.

A 'blunder' is a huge mistake. To enable referees to judge whether you have made a mistake or not, you should not hide any negative results. Be upfront (clear and honest) about the limitations of your methods and approach.

In *Why People Believe Weird Things*, author Professor Michael Shermer writes:

> In science, the value of negative findings – failures – cannot be overemphasized. Usually they are not wanted, and often they are not published. But most of the time failures are how we get close to truth. Honest scientists will readily admit their errors, but all scientists are kept in line by the fact that their fellow scientist will publicize any attempt to fudge. Not pseudo scientists. They ignore or rationalize failures, especially when exposed.

Dr. Donald Dearborn, of Bates College, comments:

> Your results may be of importance to others even though they did not support your hypothesis. Do not fall into the trap of thinking that results contrary to what you expected are necessarily "bad data". If you carried out the work well, they are simply your results and need interpretation. Many important discoveries can be traced to "bad data".

And finally, Linus Pauling, winner of two Nobel prizes and some of whose findings were later found to be majorly flawed by other scientists, is reported to have said:

> Mistakes do no harm in science because there are lots of smart people out there who will immediately spot a mistake and correct it. You can only make a fool of yourself and that does no harm, except to your pride.

Negative data are frequently commented on in the Results (17.7) and Discussion (18.6).

9.3 There will always be uncertainty in your results, don't try to hide it

The British Medical Journal (BMJ) has an extremely useful author resources section on its website. These resources are not only useful for those undertaking medical research, but can be applied to any kind of research writing. I strongly recommend accessing their site: http://www.bmj.com/about-bmj/resources-authors/article-types/research

The following extract is from the BMJ site:

> Please do not use the term "negative" to describe studies that have not found statistically significant differences, perhaps because they were too small. There will always be some uncertainty, and we hope you will be as explicit as possible in reporting what you have found in your study. Using wording such as "our results are compatible with a decrease of this much or an increase of this much" or "this study found no effect" is more accurate and helpful to readers than "there was no effect/no difference".

9.4 Be constructive in how you present your limitations

When you discuss any limitations and failures, try to do so in a constructive way so that other researchers can learn from your experiences.

However, you don't want to present your limitations in a negative light. Your results may be 'negative' for you, but for the scientific community they are not negative, rather they are helpful indicators essential for the progress of knowledge (9.2).

This means that although the results themselves may have been unexpected or appear disappointing to you, the actual way you present them should not be formulated in negative language as this might produce a negative reaction in your readers. The idea is to report everything in a neutral, subjective way.

> S1. *The limitation of this paper is that the two surveys were unfortunately not conducted in the same period. This will affect our results in terms of ...

S1 is extremely honest, but could be expressed in a way that sounds less negative, as in S2:

> S2. Although the two surveys were not conducted in the same period, this will only affect our results in terms of ...

The negative impact of S1 is reduced in S2 by:

- removing the words *limitation* and *unfortunately*. In reality, *limitation* is not a bad word to use, but if you use it more than once or twice, the reader may go away thinking that your work has more negative aspects than positive ones. If you have to refer to several limitations, another solution to reduce the possible negative effect on the reader is to use synonyms: *shortfall, shortcoming, pitfall, drawback, disadvantage* etc.

- introducing *although* and *only* – these adverbs qualify what you are saying. In this particular case, *although* immediately tells your reader that you are going to say something negative, but that something positive will immediately follow. *Only* implies a limited number of cases, thus it lessens the level of seriousness of the shortcoming

- combining two sentences into one sentence – this gives the reader less time to ponder on the negative content

Other words to avoid are adverbs such as *regrettably* and *unfortunately*, and the link word *moreover. Moreover* tends to be used when you have said something negative, and then add further negative details. On the other hand, *in addition (further, furthermore, also* etc) are used to add to any already positive or neutral comment. So I could say to my students:

S3. You are the *worst* class I have ever had. *Moreover*, you appear to understand absolutely *nothing*.
S4. You are the *best* class I have ever had. *In addition*, you appear to understand absolutely *everything*.

9.5   Clarify exactly what your limitations are

When you outline the limitations, you need to be clear what these limitations are and what exactly the implications are. S1 and S2 fail to do this.

S1. *One limitation of our research was the sample size, which was too small.
S2. *The unfortunate contamination of a few of our samples may mean that some of our conclusions are somewhat misleading.

S1 and S2 are not very helpful and are not likely to please your referees. S1 does not explain why and in what way the sample size was too small, nor what the consequences of this were. S2 does not explain why or how the samples were contaminated, nor to what extent the conclusions are misleading.

S3 and S4 provide much more information, and do so in a more positive way that does not undermine your research too dramatically:

S3. One limitation of our research was the sample size. Clearly 200 Xs are not enough to make generalizations about Y. However, from the results of those limited number of Xs, a clear pattern emerged which …

S4. Two of our samples were contaminated. This occurred because … We thus plan to repeat our experiments in future work. However, our analysis of the uncontaminated samples (24 in total) supported our initial hypothesis that …

The important thing is to be (i) honest, (ii) clear, and, if appropriate, (iii) discuss possible remedies.

9.6   Avoid losing credibility

Dr Maggie Charles is a Tutor in English for Academic Purposes at the Oxford University Language Centre. She explains the importance of admitting limitations, but doing so in a way that does not undermine your credibility:

> As a young researcher you want your scientific community to see you as credible, professional and honest, and also reasonably modest. This means that you can, and should, draw attention to limitations in your research. The community needs to know what went wrong in your research, not just for ethical reasons, but also so that others can learn from your 'mistakes'. It also means that others will see you as a reliable and honest researcher. In fact, because you have drawn attention to the problems you have had in your research, the community is more likely to accept the validity and reliability of what you describe in your paper.
>
> However, you can present these limitations in such a way that you do not have to take direct responsibility for them. You can do this by using impersonal forms. These impersonal forms distance you from the limitations of your study and at the same time they highlight for the community that you can evaluate your 'performance' in accordance with the standards of that community.

The passive form is very useful when you don't want to assume complete responsibility for what you are saying. This is because no agent is necessary with a passive.

It was found that the containers for the samples had become contaminated.

This fraction *is assumed* to originate from…

It *might be speculated* that…

Impersonal phrases beginning with *it* have the same function:

It is regrettable that the containers had become contaminated as this meant that ...

It is reasonable to hypothesize that...

It appears possible that...

These tactics give the reader the impression that the responsibility for the contamination does not rest entirely with the author. The author does not explicitly state who is doing the assuming, speculating, hypothesizing etc. This means that you can avoid losing face and so not be perceived as being incompetent (18.12).

9.7 Anticipate alternative interpretations of your data

If you want the referee and readers to accept your specific interpretation of your data, you will be more convincing if you also provide alternative interpretations. Basically you are anticipating any objections that they might have – you are playing the devil's advocate with yourself.

Let us imagine that you have stated that 'Our findings show that dogs are more intelligent than cats'. Below are some ways to hedge your claim by setting out an alternative interpretation.

S1. *Of course*, the *opposite* may also be possible. *In fact, it cannot be ruled out* that certain species of cats, for example, Siamese, show intelligence traits that are remarkably similar to those of dogs.

S2. *Other factors* besides intelligence *could be involved*, such as the visual and olfactory senses. *This implies that*, in a restricted number of cases, cats could be considered as being more intelligent...

S3. It may be *premature* to reach such conclusions, and *clearly* there may be *other possible interpretations* for our findings. *However*, we believe that our findings are evidence of...

S4. *We do not know the exact reasons for the discrepancy* between our findings and those of Santac [2013], but *it might reflect*... Feeding habits may favor intelligence, *or* they may simply be..., *or* they may result from... Future work will be devoted to investigating these three *alternative possibilities*.

S5. *Despite* this apparently clear evidence of the superiority of dogs, our findings are in contrast with those of Karaja [1999] and Thanhbinh [2012], whose experiments with Singapura and Sokoke cats apparently showed that both these species were superior to Rottweilers in terms of emotional intelligence. *However*, we believe that the species of cats involved are quite rare, and that Rottweilers were not a good choice of comparison.

S5 is an example of where you call into question the validity of a possible opposition to your findings (Sect. 8.10).

9.8   Refer to other authors who experienced similar problems

Another way to lessen the impact of the limitations of your 'bad data' is to say that other authors have experienced similar problems, as illustrated in the extract below:

> Analytic expressions for the density (1) were not derived, (2) because their interaction depends on the relative orientation of the spheres, (3) thus making integration considerably more complex. (4) Similar complications in the analytical determination of the density, using the same approach that we used, were experienced by Burgess [2018].

The strategy used in the above extract is:

(1)   explain the pitfall (i.e. the limitation in your work)

(2)   give reason for the pitfall

(3)   outline consequence of the pitfall

(4)   refer to a similar pitfall experienced by another author

However, be careful how you refer to the literature.

> S1.   The statistical tool is not able to describe all the variables involved. The same tool was used for conducting similar research with an American sample, and the results were reliable and representative.

In S1 the reference to the literature is very vague and is thus not convincing. S2 resolves this vagueness by being much more precise.

> S2.   The statistical tool may not be optimal for describing some of the variables involved. However it is optimal for x, y and z. In addition, exactly the same tool was used for conducting similar research with an American sample [Williams, 2017]. Williams' results were reliable and representative and were in fact used by the US government.

9.9 Tell the reader that with the current state-of-the-art this problem is not solvable

Your limitations may be due to the fact that current knowledge (theories, models, technologies etc.) is unable to resolve the problems you have encountered.

> (1) A full treatment of our problem using Gabbertas's theory (GT) is complicated to handle in our case, (2) *given* the complex geometry. (3) *In fact*, the expressions derived by GT are only available for a few simple geometries [Refs]. (4) *Moreover*, GT is not well suited to describing the upper regions. (5) *An additional problem* is that a theoretical description of X is still the target of active experimental and theoretical research. (6) There is little experimental or theoretical information available for the properties of X [Refs]. (7) *At the same time*, the properties of Y can be described by Burgess's model, (8) *however* its ability to account for X is still under investigation.

The strategy adopted in the above case is:

1. say that current theories (models etc.) cannot deal with your problem
2. give an explanation for (1)
3. give support for (1)
4. give more support for (1)

Note how (5–8) follow the same pattern as (1–4). The author uses link words (highlighted in italics) to give emphasis and logic to her argumentation and she provides variety by using different link words. Note however that excessive use of link words can be very tedious for readers (see Sect. 5.7).

When discussing your limitations, be consistent. Say either *this worked in 75% of cases* (affirmative approach) or *this did not work in 25%* (negative approach), then stick with just one of the two approaches. Otherwise you are in danger of confusing the reader.

Finally, only attribute your limitations to a current lack of knowledge if this really is the case – don't just use it as an excuse!

9.10   Explain why you did not study certain data

Other limitations relating to data are that i) you did not study the most recent data, ii) you did not study a sufficient amount of data. You can deal with these two limitations by writing in your Discussion or Conclusions:

> S1   Even though the data were collected two years ago, the stability of this sector means that such data have not changed significantly. In fact, in the last two years the percentage of x has remained exactly the same [Wang 2017, Chu Wa 2018]. In addition, more recent data are not currently available.
>
> S2   Our data only refer to one kind of sector. However, as far as we know there are no similar studies for this sector in South Korea. Thus we believe that this project opens the way for ...

In S1 you justify old data by saying that nothing has changed since the time that data was collected. In S2 you say that in the country that is the subject of your research (in this case South Korea), such data are not available, and you protect yourself by saying as far as we know (see Chapter 10).

9.11   Tell the reader from what standpoint you wish them to view your data

Rather than using expressions such as *in our view* and *we believe*, which clearly express your point of view, you can tell the reader from which standpoint you want them to interpret or judge your data.

This tactic works best with humanistic disciplines.

Here are some examples:

> *Viewed / Seen in this way*, the data take on a different meaning.
>
> *From this alternative perspective*, these findings shed new light on...
>
> *From an X point of view*, the results can be interpreted very differently
>
> *From such a standpoint*, our data assume a very different significance.
>
> *In this view*, these data may mean that...
>
> *Under these conditions*, it is legitimate to pose a new *perspective* on...

This technique has the effect of distancing you from your own data, and it may help to increase your credibility.

A similar approach is to make the data (or method, model, discussion, hypothesis etc.) the subject of the sentence, with no possessive adjective (i.e. no *our* or *my*), as highlighted in these examples:

These *data* indicate that...

The *evidence* favors the conclusion that...

The *model* predicted that...

From this *discussion*, it would appear that...

The *hypothesis* seems plausible because...

The *existence* of such phenomena may give confirmation of...

Here the technique is to distance yourself from your data (findings etc.) by taking a neutral stance. It seems as if the data themselves are drawing conclusions, rather than you drawing conclusions. You give the idea that you are not the only person involved in the discussion, the reader is implicitly somehow involved too. This technique is often used when you are concerned that your claims are not sufficiently important or robust.

Useful verbs in such contexts are *imply, indicate, suggest, point toward, hint at* etc.

9.12   Don't end your paper by talking about your limitations

Don't end your Discussion (or Conclusions) by talking about your limitations. End with something positive – this will be the reader's final impression. Possible endings are:

- talking about other applications for your findings

- suggesting other avenues of research for the future

- re-highlighting the benefits of your findings

See Chapter 19 Conclusions.

9.13 Summary

➢ Talk about your weaknesses not just your strengths; do not make the referees suspect any bias in your work

➢ Always mention your limitations

➢ Present your limitations using positive language

➢ Justify your limitations

➢ Ensure the final words of your paper are not about your limitations

Chapter 10

Hedging and Criticising

© Springer International Publishing Switzerland 2016
A. Wallwork, *English for Writing Research Papers*,
English for Academic Research, DOI 10.1007/978-3-319-26094-5_10

10.1 What's the buzz?

Carlsberg is a Danish beer producer and the world's fourth biggest brewer. For nearly 40 years Carlsberg ran one of the most successful advertising campaigns of any product in the world, which simply said: "Probably the best beer in the world".

However, Carlsberg's earlier adverts had had slogans such as

Lager at its best.

Unrivalled quality and flavour.

The world's best.

(1) Why do you think Carlsberg decided to use the word 'probably'?

(2) Can you see any connection between the claim made by Carlsberg and claims made by researchers in their papers?

Modern day scientific writing had its origins in England and many stylistic rules were devised by British scientists. One 'rule' is that when you present subjective or unproven propositions, you should avoid sounding arrogant or 100% certain of what you state. This approach, known as 'hedging', also spread to other scientists in other Anglo societies.

In his book 'How to be an Alien', George Mikes, a Hungarian-born British author, wrote that: *In England it is bad manners to be clear, to assert something confidently. It may be your personal view that two and two make four, but you must not state it in a self-assured way because this is a democratic country and others may be of a different opinion.*

Although Mikes was being humorous, he was making an important point. Many of the world's most important journals are based in the USA and the UK. Consequently you should consider stating your claims (i.e. things that you believe that you have proved in your experiments and propose as being possibly true, but which in the future could potentially be proved by others to be unfounded) in a slightly softer way than you may normally do in your own language.

So particularly in the Discussion and in the Conclusions you may occasionally need to use words and expressions that are not too direct and seem more tentative.

This chapter is designed to help you to:

- learn to anticipate (i.e. predict) possible objections to your claims. This means being able to make claims about your findings in a way that the referee, and subsequently the community, is more likely to accept them

- criticize the work of other authors in a constructive manner by building upon their findings rather than underlining their inadequacy

Both these skills entail the cultural concept of 'face saving'. Face saving means not putting yourself or another person in a position where others could perceive you or them as having failed.

10.2   Why and when to hedge

Hedges are central to academic argument and are abundant in research articles. Because they withhold complete commitment to a proposition they imply that a claim is based on plausible reasoning rather than certain knowledge. This protects the writer against being proved wrong while recognizing alternative ideas on the subject.

Professor Ken Hyland, Director, Centre for Applied English Studies and Chair of Applied Linguistics, University of Hong Kong

Hedging entails anticipating possible opposition by your referees and readers by not saying things too assertively or directly. A hedge was originally a fence or boundary delimiting an area of land – it was thus a form of protection from outsiders. Today, hedge has a metaphorical meaning – you protect yourself against some risk.

In your case, the risk is criticism by referees and other researchers. The idea is that you express yourself with honesty, precision and caution, and you are diplomatic in any criticisms you make of other authors.

If you learn how to hedge, it may help you to gain acceptance in your field. On the other hand, if you seem to be too sure of yourself, you might alienate the referee and potential readers.

Hedging does not mean that you should be vague. In fact, you must be as precise as possible. It is simply that you express this precision in an open-minded way that encourages other authors either to agree with your hypotheses or to postulate their own.

Here are two examples of what some referees (particularly British) might consider to be rather arrogant.

S1.   *Although many authors have investigated how PhD students write papers, *this is the first attempt* to systematically analyze all the written output (papers, reports, grant proposals, CVs etc.) of such students.

S2.   *Our results demonstrate that* students from humanistic fields produce longer written texts than students from the pure sciences and this *is due to the fact* that humanists *are* more verbose than pure scientists.

Some referees might interpret these as being arrogant because the authors leave no room for doubt. In S1 can they be sure that this is the *first* attempt? Have they read all the literature from all the world? In S2 they are only talking about their interpretation of their results that came from their sample – they cannot be sure that other researchers will not have a different interpretation or draw different conclusions from a different sample. Also, *this is due to the fact* gives the idea that this is the only possible explanation, whereas in such a subjective area there will certainly be other interpretations.

Not all referees will interpret S1 and S2 as being too assertive. In fact scientists from many parts of the world write like this in their native language. So they are unlikely to criticize it when they see it in English. In addition, not all scientists are in favor of hedging, particularly as it is a very culture-driven device (see extract by Alistair Wood in Sect. 11.3).

However, it is not difficult to hedge your propositions. Hedging is unlikely to compromise the publication of your paper and in most cases will increase it, as illustrated in S3 and S4 (which are revised versions of S1 and S2):

S3.   Although many authors have investigated how PhD students write papers, *we believe / as far as we know / to the best of our knowledge* this is the first attempt to systematically analyze all the written output (papers, reports, grant proposals, CVs etc.) of such students.

S4.   Our results *would seem to* demonstrate that students from humanistic fields produce more written work than students from the pure sciences and *this may be due to the fact* that humanists are generally more verbose than pure scientists.

Obviously you don't need to 'hedge' every time you use the verbs *show, demonstrate, reveal* etc. So for example, you can say: *Table 2 shows that X had higher values than Y.*

You only need to consider 'hedging' when you are making a big statement that could be open to interpretation or contention. In S5 the author is making a claim that goes against currently accepted knowledge (or myth) that cats are smarter than dogs.

S5.   *Our results *prove* that dogs are more intelligent than cats.

S5 would be better rewritten as one of the following:

S6. Our results would seem to indicate that dogs are more intelligent than the cats.

S7. A possible conclusion would be that dogs ...

S8. Our results may be a demonstration that dogs ...

S9. At least in terms of our sample, dogs appeared to be more intelligent ...

The examples in this subsection highlight that hedging often simply involves:

- adding a few words before making your claim: e.g. *we believe* (S3), *would seem to* (S4, S6)

- adding an adjective or adverb: e.g. *possible* (S7), *generally* (S4)

- replacing verbs that indicate 100% certainty, for example *prove, demonstrate is* (and other forms of the verb *to be*) with *may be* (S4, S8).

10.3   Highlighting and hedging

Chapter 8 dealt with how to highlight the importance of your findings. Highlighting and hedging are not contradictory skills, in fact they should be used hand in hand. Highlighting means, for example:

- helping the reader to see your findings on the pages of your manuscript (e.g. not hiding key findings in the middle of a long paragraph)

- using shorter sentences when giving important information

- using more dynamic language when drawing attention to key findings than when talking about standard issues

You can do all the above and <u>still</u> hedge where appropriate.

S1. This is a very important finding.

S2. These results suggest that this is a very important finding.

S2 gives exactly the same information as S1, but the first part of the sentence makes the author seem more modest in her claim and protects her from anyone in the future who might find that her results do not constitute an important finding. In other words the phrase *These results suggest that* is like a safety net for the author.

But S2 also qualifies as a 'highlighting sentence' because it is still a short (10 words) and simple sentence, which will attract the reader's attention. It also retains 'dynamic language' – *very important*.

S1 would be fine if you were discussing someone else's findings. It may even be acceptable if you use this to talk about your own work, provided that you then immediately explain <u>why</u> it is an important finding (i.e. you don't just tell readers that something is important, you show them as well). Without such an explanation S1 could sound arrogant. Also, you should only use such a strong declaration once or twice in an entire paper, otherwise it will lose its effect in addition to sounding arrogant.

The same is true for the use of adverbs such as *interestingly* and *surprisingly*. Such adverbs can be used in a sentence that both highlights and hedges.

> S3. Interestingly, these results prove that X is fundamental in producing Y.
>
> S4. Interestingly, these results suggest that X is fundamental in producing Y.

There is no real difference in meaning between S3 and S4, but the use of *suggest* rather than *prove* simply protects the author from any future contrasting findings or conclusions by other authors. In both S3 and S4, *interestingly* attracts readers' attention. Again, the key is not to use such words more than once or twice.

The skill is in finding the right balance of highlighting and hedging, and also in knowing how to hedge so that referees and readers perceive you as being sincere.

Sections 10.4–10.7 focus on how to tone down (i.e. reduce the strength of) various grammatical parts of a sentence to a degree that most referees would consider to be a more appropriate level of assertiveness, confidence and certainty.

10.4 Toning down verbs

There are some verbs that leave no room for doubt, for example: *is / are, means, equals, demonstrates, proves, manifests*.

> S1. This factor *is* responsible for the increase in…
>
> S2. These results *demonstrate* the importance of…
>
> S3. These findings *are conclusive proof* that x = y.
>
> S4. This problem *manifests* itself in …
>
> S5. This *means* that x = y.

S1–S5 give the reader no space to choose another possible interpretation. Such claims are very strong when used in reference to your own findings, but may be fine when talking about the literature.

Softer versions of S1–S5 are in S6–S10, respectively.

S6. This factor *may be* / *is probably* responsible for the increase in…

S7. These results *would seem to show* / *indicate* / *suggest* the importance of…

S8. These findings *provide some evidence* / *appear to prove* that x = y.

S9. This problem *tends* / *seems* / *appears* to manifest itself in…

S10. It seems *likely* / *probable* / *possible* that x = y.

S7–S9 make use of two verbs, the first (*seem, appear, tends*) reduces the power of the second (*show, prove, manifest*). Other useful verbs with a similar function are: *help, contribute, have a tendency*, and *be inclined*.

10.5 Toning down adjectives and adverbs

Some adjectives and adverbs have a very strong tone. Here are some examples:

innovation: *innovative, novel, cutting edge, seminal, pivotal*

importance: *extremely important, very significant, of central* / *vital* / *fundamental importance*

certainty: *clear(ly), obvious(ly), evident(ly), conclusive(ly), definite(ly), undeniable, undeniably, undoubtedly*

When you are referring to your own work, you need to be careful how you use the above adjectives and adverbs. You might risk being accused of being too sure of yourself. For example:

S1. *This *pivotal* approach is *particularly interesting* for physicians.

The adjective *pivotal* describes something that is of vital or central importance. An expression such as *this pivotal approach* (S1) makes the author sound rather arrogant, since it is he or she who is assessing his / her own work. Such an expression, however, would be totally acceptable if the author were using it in a review of someone else's approach. S1 also states that the author's approach will be *particularly interesting* for doctors, but perhaps the author should let the doctors decide for themselves how interesting the approach is. It would be more acceptable to write:

S2. Our approach would lend itself well for use by physicians.

S3. We hope that physicians will find our approach useful.

S2 is more modest. It does not explicitly state the importance of the approach and the conditional *would* makes the claim more tentative. S3 is even more modest.

To protect yourself from accusations that you are too certain about your findings you can use adverbs and adverbial phrases such as *somewhat, to a certain extent, relatively,* and *essentially* as well as adverbs of probability and possibility such as *probably, likely,* and *possibly.* For example, both S4 and S5 could be considered very strong claims in certain circumstances.

S4.   X is related to Y.
S5.   X is certainly related to Y.

S6 and S7 take a more indirect approach.

S6.   X is somehow related to Y.
S7.   X is likely related to Y.

S6 is a hedge on <u>how</u> X is related to Y, whereas S7 is a hedge on the <u>probability</u> of X being related to Y.

Other useful adverbs for taking an indirect approach to interpreting the level of certainty in your findings are: *apparently, presumably, seemingly.*

10.6   Inserting adverbs to tone down strong claims

Different adverbs indicate different levels of confidence. If you are talking about how visible something is or how easy it is to detect, you could say:

S1.   X was *clearly* visible.
S2.   X was *scarcely* detectable.

S1 and S2 indicate confidence at both extremes of the visibility spectrum. However, if you think that there is an element of subjectivity in this visibility you can insert another adverb or phrase to reduce the power of the main adverb. So you could say:

S3.   X was reasonably clearly visible.
S4.   X was scarcely detectable, at least in our experiments.

You can use the same techniques to describe the level of agreement, correlation or matching.

S5.   Our data fit perfectly with those of Mkrtchyan.

The confidence level of S5 could be reduced as in S6.

S6. Our data fit quite well with those of Mkrtchyan.

Words like *quite (reasonably, sufficiently, adequately, satisfactorily, suitably, appropriately)* leave your claim open to interpretation. They are vague enough to allow anyone to attach their own meaning to what you are saying. However, you don't want to use them more than once or twice, as otherwise you may risk being accused of being too evasive or equivocal.

Other words you could use to replace *quite* in S6 are *surprisingly, remarkably*, and *unexpectedly*. These words attribute a very subjective element to the interpretation of the data, and again leave readers free to give their own meaning to what exactly the author meant. However, again, you need to be careful (Sect. 9.3), and if you do use such adverbs, it helps if you say what was surprising, remarkable or unexpected about them.

Use the adverb *significantly* wisely. It is often associated with statistics and simply means that something is unlikely to have occurred by chance. So it does not have the general meaning of being important or noteworthy.

Sometimes, you need to talk about the level of completeness of an operation or activity. In such cases you can use adverbs such as *partially, in part, to some extent*, and *to a certain extent*. Again, these are rather vague expressions, if possible you should try to quantify them.

10.7   Toning down the level of probability

Another way to hedge your claims is to give readers an indication of how likely your findings are correct. There are many ways of expressing this kind of probability. The percentage probabilities in the example below should only be seen as very general indicators.

MODAL VERBS

X *must / cannot* play a role in Y. (100% certain)

Smoking *can* cause cancer. (100% – this does not mean that smoking always leads to cancer, but only that it has been proved that in certain circumstances smoking is the cause of cancer)

Future work will entail investigating X, which *should* prove whether x is equal to y or to z. (80%)

Smoking may / might cause antisocial behavior. (50–70%)

This discrepancy could / may / might be the result of contamination. (50–70%)

Could this interaction be the cause of this discrepancy? (50–70%)

NOUNS

In all *likelihood / probability* x = y. (90%)

This raises *the possibility* that x = y. (50–70%)

These results are consistent with the *possibility* that x = y. (50–70%)

ADJECTIVES

It appears *possible / probable / feasible* that x = y. (50–70%)

ADVERBS

X is *unlikely* to play a role in Y. (80–90%)

X is *probably / likely* equal to Y. (80–90%)

Possibly, X is not equal to Y. (50–70%)

X could *possibly / conceivably / plausibly / ostensibly* play a role in Y. (50–70%)

10.8   Saving your own face: revealing and obscuring your identity as the author in humanist subjects

In natural sciences, authors often adopt an objective stance by writing in an impersonal fashion. Writers in social and political sciences, on the other hand, tend to have a more personal construction of reality and thus may use the first person to persuade the reader towards their opinion.

Compare for example:

S1. *I argue* that the way 18–21 year-olds vote is influenced more by the physical appearance of the candidate than the candidate's particular political ideas.

S2. *The present study / This paper argues* that the way 18–21 year-olds vote is not uniform.

In S1, the author is stating something that may go against what other authors have previously claimed and she decides to use the first person to show that this is clearly her idea. She is saying: "I may be wrong about what I am saying. My research may not be sufficiently robust to support this idea – and this is my responsibility. So, don't worry if it contradicts what you think." By doing this she helps / hopes to make her claim more readily acceptable to the community and therefore gain credibility in her field.

Using phrases such as *I argue* is what is known as authorial voice. In many languages such a device is not used and it may sound strange, unnatural or even unimportant for you to use it. However, your decision should be based on the style permitted in your journal and the expectations of your referees and readers, rather than necessarily what would be expected in your own language.

In S2, the author is perhaps making a claim that is less controversial or already has some support in the community. Note that the verb *argue* could be replaced by *suggest, propose* or *hypothesize*.

Other verbs you could use in this context are: *infer, calculate*, and *believe*.

You can also use nouns for the same purpose:

> Our *interpretation* of these results is...

> My *perspective* on these findings is...

10.9 Saving other authors' faces: put their research in a positive light

It is fine to question other people's findings and conclusions. Even the most reputable papers sometimes include poor research. But when you do make criticisms, ensure that you <u>always</u> do so in a constructive way that still manages to put the original research in a positive light. In this way you save the original author's face, i.e. their reputation and position in the academic world.

Let's imagine that so far in the literature one hypothesis, H1, has been proposed as an explanation for a certain phenomenon x. You are proposing a different hypothesis, H2, which completely contradicts H1 and proves it to be wrong. You don't want to be overtly critical of H1, because the referee of your paper could even be the person who initially proposed H1, or at least is a big supporter of it. Equally importantly, readers will more readily accept your objections if you phrase them in a constructive way.

When you need to criticize H1, you need to do so in a way that saves the other author's (i.e. the proposer of H1) face. You can do this by providing an explanation, on their behalf, of why H1 seemed to be the right interpretation. Below are some of the types of phrases you could use:

> Since H1 was originally proposed, a lot of new data on x has been presented in the literature (Smith et al. 2010, Burgess 2011). This data would seem to indicate that ...
>
> The formulation of H1 was based on a much smaller sample size than in our study. In fact H2 is based on a sample size that is 4-fold greater than ...
>
> When proposing H1, the author admitted that the quantity of x may have been influenced by y. On this basis, we decided to investigate the impact of y, and in fact found that ...
>
> In her conclusions, the author of H1 recommended that longer follow-up times might lead to more conclusive evidence of x. This is why in our study we ...

Note that the phrases above do not undermine the credibility of the proposer of H1 and at the same time they guide your readers towards your proposition.

You will find that link words such as *although, however* and *moreover* may help you to structure your criticism. However, do not use them too often as otherwise the tone of criticism may become too negative.

You should also consider the cost to you of <u>not</u> drawing the readers' attention to some problems inherent in the work of other authors. If you <u>don't</u> draw their attention, will it really affect your argumentation?

10.10 Saving other author's faces: say their findings are open to another interpretation

Another way to indirectly call into question another author's findings is not to say that there was anything specifically wrong with their findings. You simply say that these findings are open to another interpretation (i.e. your interpretation).

> From our investigations we conclude that the data of Negovelova [2011] can be seen in a different light when the effects of hydrogen are seen in conjunction with...
>
> It would not be implausible to analyze Hedayat's data from an entirely different point of view. In fact, our analysis reveals that...
>
> Budinich's findings could also be interpreted as evidence of... Viewed in this way, Budinich's results are actually in agreement with ours.

The last example shows how you can use data that initially appeared to contradict your data to actually give support to your interpretation.

10.11 Don't overhedge

Be careful not to follow a strong positive assertion with a weak statement that undermines it (S1), and avoid having several levels of hedging (S2).

S1.   *It is *clear* that yellow *may* be preferable to red for alerting danger.

S2.   *It *may* thus, *given* these particular circumstances, be *assumed* that there is a *certain possibility* that yellow *may* be preferable to red for alerting danger.

In S1 *may* weakens the force of *clear*. In S2 four hedging words have been used, which gives the idea that the authors are not at all sure of what they are talking about. S1 and S2 could be revised as S3 and S4, respectively:

S3.   It is clear that yellow *is* preferable to red.

S4.   In these particular circumstances yellow *may be* preferable to red.

10.12 Hedging: An extended example from a Discussion section

The following is an example from the Discussion section of a paper entitled *The Archeology of Water in Gortyn,* by archeologist Elisabetta Giorgi. Her research has revealed what she believes to be a new perspective on Roman aqueducts. She takes the specific case of Gortyn, the most important Roman town on Crete. Until now it was believed that the basic function of the aqueducts in the Roman period of history was to transport water into towns for use by individual citizens in their homes. However, Elisabetta hypothesizes that the main function may have been to provide water for fountains and thermal baths. There are no Romans around today who can confirm her hypothesis, so she cannot be 100% sure of the validity of her findings. Consequently, she 'hedges' her claims, as you can see in the parts highlighted in italics.

We calculated that the minimum amount of water supplied was around 7,000 m^3 per day. On the basis of demographic estimates for that century, people (1) *may have consumed* from 25 to 50 l per day. (2) *Yet* our calculations show that, if thermal baths and fountains are not taken into account, approximately 280 l per head (3) *could have been pumped* into the town. This figure is 30 l per day higher than the daily average consumption of a post-industrial European country such as Italy.

The quantity of water that flowed along the aqueduct (4) *thus* (5) *appears to have been* much greater than was needed by the population living in Gortyn, which has been estimated as being around 25,000 [ref.]. Therefore the aqueduct was (6) *probably* built not exclusively to provide drinking water for the citizens. Other authors [ref.] contend that Roman citizens may have had running water in their houses and they cite findings at Pompeii as evidence of this. (7) *However*, our previous archeological research [ref.]. into aqueducts in other Roman towns (8) *would seem to* indicate that the aqueducts were not (9) *necessarily* built for the benefit of common citizens. (10) *In fact*, there were many cases where citizens built their own private wells and cisterns even after the construction of the aqueduct [ref.].

Elisabetta uses four types of hedging devices. The numbers below refer to the numbers in the text.

MODAL VERBS

may have + past participle (1) indicates a probability that Elisabetta is not 100% sure about, but she proposes it as being a reasonable calculation based on her (and / or others') studies of demographics.

could have + past participle (3) refers to a past capacity that she assumes would have been possible.

LINK WORDS

yet (2) means that despite the estimates made in the previous sentence, Elisabetta has evidence that may contradict these estimates. *however* (7) has a similar function, as again Elisabetta is contesting previous research.

thus (4) and *in fact* (10) are used by Elisabetta to provide further support for what she has just said. They guide the reader in following Elisabetta's gradual build up of logical evidence.

VERBS THAT INDICATE UNCERTAINTY

appears to have been (5) and *would seem to* (8) are used to precede findings that Elisabetta wishes to propose to her community. She is a young researcher and is taking a modest approach, she doesn't want to irritate the referees or readers by appearing too presumptuous. Although (5) uses the present tense and (8) uses the conditional, in reality there is only a minimal difference – the conditional just adds another 10% of softening!

ADVERBS

probably (6) and *necessarily* (9) are both used to qualify the verb *built*. Elisabetta uses these adverbs to soften the impact and implications of what she is saying. Again, she is protecting herself from possible criticism by other authors and from future research that might invalidate her theories.

Elisabetta concludes her discussion by providing evidence that the Romans could have built the aqueduct much earlier if they had wanted to, and that the real reason for the aqueduct was to supply thermal baths and monumental fountains, and to irrigate fields.

Our findings (11) *suggest* that the aqueduct in Gortyn cannot have been built earlier than the second century AD. In fact, archaeological data show that many cities, like Gortyn, had a high standard of urban, social and political life even before the Roman age.

(12) *There is thus evidence* that the aqueduct only became necessary when "Rome" decided to transform Gortyn into a Roman provincial capital, which entailed Gortyn having thermal baths, monumental fountains, theatre, amphitheatre and well-irrigated and cultivated land to supply its inhabitants.

(13) *We believe that* the present findings (14) *might help* to reassess the real effect of the Roman aqueducts on the local water supply systems and their role in the daily life of the urban populations.

(15) *To the best of our knowledge*, this is the first time that …

In the above text, Elisabetta uses a series of non-assertive verbs and soft introductory phrases in an attempt to gain credibility in her community.

suggest (11) is much less strong than verbs such as 'prove' or 'demonstrate'.

There is thus evidence (12) – this phrase manages to disassociate the author, Elisabetta, from her findings. Rather than saying *we revealed that the aqueduct only became necessary*, she opts for an impersonal expression – *there is*. The idea is to focus the reader's attention on <u>what</u> was found (i.e. the *evidence*) rather than <u>who</u> found it (*we revealed*). She uses *thus* to reinforce the logic in her argumentation.

We believe that (13) is combined with *might help* (14). This is like a double hedge. Elisabetta is making quite a controversial statement that implies a paradigm shift from previous thinking in her field. She uses this double hedge to make her claims seem more tentative.

To the best of our knowledge (15) – Elisabetta again is protecting herself against the possibility that, unknown to her, someone else has already made this finding. If she had begun her conclusion with *This is the first time that…* the tone would have been too strong, and her proposition would have left no room for doubt.

10.13 Summary

Anticipate possible opposition by your referees and readers by not saying things too assertively or directly. In practical terms, it is not difficult to insert 'we believe' and 'might' when describing key findings that could be interpreted in different ways. And if by using these hedging devices you increase your chances of having your paper accepted in a journal located in the USA or UK, then you should use them!

➢ Tone down verbs, adjectives, adverbs and your general level of certainty.

➢ Be aware that the ways you express uncertainty may simply not translate into English.

➢ Provide alternative interpretations of your data.

➢ Tell the reader from which standpoint you want them to interpret or judge your data.

➢ Use impersonal forms to distance yourself when interpreting your findings.

➢ Save your face by writing in an impersonal fashion.

➢ Try to put the work of other authors in a positive light. If appropriate, say their work is open to another interpretation (i.e. yours).

➢ Don't overhedge.

➢ Consider getting help from a native speaker when hedging your claims.

Note: There may be occasions when you really want to convince the referee that your hypothesis is essentially the only interpretation, i.e. you don't want to give the idea that there is an element of doubt. To learn how to deal with such situations, see Sect. 8.9.

Chapter 11

Plagiarism and Paraphrasing

Factoids

US screenwriter, Wilson Mizner (1876–1933), once said: *If you steal from one author, it's plagiarism, if you steal from many, it's research.*

*****

Many famous authors, artists, musicians and politicians (in their speeches) have been involved in alleged plagiarism, including Dan Brown (author of *The Da Vinci Code*), Alex Hayley (author of *Roots*), Andy Warhol (US artist), Damien Hirst (British artist), John Lennon and George Harrison (The Beatles), and Led Zeppelin (British rock band).

*****

According to the website of plagiarism-detector software producers, iThenticate, one in three editors regularly encounters plagiarism, and nine in ten editors say that plagiarism software is effective in revealing cases of plagiarism.

*****

In 2001, thirty-one students at Carleton University (Ottowa, Canada) were caught submitting essays that they had taken from websites, in one case a student had only changed four words from the original essay.

*****

A study by Donald McCabe conducted at Rutgers University (Newark, USA) showed that only 6% of professors report cheating regularly (54% rarely, 40% never). The study highlighted that in an era of political corruption, drug-taking athletes, and illegal downloading (of movies, music and books), students are not able to understand that cheating and plagiarism are wrong.

*****

Wikipedia cites around 20 famous cases of plagiarism in academia, a Rumanian mathematician and computer scientist claims to have published more than 400 papers, a number of which have been shown to be duplicates of papers previously published by other researchers.

© Springer International Publishing Switzerland 2016
A. Wallwork, *English for Writing Research Papers*,
English for Academic Research, DOI 10.1007/978-3-319-26094-5_11

11.1   What's the buzz?

1) What do you understand by the term 'plagiarism'? How serious a problem is it?

2) Choose two of the quotations below. Imagine you wanted to cite them in your paper, but using your own words (i.e. paraphrasing) – what would you write?

What science cannot tell us, mankind cannot know. Bertrand Russell (British philosopher, mathematician, historian, social critic, and political activist)

Science knows only one commandment – contribute to science. Bertolt Brecht (German poet, playwright, and theatre director)

Science cannot stop while ethics catches up – and nobody should expect scientists to do all the thinking for the country. Elvin Stackman (US plant pathologist)

Science has done more for the development of Western civilization in one hundred years than Christianity did in 18 hundred. John Burroughs (US naturalist)

That is the essence of science: ask an impertinent question, and you are on the way to a pertinent answer. Jacob Bronowski (Polish-born British historian of science)

3) Using your own words, write two or three sentences combining and summarizing what is said in the two quotations below.

Plagiarism is unacceptable under any circumstances but, despite this universal disapproval, it is one of the more common faults with student papers. In some cases, it is a case of downright dishonesty brought upon by laziness, but more often it is lack of experience as how to properly use material taken from another source. ... Plagiarism in professional work may result in dismissal from an academic position, being barred from publishing in a particular journal or from receiving funds from a particular granting agency, or even a lawsuit and criminal prosecution. (Prof. Ronald K. Gratz)

Conventions with regard to what constitutes plagiarism vary in different countries and not infrequently clash with commonly accepted practice in most international journals. It is vital that authors ensure that they credit the originator of any ideas as well as the words and figures that they use to express these ideas. Copying without proper acknowledgement of the origin of text or figures is strictly forbidden. Small amounts of text, a line or two, are usually ignored. Plagiarism includes self-plagiarism, which is, in effect, publishing the same work twice. (Prof. Robert Adams)

****

Plagiarism in its simplest terms means cutting and pasting from other studies and papers. It also means taking credit for work that others have done.

Plagiarism includes plagiarizing your own work. In fact, some journals stipulate that you cannot use more than five consecutive words from another paper that you have written.

If a referee thinks you may have plagiarized other people's work or your own, then there is a very high probability that he or she will recommend rejecting your paper. If you commit plagiarism within your university or institute, then you may risk expulsion.

This chapter is designed to help you understand what is and what is not plagiarism, and how to paraphrase other people's work (but always giving a reference). Paraphrasing is also useful for avoiding repetition within your manuscript, and as a means to avoid writing words or phrases that you are not sure are correct.

11.2 Plagiarism is not difficult to spot

Plagiarism is very easy to identify, particularly in papers written by non-native speakers. Plagiarism is particularly evident if you copy phrases from the Internet that contain examples of non-scientific English (e.g. that come from advertisements describing the technical features of a product) or that contain the second person pronoun 'you'. There are many different forms / registers of English (e.g. scientific, commercial, colloquial), and you should not mix them. The problem is that you may not be able to recognize which register a text is in.

I revise a lot of research papers from my PhD students. Sometimes I read a paragraph that contains a considerable number of mistakes in the English (grammar, vocabulary, spelling etc.) and then suddenly there is a sentence written in perfect English! If I then Google the sentence, I very frequently discover it comes from a published paper.

What I do using Google, editors can do using specific software. One such software provider is iThenticate, whose website (http://www.ithenticate.com/) contains much useful information about plagiarism, including a survey amongst academics on what constitutes plagiarism.

The iThenticate survey identified 10 types of plagiarism, including: resubmitting the same paper to many different journals so as to get it published more than once; self-plagiarism (i.e. if you re-use your own work without saying so); not referencing other works correctly; and taking someone else's words and making them seem like your own and without any attribution. The worst case is taking someone else's manuscript and submitting it under your own name.

Clearly, it is not just editors that can benefit from such software. If you are worried that you might have unintentionally plagiarized someone's work (particularly when you are using text that you may have written many months or years ago), then you can use software to check (other tools include CrossCheck, Turnitin, and eBlast).

11.3   You <u>can</u> copy generic phrases

It is perfectly normal to copy phrases from other people's papers. However, these phrases must be generic. In fact, such phrases may even help you to improve your English.

Let's look at what you <u>can</u> paste from another paper.

Here is an example from the literature review of a very interesting paper entitled *International scientific English: Some thoughts on science, language and owner-ship* by Alistair Wood of the University of Brunei Darussalam. In the extract below Wood talks about different styles of scientific writing around the world and how non-native authors may be at a disadvantage with respect to native authors.

Let's imagine that you work in the same field of research as Wood. I have high-lighted phrases in italics that would be perfectly acceptable to paste into your own paper. In fact, these phrases are completely generic.

> *In fact* there is some cross-linguistic contrastive research *to suggest that* the foreigner is *at a disadvantage. Even where* the grammar and vocabulary *may be perfectly adequate, it seems to be the case tha*t a non-native *may tend* to transfer the discourse patterns of her native language to English. *It has been suggested, for example, that* Asian languages such as Chinese, Japanese and Korean have different patterns of argument to English [3]. Thus *one study found that* those Korean academics trained in the United States wrote in an 'English' discourse style, while their colleague who had trained and worked only in Korea, with *a paper published in the same anthology,* wrote in a Korean style *with no statement of purpose* of the article and a very loose and unstructured pattern *from the English point of view* [4]. *More generally* Hinds *has put forward* a *widely discussed position that* Japanese has a different expectation *as to the degree of* involvement of the reader *compared to* English, with Japanese giving more responsibility to the reader, English to the writer [5].

> *It might be objected though that* this is relevant only to languages and cultures which *differ greatly to* English. *However,* research on German *has shown* that German academic writing in the social sciences has a *much less linear structure* than English, *to the extent that* the English translation of a German textbook was criticized as haphazard or even chaotic by American reviewers, *whereas* the original had received no such reviews on the European continent [6]. Academic respectability in English *is evidenced by* the appropriate discourse structure but in German *by the appropriate level of abstraction* [7]. *Similarly,* academic Finnish texts *have been shown to* differ in the way they use connectors and previews and are much less explicit than English in their *drawing of conclusions.* Spanish also has *a similar pattern* [8]. English, *therefore, would seem to be a more* 'writer-responsible' language *than at least some other* European languages.

Note how none of the phrases in italics contain unique information. The phrases could be used in many other contexts.

The above extract is also a good example of how to write a literature review (15.2).

11.4   How to quote directly from other papers

If you use any of the parts of Wood's text that are not in italics without any acknowledgement you are committing plagiarism.

Let's imagine you wanted to quote from the last line of Wood's paper, which concludes as follows:

> The owners of international scientific English should be international scientists not Englishmen or Americans.

You can cite the exact phrase or sentence used by putting it in quotations marks. Then reference the author.

> As noted by Wood [1997]: "The owners of international scientific English should be international scientists not Englishmen or Americans".

As an alternative to *As noted by Wood [1997]* you could say:

> Wood [1997] concludes:
>
> As Wood [1997] states:
>
> As Wood states in his 1997 paper:
>
> In his Conclusions, Wood [1997] writes:

How you make the reference to Wood's paper will obviously depend on your journal's style.

Putting quotation marks ("...") around an unaltered sentence and giving the proper citation for the origin of the work does not technically constitute plagiarism. But it may indicate to supervisors and referees that you have not actually understood what you have written – it is not your own work.

The following comment comes from Dr Ronald K. Gratz's very useful online article *Using Another's Words and Ideas.*

> It is important that you understand the work you are using in your writing. Quoting someone's sentences does not necessarily require this understanding. On the other hand, you must understand the author's meaning if you are going to be able to paraphrase correctly. This is not to say that one should never quote a reference exactly. Exact quotes have value when it is important to give the precise wording used by the original author. It is unacceptable when it is used to make up the bulk of a paper, or of a part of a paper. It is also unacceptable when it is used to avoid the work of putting the ideas into your own words.

However, using quotation marks is acceptable when you are reporting another author's definition or a philosopher's statement.

11.5 How to quote from another paper by paraphrasing

Rather than quoting directly, you can paraphrase Wood's sentence using your own words. But you must still reference Wood, otherwise it would appear that these are you own conclusions. S1 is Wood's original sentence, S2 and S3 are paraphrased versions.

S1. The owners of international scientific English should be international scientists not Englishmen or Americans.

S2. International scientific English belongs to everyone in science [Wood, 1997].

S3. International scientific English does not just belong to native English speakers but to the whole scientific community [Wood, 1997].

Let us now compare the versions.

	WOOD'S ORIGINAL VERSION (S1)	PARAPHRASED VERSIONS (S2 AND S3)
(1)	owners	belongs
(2)	International scientific English	International scientific English
(3)	international scientists	everyone in science
		the whole scientific community
(4)	not Englishmen or Americans	not just … native English speakers

Below is an analysis of the four items in the table.

- Wood uses a noun, the paraphrased version (PV) uses a verb. Switching parts of speech (e.g. noun to verb, noun to adjective) is a great way to paraphrase and 'disguise' the original.

- The only item in Wood's sentence that has not been paraphrased is international scientific English (ISE). This is because ISE is not an expression that was coined (i.e. used for the first time) by Wood. It is a recognized expression that people in the field of teaching English as a foreign language will be aware of.

- Wood uses a noun that refers to a person (scientist), the PV uses the root word (science) and the adjective (scientific). This method of using the same root, but changing the part of speech is very common. A similar combination would be: photographer, photography, photographic.

- Wood made a contrast between two groups of people – all those involved in science (international scientists), and just the English and Americans (and by implication, Canada, Australia etc.). The PV changes the focus slightly and interprets this contrast as being between non-native speakers (international scientists) and native speakers of English.

Now let's look at another example. This time let's imagine you wanted to paraphrase the first line (S4) of Dr Gratz's comments in Sect. 11.4. S5–S8 are possible paraphrased versions, which are in order of increasing difference.

S4. It is important that you understand the work you are using in your writing.

S5. *It is crucial that you completely understand the works you use in your paper [Gratz 2006].

S6. You must have a clear understanding of the reference papers that you quote from in your own manuscript [Gratz 2006].

S7. If you cite any works by other authors in your own paper, it is vital that you really understand the full meaning of what the other authors have written [Gratz 2006].

S8. Researchers should ensure that they fully grasp the meaning of any of the literature that they cite in their papers [Gratz 2006].

Here is an analysis of the types of changes made in each PV. This should help you see the many devices that can be used in paraphrasing.

S5: *crucial* is a synonym for *important*; *completely* is redundant but is a modification of the original; *work* (singular) vs *works* (plural); the present continuous (*are using*) vs present simple (*use*); *writing* (an – ing form used to indicate an activity) vs *your paper* (a noun). S5 is an example of what Gratz would define as 'unacceptable' (Sect. 11.4) because it is essentially identical to the original. Nevertheless, the devices used (synonyms, change of tense etc.) are very useful when paraphrasing.

S6: the concept of *important* (adjective) has been replaced by *must* (a modal verb); *understand* (verb) vs *understanding* (noun); *works you use in your paper* vs *reference papers that you quote from in your own manuscript* (three synonyms for three nouns). S6 might still be considered unacceptable by some experts.

S7: the order in which the information is presented in the original is reversed in the PV. Similar devices to those used in S5 and S6 have also been exploited. S7 is, in my opinion, an acceptable paraphrase.

S8: the major change here is in the way readers are addressed (*you* vs *researchers*), this factor along with the other changes make the sentences almost unrecognizable compared to Gratz's original sentence. However, Gratz is still referenced at the end of the sentence. This is because the concept contained in the sentence still 'belongs' to Gratz. S8 is certainly an acceptable paraphrase.

You may be thinking that paraphrasing is a pointless exercise particularly if you quote the original reference to indicate that the concepts contained are not yours. However what I have outlined above is generally considered to be good practice in the international community. In addition, to be able to paraphrase as in S7 and S8 means that you really have to understand the original sentence, which is clearly beneficial for you.

Note also that you may wish to paraphrase your own writing within the same paper, i.e. to not repeat in the Conclusions the same phrases you have used in the Abstract (Sect. 19.5).

11.6   Examples of how and how not to paraphrase

The following examples and explanations are taken from Dr Gratz's article *Using Another's Words and Ideas*. They are more technical than the examples given in 11.5 and also highlight unacceptable paraphrasing.

S1 is the original version of a sentence from one of Gratz's works, published in 1982.

> S1.   Bilateral vagotomy resulted in an increase in tidal volume but a depression in respiratory frequency such that total ventilation did not change.

A *vagotomy* is a surgical procedure, and *tidal volume* is the lung volume representing the normal volume of air displaced when breathing in and out. Here are three examples of <u>unacceptable</u> attempts to rewrite S1.

> S2.   *Gratz (1982) showed that bilateral vagotomy resulted in an increase in tidal volume but a depression in respiratory frequency such that total ventilation did not change.
>
> S3.   *Gratz (1982) showed that bilateral vagotomy produced an increase in tidal volume and a depression in respiratory frequency so that total ventilation did not change.
>
> S4.   *Gratz (1982) showed that following vagotomy the snakes' lung volume increased but their respiratory rate was lowered. As a result, their breathing was unchanged.

S2 is identical to S1 except that the author is attributed. A couple of words have been changed in S3, but this does not alter the fact that S3 is still substantially the same as S1.

S4 is more serious because the paraphrased version has attempted to find synonyms for key technical words: *lung volume* is not the same as *tidal volume*, and *breathing* is not the same as *total ventilation*. Moreover, dropping the adjective "bilateral" alters the sense of the experimental technique.

S5 is what Dr Gratz would consider as an acceptable paraphrase of his sentence. Although the same information is presented, the sentence structure and word order have been substantially altered.

> S5   Gratz (1982) showed that following bilateral vagotomy the snakes' tidal volume increased but their respiratory frequency was lowered. As a result, their total ventilation was unchanged.

11.7   Paraphrasing the work of a third author

Another case is where you want say the same thing as another author (Wood, in S1), regarding a finding that does not belong to Wood but to a third author's work (Hinds, in S1) which Wood refers to. In this case Wood is discussing the literature, rather than his own personal ideas.

S1.   More generally Hinds has put forward a widely discussed position that Japanese has a different expectation as to the degree of involvement of the reader compared to English, with Japanese giving more responsibility to the reader, English to the writer [Ref 5].

You could paraphrase S1 as follows:

S2.   Many authors, for example Hinds [Ref 5], have proposed that the level of expected reader involvement in Japanese writing is higher than in English.

S3.   It is generally accepted that Japanese writers expect their readers to be more involved than do English writers [Ref 5].

S2 retains the name of the author mentioned by Wood. S3 is stronger and suggests that what Hinds originally proposed has now become generally accepted (an alternative expression is *it is well known that*). This is commonly the case. In fact, Wood's article was published in 1997, since then several other papers and books have been published on the topic, which have reinforced what Hinds proposed.

11.8   Paraphrasing: a simple example

Albert Einstein has been quoted as saying: *The true sign of intelligence is not knowledge but imagination.*

How could you paraphrase Einstein's quotation? [NB: 1935 in the examples below is just my guess as to the year when Einstein made his claim].

SYNONYMS

verbs: Einstein proposed / suggested / stated / found / revealed that ... (1935).

nouns and verbs: A clear indicator of someone's power of intellect is not how much they know but how well their imagination functions (Einstein, 1935).

ACTIVE TO PASSIVE

It has been claimed / proposed / suggested / stated / found / revealed that ... (Einstein, 1935)

DIFFERENT WORD ORDER

> According to (Einstein, 1935), it is imagination rather than knowledge that is the real sign of intelligence.

> Intelligence should be judged in terms of imagination rather than knowledge (Einstein, 1935).

Note how the three key words – *intelligence, knowledge* and *imagination* – have not been paraphrased into words such as *smartness, knowhow* or *fantasy*. None of these three words are exact synonyms and they do not have the same semantic roots. It is important that key words remain as they are. However saying *power of intellect* and *how much they know* is approximately equivalent to saying *intelligence* and *knowledge* and is thus probably acceptable.

The words that can be paraphrased are the more generic words such as *indicator* for *sign*.

11.9 Paraphrasing: how it can help you write correct English

Paraphrasing avoids:

- plagiarism (at least to some extent)

- repetition of phrases within your paper (e.g. not repeating sentences in the Conclusions that you already wrote in the Abstract)

But paraphrasing is also very useful when you are not sure that a sentence you have written is correct English. You can simply paraphrase the sentence using a form that you know is correct. A great rule for writing in English is:

> "Only write what you know is correct".

Let's imagine that you write S1 but you are not sure whether you can begin a sentence with such a time clause (*It is six years that ...*) or whether you have used the correct tense for the second verb (i.e. should it be *is* or something else?).

> S1. *It is several years that* this technology *is* available on the market.

Think about how else you could write the phrase. Here are three other possibilities.

> S2. This technology *was introduced* onto the market *in 2015*.
> S3. This technology first *became* available *several years ago*.
> S4. This technology *has been* on the market *for several years*.

The idea is that you think about various alternatives, and then choose the one that you are most confident about. S2 and S3 contain very simple constructions. S4 is more complex, as this use of the present perfect is almost unique to English.

This technique should help you not only in writing manuscripts, but also in your correspondence with editors (emails and letters), and when writing proposals and reports.

11.10   Plagiarism: A personal view

It is easy to become obsessed by plagiarism, particularly given that you can be 'discovered' by software.

But there is a danger that the anti-plagiarists become unnecessarily rigid.

In my view, plagiarism is unacceptable under three main circumstances:

- plagiarism of others: when you try to deceive editors and readers that some findings are yours when in reality they are someone else's and you have made no attribution to the original author

- quoting directly from another author (and referencing the quotation), but regarding a context that the original author did not intend. This is known as 'quoting out of context', i.e. where someone doesn't report fully what the 'author' meant but just uses a particular part of what was said in order to make a completely different point.

- self-plagiarism: when you try to publish essentially the same paper in more than one journal

However, what I personally feel is acceptable self-plagiarism is in cases where you:

1. repeat the methods that you reported in a previous paper, if the method is exactly the same (but see 16.6 for sensible ways of avoiding this)
2. use text from your own previous works but for a totally different audience

We should use common sense to understand (i) whether we or someone else has committed plagiarism, and (ii) whether such plagiarism will really have a negative impact on someone else.

And finally … I am a native speaker and English language teacher. I am very well equipped to paraphrase. This is not the case for non-native speakers who simply may not have the tools to do so – lack of vocabulary, lack of awareness of possible other grammatical structures. In addition, the education system of many countries is based around children and students studying texts and regurgitating them almost word for word during a written exam or oral test. 'Plagiarism' in this form is ingrained into societies and cultures, so it is hardly surprising that it finds its way into research papers.

11.11   Summary

➢ Plagiarism is a serious issue in international science, even though it may not be considered so in your country of origin. It is easy for native speakers to spot it in the work of non native speakers. If you commit plagiarism your credibility and reputation will be seriously compromised. If you not sure whether you have plagiarized your own or someone else's work, use plagiarism software

➢ Copying phrases from other people's work is perfectly acceptable and is a good way to learn useful phrases in English that you can then use in your own work. However, such phrases must be 100% generic in the sense that they hold absolutely no hard information

➢ Use direct quotations sparingly. The problem is that the referee (or your professor) cannot be sure that you have fully understood the quotation

➢ Typical ways to paraphrase:

- use of synonyms for non key words (especially verbs, adverbs and adjectives)

- change of part of speech, for example: from noun to verb, from noun to adjective, from one category of noun to another category of noun (e.g. *science* to *scientist*)

- change of nouns and pronouns from singular to plural and vice versa

- change of verb form, for example: from *–ing* form to infinitive, from simple to continuous, from active to passive

- change of style from personal to impersonal

- reversal of the order in which information is presented

➢ Never paraphrase technical words

➢ If the original contains ideas that in some sense 'belonged' to the original author, then this author should be acknowledged. This is true even if you have radically changed the original so that it is now unrecognizable

➢ When quoting the work of a 'third' author, cite the reference to that third author's paper

➢ If you are worried that you might have committed plagiarism check with your professor and co-authors

Part II
Sections of a Paper

Chapter 12

Titles

Factoids: Great titles of real papers

❖ Describing the Relationship between Cat Bites and Human Depression Using Data from an Electronic Health Record

❖ Dogs are sensitive to small variations of the Earth's magnetic field

❖ Aesthetic value of paintings affects pain thresholds

❖ Response Behaviors of Svalbard Reindeer towards Humans and Humans Disguised as Polar Bears on Edgeøya

❖ Holy balls!

❖ $10 = 6 + 4$

❖ A minus sign that used to annoy me but now I know why it is there

❖ Can One Hear the Shape of a Drum?

❖ A Midsummer Knot's Dream

❖ College Admissions and the Stability of Marriage

❖ On what I do not understand (and have something to say)

❖ A Smaller Sleeping Bag for a Baby Snake

© Springer International Publishing Switzerland 2016
A. Wallwork, *English for Writing Research Papers*,
English for Academic Research, DOI 10.1007/978-3-319-26094-5_12

12.1   What's the buzz?

1) Match each title (all fictitious) with one or more of the typical complaints by referees. If you think the title is acceptable as it is, then mark it d).

Titles:

1. An in-depth investigation into the overall possibilities of becoming an Olympic medal holder vs getting a well-paid position in academia
2. Inside the right-wing brain: the right hemisphere fails to fulfill abstract reasoning skills and focuses exclusively on self promotion rather than empathy
3. In-car cellular phone usage as a car accident determinant measurement
4. Measuring the sense of humor of various nations as revealed by feedback and comments left on Facebook
5. Observations on the correlation between post office queue length and a country's GDP
6. A novel approach to spam-content determination
7. Should anyone 'own' the world? Is mass emigration a crisis or an opportunity for global integration and understanding?

Referee complaints:

(a) The title is too generic – it should be more informative of the content of the manuscript
(b) Much of the title is redundant: remove non-essential words to allow the key words to stand out. In this way the paper will be more searchable.
(c) As it stands, the title is just a sequence of nouns. I only understood the meaning of the title after I had read the abstract and introduction.

2) Which of the titles above would inspire you to read the whole paper? Which paper do you think would be the most interesting?

3) What is the main finding of your research? Invent a title that encapsulates this finding. Make sure your title is as specific as possible by using the key words that make your research unique. Remember that the more specific your title is, the greater chance that it will be found by indexing and abstracting services.

****

Browsers on the Internet looking for a paper may read hundreds of titles before they select an Abstract to read. According to one of Britain's top editors, writing good headlines represents about 50% of the skills vital to article writing. For this reason the gurus of research writing tend to dedicate more pages to discussing the importance of the title than they do to any section in the paper itself.

Every word in your title is important. So the key is to devise a title that:

1. will immediately make sense to the referee
2. will easily be found by a search engine or indexing system
3. will attract the right kind of readers rather than discouraging them, and will also catch the attention of browsers. Note 'attraction' does not mean resorting to newspaper-like headlines, but simply containing those words that readers in your field would expect to find
4. does not consist of a string of nouns and will be immediately comprehensible to anyone in your general field
5. is reasonably short
6. has a definite and concise indication of what is written in the paper itself. It is neither unjustifiably specific nor too vague or generic

The rules for writing good titles reflect the rules on writing skills in Part 1 of this book.

Note that all the rules relating to titles given in this chapter are also valid for headings, subheadings, and legends / captions. They are also valid for book titles and chapter titles.

12.2   How can I generate a title? How long should it be?

Think about the following questions:

- Which of my findings will attract attention?

- What is new, different and interesting about my findings?

- What are the 3–5 key words that highlight what makes my research and my findings unique?

On the basis of your answers you should be able to formulate a title. If your paper is not about results but proposes a particularly methodology, then your title should encapsulate why your methodology is novel and useful.

Some research (see References for 12.2) has shown that 'journals which publish papers with shorter titles receive more citations per paper'. However, not all researchers have reached the same conclusion, and the best advice is probably to go for a title of intermediate length.

Other research (see References for 12.2) has found that, in some fields, the amount of humor in titles has increased over the years.

One thing everyone agrees on is that the title should be clear and understandable, and be a true reflection of the content of the paper.

12.3   Should I use prepositions in my title?

Most titles of more than about five words require prepositions. The table below explains the typical meanings of prepositions in titles, and gives some examples with and without prepositions.

	MEANING	POOR / INCORRECT ENGLISH	GOOD ENGLISH
by	how something is done	Fast computing machines equation of state calculations	Equation of state calculations *by* fast computing machines
for	for the purpose of	Depression measuring inventory	An inventory *for* measuring depression
from	the origin of	Antonio Gramsci prison notebooks selections	Selections *from* the prison notebooks of Antonio Gramsci
in	where something is located,	Vertical flux of ocean particles	Vertical flux of particles *in* the ocean
	what something regards	Classical theory of elasticity crack problems	Crack problems *in* the classical theory of elasticity
of	belonging to, regarding	Reality social construction	The social construction *of* reality
		Model dimension estimation	Estimating the dimension *of* a model
		Cancer causes: cancer avoidable risks quantitative estimates	The causes *of* cancer: quantitative estimates *of* avoidable risks *of* cancer

Even if you don't understand the exact meaning of the above titles, the important thing to note is that the use of prepositions helps the reader to understand how the various elements in the title are related to each other. Also note that rewriting a title so that it contains prepositions may involve adding *a/an* or *the*. Such cases are underlined in the table.

I have given more examples of the preposition *of* than for the other prepositions because the non-use of *of* tends to create more difficulties for the reader than any other preposition.

Do not worry if you use the same preposition more than once in the same title. For example *of* is used three times in the last title in the table above. This is perfectly acceptable and is not considered bad style in English.

12.4   Are articles (*a / an, the*) necessary?

Although a title is not generally a complete sentence, it does have to be grammatically correct. This means that it must have articles where necessary, even though this will increase the length of the title.

S1.   *Survey of importance of improving design of internal systems
S2.   A survey of the importance of improving the design of internal systems

S1 is not correct English. A general rule of English is that a countable noun that is in the singular must be preceded by an article. In S1, *survey* is a singular countable noun, so it must be preceded by either *a* or *the*. In S2, *a* is the correct choice because we are not referring to a survey that the reader already knows about. An example of where *the* would be necessary is in S3, which is part of a literature review:

S3.   Two surveys on x have been reported in the literature: *the* survey conducted by Williams is more comprehensive than *the* survey carried out by Evans,

In S3, the author is referring to specific surveys, so *the* is obligatory.

Going back to S1, another general grammatical feature of English is that if you have the following sequence of words: *noun1* + *of* + *noun2*, then noun1 is preceded by *the*. This is because noun1 is used to specify noun2. This means that we need *the* before *importance* and before *design*.

The last noun in S1 is countable but it is plural (*systems*) and unspecified (we know that the systems are *internal*, but we do not know which *internal systems* they are). In such cases, no article is required.

No *the* is required for uncountable nouns (i.e. *lack, feedback* and *equipment* in S4–S6).

S4.   Lack of protective immunity against reinfection with hepatitis C virus
S5.   Feedback and optimal sensitivity
S6.   Vibration analysis for electronic equipment

There are some cases where the use or non-use of *the* changes the meaning of the title.

S7.   The factors that determine depression
S8.   Factors that determine depression

S7 gives the idea that the author has made a comprehensive survey of depression and has identified <u>all</u> those factors that lead to depression. This makes the paper sound like the final word on depression, i.e. this is the definitive article on depression.

S8 is not all-inclusive. The reader will expect to learn about <u>some</u> factors. This makes the paper sound much more modest.

Sometimes the use of *the* does not follow the same rules as in general English. For example, the first word in S9–S11 is a countable noun in the singular and as such would normally require *the*.

S9. Effect of clinical guidelines on medical practice

S10. Influence of education and occupation on the incidence of Alzheimer's disease

S11. Association of exogenous estrogen and endometrial carcinoma

S12. Measurement of protein using bicinchoninic acid

Such non-use of *the* seems to be very common in medicine, biology and chemistry. S9 and S10 could also be written as *The effect of...* and *The influence of* with no change in meaning.

Given that the rules of the use of *the* are rather mysterious, the best thing to do is to use Google Scholar to compare your draft title with similar titles. For more explanations of the usage of articles, see Sect. 6.16.

12.5   How do I know whether to use *a* or *an*?

The difference between *a* and *an* in a title follows normal usage.

Use *a* before all consonants, before *eu*, and before *u* when *u* has the sound as in *university* and *unit*.

Use *an* before *a, i* and *o*. It should also be used before *e* except before *eu*, and before *u* when *u* has the sound as in *unusual* and *understanding*. Use *an* before *h* only in the following cases: *hour, honest, honor, heir.* Some authors use *an* before *historical* too.

These rules mean that the following are <u>wrong</u>:

S1. *An hybrid approach to X.

S2. *An unique approach to Y.

S1 should be *a hybrid* (the *h* in *hybrid* is aspirated). S2 should be *a unique*, because the *u* in *unique* is pronounced like *you*.

Note also the words in italics in the following examples:

S3. GNRA tetraloops make a U-turn

S4. The evacuation of the Machault, an 18th-century French frigate

S5. An NLP application with a multi-paradigm architecture

u as a separate letter is pronounced *you*, *18th* stands for *eighteenth* (i.e. beginning with an *e*), and *N* is pronounced *en*.

12.6   Should I try to include some verbs?

Where possible use the *-ing* form of verbs rather than abstract nouns. This will make your title more readable as well as making it 2–3 words shorter.

ABSTRACT NOUNS	VERBS
The *Specification* and the *Evaluation* of Educational Software in Primary Schools	*Specifying* and *Evaluating* Educational Software in Primary Schools
Methods for the *Comparison* of Indian and British Governmental Systems in the 19th century	Methods for *Comparing* Indian and British Governmental Systems in the 19th century
A Natural Language for Problem *Solution* in Cross Cultural Communication	A Natural Language for *Solving* Problems in Cross Cultural Communication
Silicon Wafer Mechanical Strength *Measurement* for Surface Damage *Quantification*	*Quantifying* Surface Damage by *Measuring* the Mechanical Strength of Silicon Wafers

The key words in your title are likely to be nouns. So choose these nouns very carefully. The key words in the first title above are *educational software* and *primary schools*.

Try to choose adjectives that indicate the unique features of your work, e.g. *low cost, scalable, robust, powerful*. Adjectives such as *reliable* should only be used if work in your field has so far only produced an unreliable system or unreliable results.

12.7 Will adjectives such as *innovative* and *novel* attract attention?

The problem with *novel* and *innovative* is that they give no indication as to how something is novel. For example, what does *novel* mean in the following title?

> A novel method for learning English

If your research is not novel then no one would want to read about it anyway. You need to explain to readers what makes it novel. More explicit adjectives to replace *novel* could be: *computerized, guaranteed, high-performance, low-cost, minimal-stress, no-cost, pain-free.*

Finally, no one is likely to include the words *novel* or *innovative* when Googling papers in their field.

12.8 Is it a good idea to make my title concise by having a string of nouns?

The title in S1 is almost incomprehensible for a reader.

> S1.   *Cultural heritage audiovisual material multilingual search gathering requirements

However, for the author S1 will be perfectly clear. You, as an author, know exactly what your title means and so for you it does not seem a problem to put lots of nouns together with no prepositions or verbs. Some of my students have even told me that to them it seems "more English and more elegant". This is simply not the case.

A much clearer version of S1 is S2.

> S2.   Gathering requirements for multilingual searches for audiovisual materials in the cultural heritage

S2 contains prepositions and the definite article, which help to make the meaning much clearer for readers.

Below are some more examples.

ORIGINAL VERSION (OV)	REVISED VERSION (RV)
Educational software specification definitions trends	Trends in defining the specifications for educational software
Examining narrative cinema fiction and fact boundaries	Examining the boundaries between fiction and fact in narrative cinema
New archaeological research and teaching technologies	New technologies for research and teaching in archaeology

What the RVs highlight is that the order of the nouns has been reversed. In the OVs there is a series of nouns that premodify (describe) the final noun. However, these final nouns (*trends, boundaries, technologies*) are not usually used in English in combination with another noun.

Melanie Bell, who researches English language at the University of Cambridge, comments:

> Although native speakers string nouns together, especially when coining terms in technical language, it's probably safer to avoid creating multiword compounds of more than two, or perhaps three, words. English tends to be clearer if nouns are not used in a long string but are broken up by the use of prepositions and verbs that show how the nouns are related to one another.

The OVs are examples of concatenations of nouns, and the RVs represent phrasal options. By 'coining terms' Bell means creating a combination of nouns that has never existed before: *specification definitions trends* and *fact boundaries* are examples of such combinations. The difference between a native speaker and a non-native speaker, is that a native speaker intuitively knows whether a combination sounds right or not, whereas a non-native rarely has this ability. If you are not sure whether a combination exists or not, then check with Google Scholar. If you are combining relatively common words (including technical words) and you don't get at least 100,000 returns, there is a good chance that your combination of nouns does not exist. In such cases you can simply adopt the method highlighted in the RVs. This method involves using verbs (Sect. 12.6) and prepositions (Sect. 12.3).

However, strings of nouns and adjectives must be used if they are names of pieces of equipment or procedures. Here are some examples taken from the Methods section of three papers.

An Oxford Link SATW ultra-thin window EDX detector

A Hitachi S3500N environmental scanning electron microscope

A recently developed reverse Monte Carlo quantification method

For more on this topic see 2.15 and 2.16.

12.9 What other criteria should I use to decide whether to include certain words or not?

You can use an Advanced Scholar Search to check how frequently a word in your title is used. Under the form 'Find articles' insert your word or combination of words into the 'with the exact phrase' field. Then in the 'where my words occur' field, choose 'in the title of the article'.

If the word you choose gets less than a few thousand returns and it is not specifically technical then you should check whether the authors:

- are native speakers

- use the word in the same way and in the same kind of context as you do

If the answer to either of the above is 'no', then you need to think of another word.

For example, the title below may make sense in the native language of the author, but when translated into English it sounds rather strange:

A study on the use of oils and colorants in Roman cosmetics: a witness of make-up preparation

The problem word is *witness*, which is here being used to mean *evidence* or *example*. A search on Google Scholar for "a witness" only gives 1,300 returns, which is very low given that the concept of evidence and examples is very common in research. Also, a quick look at the titles in which the term *witness* appears quickly indicates that *witness* is generally confined to a legal context meaning someone who sees something, it thus refers to a human subject whereas *make-up* is inanimate. You can also see words in context on wordnik.com.

12.10   How should I punctuate my title? What words should I capitalize?

There are two common standards for punctuating titles. Both standards are exemplified in the Factoids at the beginning of this chapter. Check which system is used in your chosen journal.

You can capitalize the first letter of every word except for articles (*a, the, an*), and prepositions and conjunctions:

> Describing the Relationship between Cat Bites and Human Depression Using Data from an Electronic Health Record

> College Admissions and the Stability of Marriage

Or you can just capitalize the first word.

> Aesthetic value of paintings affects pain thresholds

> On what I do not understand (and have something to say)

Note that some words require an initial capital letter if they are proper nouns:

> Does the fact that there are three different electric plug sizes in Italy indicate the level of chaos in the Italian government or economy?

The above title also indicates that the title can end with a question mark. However no other punctuation is required at the end of the title.

Two-part titles may contain a colon:

> The causes of cancer: quantitative estimates of avoidable risks of cancer

For more precise rules, see 24.1 in *English for Research: Grammar, Usage and Style*.

12.11   How can I make my title shorter?

Titles are often constricted by the number of characters that can be used (check with your journal to see how many words or characters you can use). In some cases you can keep your title as it is but reduce it in length simply by replacing the non-key words with shorter synonyms.

LONG VERB	SHORT VERB	LONG NOUN	SHORT NOUN
achieve	gain	advantages	gains, benefits, pros
apportion	allot	examination, investigation	study
calculate, evaluate	assess, rate	improvement	advance
demonstrate, display, exhibit	show	modification	change
determine	fix	LONG ADJECTIVE	SHORT ADJECTIVE
facilitate	ease	accurate	exact
guarantee	ensure	fundamental	basic
prohibit	block	important	key, top
require	need	innovative	novel, new
support	aid	necessary	needed
utilize	use	primary	main

The most obvious ways to make your title shorter are to:

- choose the shortest word (5.8 and 5.9)

- remove redundant words (5.3)

- use verbs rather than nouns (5.13 and 5.14)

12.12 How can I make my title sound more dynamic?

Every word (apart from articles and prepositions) included in the title should add significance. The following words in italics rarely add value.

S1.   *A study of* the factors affecting the trihyroxyindole procedure for the analysis of deoxyribonucleic acid

S2.   *An investigation into* some psychological aspects of English pronunciation

The first seven words in S1 give the reader no information. S1 and S2 might be more dynamic and more concise if the initial redundant words were removed.

S3.   Factors affecting the trihyroxyindole procedure for the analysis of deoxyribonucleic acid

S4.   Some psychological aspects of English pronunciation

Similar words that are often redundant are: *inquiry, analysis, evaluation,* and *assessment.*

However, words such as *study* and *investigation* may be useful to make your research sound less conclusive. S5 sounds like the authors have made the definitive study (i.e. the final settlement or decision) of customer satisfaction, whereas S6 sounds less arrogant and more open.

S5.   *The determinants of customer satisfaction

S6.   An investigation into the determinants of customer satisfaction

However, simply replacing *the* with *some* (S7) or removing it completely (S8) would also make the research seem less definitive.

S7.   Some determinants of customer satisfaction

S8.   Determinants of customer satisfaction

Another occasion where words such as *study* and *investigation* may be useful is in two-part titles. For example:

S9.   Old age: A study of diversity among men and women

However, S9 might have more impact as follows:

S10.   Old age: diversity among men and women

S10 could also be rewritten as a question.

S11.   What factors affect diversity among men and women in old age?

But S11 still contains redundancy and is not particularly eye-catching. Better might be:

S12.   Will women always live longer than men?

12.13 Can I use my title to make a claim?

Many referees and journals editors do not appreciate authors who use the title to present their major conclusion and thus perhaps overstate the importance of their findings. For example:

> The consumption of one apple per day precludes the necessity of using medical services

The above is what is known as a declarative title. It summarizes the author's most important findings, as a complete sentence (i.e. with subject – verb – object). It does so in a way that there seems to be no element of doubt. However, if the author's conclusions are only speculations, then such declarative titles are dangerous. This is because they give readers the initial idea that the issue has been settled and that what the author asserts is now scientific fact.

Such titles are increasingly common in medicine and biology, and may be acceptable if well documented. Such titles also get your paper noticed and potential readers may thus become stimulated into reading your paper. The important thing is to ensure that the title reflects the truth and is supported by the rest of the paper.

Before using a declarative title check with other titles in your chosen journal.

12.14 Are questions in titles a good way to attract attention?

The titles below highlight that a question can be formulated using an auxiliary (e.g. *does, would, can, will*) and using question words (e.g. *why, when, what, which, who*).

> Does the ocean-atmosphere system have more than one stable mode of operation?

> If homo economicus could choose his own utility function, would he want one with a conscience?

> Why Do Some Countries Produce So Much More Output Per Worker Than Others?

> When do foreign-language readers look up the meaning of unfamiliar words? The influence of task and learner variables

> What do bosses do? The origins and functions of hierarchy in capitalist production

> Who would have thought it? An operation proves to be the most effective therapy for adult-onset diabetes mellitus.

Titles with questions also work particularly well for abstracts submitted to conferences. They are generally much more informal and because of their question form they immediately get readers thinking about what the answer might be. They can also be original and fun, as highlighted by the last title. They thus tend to stand out from other titles and are more likely to attract attention.

12.15　When is a two-part title a good idea?

In some cases the first part poses a question, expressed in an informal manner to attract the attention of readers. The second part gives a more technical description of the content of the paper. For example (see 12.14):

What do bosses do? The origins and functions of hierarchy in capitalist production

Who would have thought it? An operation proves to be the most effective therapy for adult-onset diabetes mellitus

In other cases the second part acts as an explanation for the first part:

Consequences of erudite vernacular utilized irrespective of necessity: problems of using long words needlessly

The role of medicine: dream, mirage or nemesis

Telling more than we can know: Verbal reports on mental processes

Given that two-part titles are much less common than other titles they generally attract more attention, and like questions work well for abstracts submitted to conferences.

12.16　How should I write a title for a conference?

Try to ensure that your abstract will not just be enticing for the editorial board, but also that it will be suitable for publishing in the conference handbook / proceedings. Your title should be interesting but not too obscure or too colloquial / witty. It can be less 'technical' than a title for a journal, and may contain a question (12.14) or two parts (12.15) – the first part is technical, and the second part contains a more informal interpretation of the first part. Or vice versa – the first part is more fun, and the second more serious.

12.17   What is a running title?

Many journals require that a running title, also known as a running head or short title, be included in submitted manuscripts. This shortened form of the main title, usually cited at the top of each published page of an article, serves to guide readers browsing a print journal, shuffling loose printed pages, or toggling between multiple papers in PDF form. The running head may also be used in RSS feeds and mobile applications instead of the frequently more unwieldy main title.

Requirements for running titles vary between journals, but generally, they must be 50–60 characters long at most, often including spaces. To achieve brevity, these titles typically include abbreviations, even if the main title does not (or cannot, based on journal guidelines). Articles (the, a, an) may also be omitted to conserve characters, and wordy phrasing, including filler phrases, should be minimized. However, if the main title is brief enough, it can function as the running head as well.

Unlike for the manuscript title itself, being catchy is not a priority for a running title. Rather, because it is so abbreviated, clarity and accuracy should be priorities. Some also suggest that as much content as possible should be preserved from the main title, although in practice, this approach is not widespread; authors instead tend to include only what they deem most important to highlight.

The following is an example of effective title abridgment, drawn from a recently published article (Lambert et al., 2013):

Manuscript title: *Dendritic Cell Immunoreceptor Is a New Target for Anti-AIDS Drug Development: Identification of DCIR/HIV-1 Inhibitors* (117 ch with spaces, 103 ch without spaces)

Running title: *Inhibitors of DCIR Limit HIV-1 Infection* (40 ch with spaces, 35 ch without spaces)

The authors combined a few strategies here to reduce the title length by two thirds, applying the abbreviation "DCIR", omitting articles ("DCIR" instead of "the DCIR"), and focusing on what they judged to be the central concept (the limitation of HIV-1 infection by the inhibitors, rather than the novelty of the target, the application in drug development, or the identification process). Of course, this task may be easier for papers with a narrower and more descriptive focus, such as review articles.

I would like to acknowledge the professional manuscript information of American Journal Experts and their excellent online resource (https://www.aje.com/en/author-resource) from which this entire subsection, written by Michaela Panter, was taken verbatim.

12.18   Is using an automatic spell check enough?

No, it isn't! The following titles contain spelling mistakes and typos (e.g. inverted or missing letters) that spell checkers are not able to find.

S1.   *Incidence of Hearth Attacks and Alzeimer's Disease among Women form East Asia

S2.   *An atmospheric tape reorder: rainfall analysis trough sequence weighing

In S1 there are two errors that a spell checker cannot find – *hearth* and *form* (*heart* and *from*). This is because these words exist and will be in the spell checker's vocabulary. Likewise in S2 *reorder, trough* and *weighing* (*recorder, through* and *weighting*) are words that exist.

A spell checker would certainly highlight *Alzeimer's* (S1) as not being correct, but many authors ignore technical words that are highlighted by mistakenly thinking that they are simply not in the spell checker's vocabulary. Often this is the case, but not here. The correct spelling is *Alzheimer's*.

The problem in this case is that you as the author may be incredibly familiar with the title of your paper, it may even have been the title of your Masters or PhD thesis. This means that you are unlikely to check for possible errors. Given that you may be unable to see your own spelling mistakes, it is a good idea to show your title to several other people, firstly to get them to check the spelling but more importantly to get some feedback on whether your title is clear and explicit enough.

In a research paper, poor spelling gives the idea that you did not make the effort to check your paper. By extension, if you did not check your spelling there is a chance you did not check your data. Perhaps for this reason referees seem obsessed with finding and reporting spelling mistakes. If they find more than one or two this may cause them to recommend that publication of your paper should be delayed until the paper has been thoroughly proof read.

Another major reason for checking the spelling in your title, is that if a key word (e.g. Alzheimer's) is misspelled or not punctuated correctly (note the apostrophe before the *s*), then search engines will not be able to find it.

12.19 Summary: How can I assess the quality of my title?

➤ You need to check that your title is:

- o in correct English – in terms of syntax, vocabulary, spelling and capitalization

- o understandable (no strings of nouns)

- o eye-catching and dynamic (through effective use of vocabulary and even punctuation)

- o sufficiently and appropriately specific

- o a reflection of the content of your paper

- o expressed in a form that is acceptable for a journal

➤ You can check the syntax and the level of understandability by consulting with a native speaker. Generally speaking titles that contain at least one verb and one or more prepositions tend to be much easier to understand.

➤ You can check the vocabulary and spelling using Google Scholar. Remember that an automatic spell check is not enough.

➤ The best way to decide whether it is eye-catching and sufficiently specific is to prepare several titles (including ones in two parts, and in the form of a question) with various levels of specificity and ask colleagues to choose their favorite.

➤ Unless you get someone to read the whole paper for you, you are probably the best judge of whether your title reflects the actual content of your paper. If it doesn't, the referees will probably tell you.

Chapter 13

Abstracts

Factoids: Unusual abstracts

In their paper *Can apparent superluminal neutrino speeds be explained as a quantum weak measurement?* the authors wrote possibly the shortest abstract ever: *Probably not.*

*****

Not quite as short as the Abstract above is this: *A zipper-entrapped penis is a painful predicament that can be made worse by overzealous intervention. Described is a simple, basic approach to release, that is the least traumatic to both patient and provider.* The key words to the paper are: *zipper; foreskin/ penile skin; bone cutter.*

*****

A paper published in 2014 was co-authored by four economists all with the same surname – Goodman. Their 3-sentence abstract was: *We explore the phenomenon of coauthorship by economists who share a surname. Prior research has included at most three economist coauthors who share a surname. Ours is the first paper to have four economist coauthors who share a surname, as well as the first where such coauthors are unrelated by marriage, blood or current campus.*

*****

God does not play dice. He flips coins instead. So began Carlos Mochon's abstract to his paper entitled *Quantum weak coin flipping with arbitrarily small bias.*

*****

The Socceral Force by Norbert Bátfia began: *We have an audacious dream, we would like to develop a simulation and virtual reality system to support the decision making in European football (soccer).*

*****

The abstract to a paper entitled *Pressures produced when penguins pooh– Calculations on avian defecation* ends as follows: *Whether a bird chooses the direction into which it decides to expel its faeces, and what role the wind plays in this, remain unknown.*

*****

The last line of the abstract to a paper entitled *Fractcal Analysis of Deep Sea Topography* is: *No attempt has been made to understand this result.*

© Springer International Publishing Switzerland 2016
A. Wallwork, *English for Writing Research Papers*,
English for Academic Research, DOI 10.1007/978-3-319-26094-5_13

13.1   What's the buzz?

1) Below is a structured abstract (13.10) entitled *Language and publication in Cardiovascular Research articles* and was published in the international journal *Cardiovascular Research*. The author, Robert Coates, talks about the reasons why papers are and are not accepted for publication.

Read the abstract and think about:

- how it is structured and what information is contained in each of the four parts

- how relevant Dr Coates' research is in terms of you writing a manuscript for publication in an international journal

- what kinds of English language errors you tend to make when writing papers and how you could avoid them

BACKGROUND: The acceptance rate of non-mother English tongue authors is generally a lot lower than for native English tongue authors. Obviously the scientific quality of an article is the principal reason for publication. However, is editorial rejection *purely* on scientific grounds? English mother tongue writers publish *more* than non mother-tongue writers—so are editors discriminating linguistically? We therefore decided to survey language errors in manuscripts submitted for publication to *Cardiovascular Research* (CVR).

METHOD: We surveyed language errors in 120 medical articles which had been submitted for publication in 1999 and 2000. The language 'error' categories were divided into three principal groups: grammatical, structural and lexical which were then further sub-divided into key areas. The articles were corrected without any knowledge of the author's nationality or the corrections made by other language researchers. After an initial correction, a sample of the papers were cross-checked to verify reliability.

RESULTS: The control groups of US and UK authors had an almost identical acceptance rate and overall 'error' rate indicating that the language categories were objective categories also for the other nationalities. Although there was not a direct relationship between the acceptance rate and the amount of language errors, there was a clear indication that badly written articles correlated with a high rejection rate. The US/UK acceptance rate of 30.4% was higher than for all the other countries. The lowest acceptance rate of 9% (Italian) also had the highest error rate.

DISCUSSION: Many factors could influence the rejection of an article. However, we found clear indications that carelessly written articles could often have either a direct or subliminal influence on whether a paper was accepted or rejected. On equal scientific merit, a badly written article will have less chance of being accepted. This is even if the editor involved in rejecting a paper does not necessarily identify language problems as a motive for rejection. A more detailed look at the types and categories of language errors is needed. Furthermore we suggest the introduction of standardized guidelines in scientific writing.

2) What key information is missing in the Abstract below?

The aim of our research was to discover whether it is possible to transform recycled plastic into pure 100% gold. *Background information.* This paper describes how recycled plastic provided by local industries was fused and then mixed with an innovative mixture of water and air. Tests were then carried out over a six-month period. Future work will involve repeating the same tests to see whether platinum can be produced with the same procedure.

****

The first fourteen subsections of this chapter explain what an Abstract is, what tenses and style to choose (Sects. 13.8 and 13.9), and what the various types of Abstracts are (structured, extended, video). Sections 13.15–13.19 explain how to begin an abstract, what to include and how to raise its impact. Sections 13.20–13.22 outline some typical pitfalls of badly written abstracts. Sections 13.23–13.24 highlight how abstracts may vary from discipline to discipline. Sections 13.25–13.28 discuss abstracts for review papers and conferences. The final section (13.29) indicates how editors and reviewers evaluate an abstract.

Note that the sources of the many abstracts mentioned in this chapter can be found in the References.

13.2 What is an abstract?

An Abstract is like a mini paper. It accurately summarizes all the sections of your paper. It will be judged in isolation from the accompanying paper. Abstracts are sometimes called Summaries.

Abstracts are found before a full article in a journal, standalone in databases of abstracts, and in conference programs.

The structure of an abstract and its length will depend on the journal or conference, as well as on your field of research. Make sure you read their instructions to authors (13.7) before you begin writing.

An Abstract generally answers at last the first three of the following questions, and generally in the following order. You can use the answers to these questions to structure your Abstract.

- Why did I carry out this project? Why am I writing this paper?

- What did you I, and how?

- What were my results? What was new compared to previous research?

- What are the implications of my findings? What are my conclusions and/or recommendations?

Although most Abstracts shouldn't concentrate on the methods but more on the results, some scientists (e.g. chemists, physicists, biologists) who are presenting some new instrumentation may want to focus not on what they found, but on what the benefits of their apparatus are and how well it performs.

To decide what to include in your Abstract, go through your paper and highlight what you consider to be the most important points in each section.

Remember that an Abstract is NOT an Introduction to your paper, it is a summary of ALL your paper.

13.3   How important is the Abstract?

Incredibly important.

Editors may decide whether or not to send your paper for review exclusively on the basis of your Abstract.

Reviewers will probably read your Abstract first before reading any other parts your paper. Ensuring that they have a positive reaction is essential. If they don't like your Abstract they may simply stop reading and reject the paper, rather than wasting their time reading and evaluating the rest of the paper. In fact, a poor Abstract is very often the sign of a poor paper.

Research has proved that what you experience first will condition how you perceive what comes after – we tend to judge everything in comparison with something else, i.e. something that came before. This means that if your Abstract is clearly written, you will set up a positive expectation amongst your readers – they will think that if the Abstract is easy to understand then the rest of the paper is likely to be easily understood too. This will certainly encourage them to read on.

Your title and your Abstract will generally be the only parts of your paper that are available online at no cost. So when a potential reader finds your paper, they will use your Abstract to help them decide whether to buy the full version of your paper and / or read the rest of the paper.

13.4   Where is the Abstract located?

A typical first page of a research paper for publication in an international journal contains the following headings, generally in this order:

1. Title
2. Abstract
3. Highlights
4. Key words

Not all journals require Highlights and Key Words.

13.5   What are 'highlights'?

Some journals require you to write between three and five bullet points reporting the core findings of your paper. The 'instructions to the author' (see Sect. 13.7) will tell you how many bullets and how many characters per bullet. For example, the highlights of the paper in 13.1 could be:

► We surveyed grammatical, structural and lexical errors in 120 medical articles.

► Badly written articles correlated with a high rejection rate.

► On equal scientific merit, a badly written article will have less chance of being accepted.

► Rejection may be due to language errors, though editors may not identify this as the cause.

► We suggest the introduction of standardized guidelines in scientific writing.

The Highlights are generally located immediately below the Abstract and immediately above the Key Words.

13.6 How should I select my key words?

In most journals, directly below the Abstract there is a list of key words. These are for indexing purposes and will help your paper be identified more easily and thus cited more frequently.

Ensure you check with your journal's 'instructions to authors' to see how many key words to include, and whether or not these can also be words that appear in the title of your paper.

1. Read through your paper and underline the 'technical' terms that you've used most frequently.
2. Check that the terms you've listed in (1) match the key technical terms used in your specific field
3. Consider including variants / alternatives of some of the terms, and also their acronyms
4. Include common abbreviations of terms (e.g., HIV).
5. Meet the criteria of indexing and abstracting services (see en.wikipedia.org/wiki/Indexing_and_abstracting_service)
6. Type your chosen keywords into Google Scholar (or a similar search engine). Do the results match your topic?

There is a lot of mystery around how Google and other search engines use key words when indexing websites and articles. In any case it makes sense to have key words in your abstract (and title too) because it forces you, the author, to decide what words in your paper really are important. The key words are also the words that readers are looking for in their initial search and then when they actually scan your abstract. General consensus seems to be to not repeat the key words more than three times in the abstract. This can be tedious for the reader. More importantly, 'keyword spamming' may lead to the web page being rejected by the search engine.

13.7 Why should I download the instructions to the author? Isn't it enough to check how other authors for the same journal have structured their abstract?

You cannot tell from looking at a published abstract in your journal of choice exactly what the editors want and do not want. This information can only be obtained by downloading the journal's "instructions to authors". These instructions will tell you whether:

- there is a limit on the word count

- you can use the active or passive (7.4), and whether you can use *we*

- references are allowed

- you can use a note-like form in some items of a structured abstract (13.10), but full sentences are required in the results and conclusions

- you can change and/or delete the headings in a structured abstract

It is not possible to glean the information above simply by looking at another author's abstract.

13.8 What style should I use: personal or impersonal?

There are four possible styles for writing abstracts and papers:

STYLE 1   I found that x = y.
STYLE 2   We found that x = y.
STYLE 3   It was found that x = y.
STYLE 4   The authors found that x = y.

The style you use will depend on your discipline and on the requirements of the journal. Using the first person singular (Style 1), is generally only found in humanistic fields where the author's opinions are often outlined. Here is an example – an abstract from a paper entitled *International scientific English: Some thoughts on science, language and ownership.*

STYLE 1 The intention of this paper is to raise some questions about the 'ownership' of scientific English. Its author is a native speaker of English and a teacher of scientific English, but it aims its arguments at the international scientific community communicating in English. The paper is deliberately somewhat provocative in parts in an attempt to raise some questions about 'scientific English' which *I think* are important but which have not been faced to date.

Style 2 is found in all fields. Here is an example of the beginning of an abstract from a physics paper entitled *Tumbling toast, Murphy's Law and the fundamental constants*.

> STYLE 2 *We investigate* the dynamics of toast tumbling from a table to the floor. Popular opinion is that the final state is usually butter-side down, and constitutes prima facie evidence of Murphy's Law ('If it can go wrong, it will'). The orthodox view, in contrast, is that the phenomenon is essentially random, with a 50/50 split of possible outcomes. *We show* that toast does indeed have an inherent tendency to land butter-side down for a wide range of conditions.

Style 3 is also very common and many journals insist on this style. For an example of this style see the abstract in 13.23. For the problems associated with this style see 7.4.

Style 4 is the least common style. Here is an example of the beginning of an abstract from a fascinating psychology paper entitled *Unskilled and unaware of it: How difficulties in recognizing one's own incompetence lead to inflated self-assessments*

> STYLE 4 People tend to hold overly favorable views of their abilities in many social and intellectual domains. *The authors* suggest that this overestimation occurs, in part, because people who are unskilled in these domains suffer a dual burden: Not only do these people reach erroneous conclusions and make unfortunate choices, but their incompetence robs them of the metacognitive ability to realize it. Across 4 studies, the authors found that ...

For links to these papers see References.

To give you an idea of the different effects that using different styles can have, below is an abstract written in a personal style (see Sect. 13.16 for a version of the same abstract with an impersonal style).

> We have developed an analytical model which predicts the relationship between the number of times a 5G cellular phone battery is recharged, the length of time of each individual recharge, and the duration of the battery. We validated this model by comparison with both experimental measurements and finite element analyses, and it shows strong agreement for all three parameters. The results for the proposed model are more accurate than results for previous analytical models reported in the literature for 5G cell phones. The new model can be used to design longer lasting batteries. It can also lead towards further models that can predict battery failure.

The benefits of using *we* rather than the impersonal passive form are:

- it is more reader friendly and easier to follow

- it is more direct and dynamic

- the word count is reduced and sentences tend to be shorter

- it is much easier for you, the author, to write

I suggest that if given the choice you opt to use *we / our*.

13.9   What tenses should I use?

The most commonly used tenses in all kinds of abstracts are the PRESENT SIMPLE (*we show*) and the PAST SIMPLE (*we showed*).

The author of the "tumbling toast" abstract (Style 2) uses the PRESENT SIMPLE to:

- describe the contents of his paper (*we investigate, we show*).

- describe the common opinion that he is trying to question (*the phenomenon is essentially random*)

- refer to what he did during his experiments (*We show that toast does indeed have an inherent tendency*)

- give his conclusions – not shown here – (*Murphy's Law appears to be an ineluctable feature of our universe*)

In fact he uses <u>only</u> the PRESENT SIMPLE . Even though his research has already been done (thus the investigation is complete), he uses the PRESENT SIMPLE because he wants to make his abstract sound more dynamic and his conclusions more convincing. However, in the paper itself he uses the PAST SIMPLE to describe what he did and found.

In the "incompetence" abstract (Style 4), the authors use the PRESENT SIMPLE to:

- talk about a well-known situation (*people tend to hold overly favorable views*)

- explain their opinion on this well-known situation (*the authors suggest that …*)

They then use the PAST SIMPLE to describe what they did / achieved and what conclusions they reached (*the authors found that ..*). This is the standard way to use tenses in abstracts.

The author of the "scientific English" abstract (Style 1) ends his abstract by using the PRESENT PERFECT (*which have not been faced to date*). You can use the PRESENT PERFECT and the PRESENT PERFECT CONTINUOUS when you describe a situation that began in the past and is still true now. This is typical when you are giving the context / background.

In the last few years there *has been* considerable interest in …

Since 2015 attention *has focused* on …

To date, there *has not been* an adequate analytical model …

For more than a decade data analysts *have been developing* new ways to …

Note: the underlined parts highlight the past-to-present timeframe. For example, *in the last few years* means a situation or action that began a few years ago and is still true today. *To date* means so far in the history of this particular branch of study.

Some authors also use the PRESENT PERFECT (in the active or passive) to describe what they achieved during their research.

We *have found / devised / developed* a new approach to X. We *have demonstrated / proved / validated* the effectiveness of this approach by …

A new approach to X *has been devised.* The effectiveness of the approach *has been demonstrated* …

Important note: Beginning your Abstract with a phrase such as *In the last few years* or *Recently there has been* is both uninspiring and unnecessary.

13.10   What is a structured abstract?

A structured abstract is an abstract with distinct, labeled sections. Here is an example from a fictitious paper entitled *Do selfies induce selfish behavior?*

Background The selfie gene (NARC1 *egophilia*) ensures that individuals try to maximize their own success, even if this impacts negatively on other members of society and on the natural environment. For example, smoking, particularly in public places, is considered to be a selfish act as well as polluting the local atmosphere.

Objective We investigated the possible correlation between smoking and four specific acts of selfish behavior: use of selfie sticks in confined public places, litter throwing, spitting chewing gum, and double parking.

Methods Closed-circuit TV (Canon VB S30D Dome CCTV cameras) were strategically located outside bars, in the street, in football stadiums and tourists sites. A total of 10,000 hours of film footage, collected from cameras located in five European cities, were analysed using SeeSeeTV v. 2.1.

Results Smokers were found to be much more likely to indulge in acts of selfish behavior compared to non-smokers: double parking (+80%), litter throwing (+57.33%), and spitting chewing gum onto the pavement (+34%). No correlation was found between male smokers and the use of selfie sticks, whereas female smokers showed a five-fold greater prevalence of selfie stick usage with respect to female non-smokers.

Conclusions Selfish behavior is a clear form of self promotion, benefitting the individual in terms of saving time (double parking, leaving litter and spitting gum) and image with other friends (obsession with selfies). Moreover, it impacts negatively on the environment, ultimately destroying the beauty of the world for the rest of the population. Such behavior should be addressed by educationalists in school curricula. Future work will investigate the link between smoking and the following three factors: tax avoidance, non-collection of owner's dog excrement, and drink driving.

As highlighted on the website of the U.S. National Library of Medicine:

Structured abstracts have several advantages for authors and readers. These formats were developed in the late 1980s and early 1990s to assist health professionals in selecting clinically relevant and methodologically valid journal articles. They also guide authors in summarizing the content of their manuscripts precisely, facilitate the peer-review process for manuscripts submitted for publication, and enhance computerized literature searching.

Structured abstracts tend to be used most in medical journals:

Approximately 30% of all abstracts currently added to MEDLINE® in PubMed are structured. Structured abstracts perform better than unstructured abstracts for the discovery of corresponding MeSH (Medical Subject Headings®) terms using the Medical Text Indexer (MTI) software application.

If you are a medical researcher you can learn more about the different types of abstract from the British Medical Journal's website: www.bmj.com/about-bmj/resources-authors/article-types/researchStructured abstract

Below are some more typical headings for structured abstracts in the medical field:

Background / Context / Purpose – Methods – Results / Findings – Conclusions

Context – Aim / Objective – Design – Setting – Patients (or Participants) – Interventions / Treatment – Main Outcome Measure(s) – Results – Conclusions

Context – Objective – Data Sources – Study Selection – Data Extraction – Results – Conclusions

And here are some from other disciplines:

From a journal of vegetation sciences:

Question – Location – Methods – Results – Conclusions

From an economics journal:

Purpose – Design / Methodology / Approach – Findings – Practical implications – Originality / Value – Keywords – Paper type

Another example of a structured abstract can be found in 13.1.

13.11 I am not a medical researcher, can I still use a structured abstract?

The type of abstract you opt for does not depend on you, but on the journal – so have a look at other papers in your chosen journal to see what the typical style is. In any case you should always download the instructions to the author (see Sect. 7.2).

A structured abstract could really be used for any piece of research, given that all research should have (1) a context, (2) an aim, (3) a method, (4) some results, (5) an interpretation of the overall meaning, possible applications, and ideas for how the research might be continued.

So even if your journal does not require a structured abstract, you will certainly write a much more effective abstract if you at least include the same information in the same order (though you can invert points 1 and 2)

13.12 What is an Extended Abstract?

An extended abstract is like a mini research paper, whose ideas and significance can be understood, according to William Pugh, professor of Computer Science at the University of Maryland, "in less than an hour". Professor Pugh says:

> An ideal submission should have a reviewer intrigued within the first 5 minutes of reading, excited within 15 minutes and satisfied within 45 minutes. If your abstract fails any of these tests, it might be rejected no matter how good the research is. Committee members may spend more than 30–45 minutes on your abstract, but you shouldn't rely on it.

Some journals will not require an extended abstract to contain complete details of methodology / proofs and future work. However, they will expect comparisons with related work, the key aspects of the methodology, results and some kind of discussion of the results.

If you are short of space, then you may be allowed to use an appendix, but bear in mind that many reviewers simply won't have the time to read appendices.

13.13 What is a video abstract? How can I make one?

A video abstract, as explained by expert Karen McKee (see References), is a brief description of a technical paper in which you explain your work on camera, physically demonstrate your methods, use animations or simulations to illustrate concepts, and/or discuss the implications of your findings. By using video and other multimedia, you can explain your work in a way that the print article cannot. This approach provides a richer, more accessible and more diverse experience for the readership.

There are several reasons for using a video abstract:

* have more flexibility to describe and explain your work

* gain greater visibility for you and your research, particularly if you post your video on the internet (e.g. YouTube)

* increase readership for your printed article

* exploit search engines which tend to rank video high in relation to text-based descriptions, so a video abstract can make your work more visible and accessible to fellow researchers searching for papers on that topic

The British Medical Journal (BMJ) encourages authors to create video abstracts lasting up to four minutes to accompany accepted research articles. The BMJ's website (www.bmj.com/about-bmj/resources-authors/article-types/research) gives some great advice:

> Video abstracts enable authors to go beyond the constraints of their written article to personally explain the importance of their work to *The BMJ*'s global audience. ... In the simplest kind of video abstract the author(s) talks directly into the camera and, perhaps, presents a slideshow. In the interest of maximising engagement and visibility, however, we encourage authors, where appropriate, to combine footage of themselves with other relevant visual and audio material (such as animations, video clips showing how the study was conducted and any intervention was delivered, audio, still photographs, figures, infographics).

When using materials from previously published work, ensure you have the relevant permissions.

13.14 My aim is to have my paper published in *Nature*. Is a *Nature* abstract different from abstracts in other journals?

In *Nature* an abstract is called a 'summary paragraph'. On their website, *Nature* recommends the structure below, which you can also use to good effect if you are submitting your manuscript to another journal:

- One or two sentences providing a basic introduction to the field, comprehensible to a scientist in any discipline.

- Two to three sentences of more detailed background, comprehensible to scientists in related disciplines.

- One sentence clearly stating the general problem being addressed by this particular study.

- One sentence summarising the main result (with the words "here we show" or their equivalent).

- Two or three sentences explaining what the main result reveals in direct comparison to what was thought to be the case previously, or how the main result adds to previous knowledge.

- One or two sentences to put the results into a more general context.

- Two or three sentences to provide a broader perspective, readily comprehensible to a scientist in any discipline, may be included in the first paragraph if the editor considers that the accessibility of the paper is significantly enhanced by their inclusion. Under these circumstances, the length of the paragraph can be up to 300 words.

For an example of this structure taken from a summary paragraph in Nature see: www.nature.com/nature/authors/gta/Letter_bold_para.doc

13.15 How should I begin my Abstract?

When you read an advertisement for a product it never begins *The objective of this advertisement is to convince you to buy* ... Instead advertisers go straight to the point. Abstracts are like advertisements for your paper.

You want your abstract to stand out so that there will be a better chance someone will notice it and read it. If you begin your abstract with commonly used phrases (by both native and non-native English speakers) such as *This paper deals with* ... *The aim of this paper* ... *This article explores* ... *We report* ... you are not differentiating yourself from the others. In fact, some journals advise against using such expressions.

Below are some examples taken from abstracts (the first and third are fictitious) in very different fields. In the OVs readers have to wait for up to 15 words (i.e. until //) before reaching a key word that enables them to understand the potential relevance of the topic. They are forced to read words and expressions that they have read thousands of times before and which add absolutely no value to the abstract. In the RVs, the reader learns either immediately or very quickly how the author has filled the knowledge gap.

ORIGINAL VERSION (OV)	REVISED VERSION (RV)
1 In this paper we present the design and development of a *highly innovative* software application //, Transpeach, which allows *mobile phone users* to use their own native language when speaking to someone of another native language. The prototype version enables a Japanese mobile phone user ...	*Transpeach* extends automatic translation from written to oral communication. This software allows, for instance, a *Japanese mobile phone* user to talk to a Greek counterpart in Greek, likewise the Greek's words are automatically translated into Japanese .

RV1: In the first sentence the author manages to combine both the background (automatic written translation) with the new information (automatic oral translation). The words *highly innovative* have been removed. More concrete examples are given, which reflect what the prototype does.

2 We present a procedure for the analysis of the content of // organic materials present in archeological samples. The procedure allows the identification of a *wide variety* of materials within the same micro sample.	Archeological samples used for identifying organic materials are by necessity extremely small. We have found a way, which *we believe* is the first of its kind, to accurately identify *glycerolipids, natural waxes, proteinaceous, resinous and polysaccharide* materials within the same micro sample.

RV2: The abstract now begins with *archeological samples*, so that the reader can immediately understand the general topic of the paper. The vague phrase *a wide variety of materials* has been replaced with concrete examples of these materials. This makes the RV slightly longer than the OV, but it now has a much stronger impact.

Going back to RV1, rather than telling your readers that what you have done is *highly innovative*, it might be more effective if you demonstrate the innovation element so clearly that readers reach this conclusion by themselves. This does not mean you always have to be modest about your achievements. In fact in RV2 the phrase *which we believe is the first of its kind* has been added to draw the reader's attention to the contribution of the paper. The term *highly innovative* is subjective, *first of its kind* is informative.

3	In this article we conduct an exploration of the crucial role of the // invention of the steam engine in the Industrial Revolution, and specifically the modified version created by James Watt, the Scottish inventor born in 1736. However, *we contend that the merit* for the success of the steam engine should be ...	James Watt's modified steam engine is widely acknowledged as paving the road to the Industrial Revolution. But was this Scottish inventor really the brains behind the steam engine? We *contend that Henry Wallwork*, a little-known Mancunian foundry entrepreneur, should be given more credit for ...

RV3: The abstract now gets straight to the point without the initial redundancy of the OV. The OV contains a detail – the birth date of James Watt – that serves no purpose for the reader and has thus been removed in the RV.

4	Several authors have highlighted the high yields and low environmental impacts associated with the cultivation of // perennial rhizomatous grasses (PRGs).	Perennial rhizomatous grasses (PRGs) tend to have a high yield combined with a low environmental impact.

RV4: Redundancy has been removed. The abstract now begins with the key word (PRGs), which are also the main topic of the paper. This leads to an opening sentence – describing the background to the research – that is both clear and incisive.

5	All of us, you and I, have individual abilities and disabilities in a physical and mental as well as a social and economic sense.

RV5: The reviewer told the author to delete the phrase, giving this explanation:

The opening statement is both casual and contentious and is thus unsuitable for publication in *<name of journal>*. Start by giving the aims of the paper and how they will be achieved.

Note that what the reviewer says is not in contradiction to what I outlined at the beginning of this section (i.e. not saying *The aim of the paper is to ...*). She is simply recommending that the author begin the abstract by writing something like: *We investigated the physical and mental disabilities of a sample of ...*

13.16   How much background information should I give?

An Abstract is not an introduction to your paper. This means that context setting should never take up more than 25% of the whole abstract, as it probably contains information that the reader already knows. The background information in the abstract (fictitious) below represents about four fifths of the total abstract – this is too much.

In the last few years 5G cellular batteries have become increasingly popular in the telecommunications and computer industries. Many authors have studied the various features of such batteries and noted that the lifetime of a 5G cellular battery, in particular those used in the most recent generations of mobile phones, may be subject to the number of times the battery is recharged and how long it is charged for. In addition, it has been found that there is no adequate analytical model to predict this lifetime. Such an accurate model is necessary in order for producers and consumers alike to be able to predict how long the batteries will last and also, in some cases, how they can be recycled. In this work, an analytical model is developed which describes the relationship between the number of times a battery is recharged, the length of time of each individual recharge, and the duration of the battery.

Your readers want new information, not old information. Remember that the reader may be a referee who has to read hundreds of abstracts to decide which to include for a conference or in a journal. He / She wants to know immediately what the topic is and will be negatively affected if forced to wait several lines before understanding this. Of course, you can (and should) give more background details in the Introduction.

Also, the extract above does not describe the methodology or the results, nor what can be concluded from the model the authors have developed. A much better solution is given below:

(1) The lifetime of a 5G cellular phone battery may be subject to the number of times the battery is recharged and how long it is charged for. To date, there has not been an adequate analytical model to predict this lifetime. (2) In this work an analytical model is developed which describes the relationship between the number of times a battery is recharged, the length of time of each individual recharge, and the duration of the battery. (3) This model has been validated by comparison with both experimental measurements and finite element analyses, and shows strong agreement for all three parameters. (4) The results for the proposed model are more accurate than results for previous analytical models reported in the literature for 5G cell phones. (5) The new model can be used to design longer lasting batteries.

Below is the structure of the above abstract and the questions it aims to answer. The numbers refer to the numbers in the abstract.

1. The problem that this paper is trying to resolve set in the context of the current situation. Why did you carry out your project and why are you writing this paper? What gap in the current knowledge do you hope to fill?
2. New solution given by authors of the paper. What is the innovative contribution of your work? What did you do and achieve? What makes it different from previous research?
3. Validity of the model. Does it really do what you say it does?
4. Results. What is new compared to previous results?
5. Implications and future work. What does this all mean? What are your conclusions and recommendations? What do you plan to do next?

This abstract only has a minimal amount of background information (two lines). This background information is given so that reader can understand the context of the author's research.

13.17   Should I mention any limitations in my research?

You should certainly mention the limitations of your research at some point in the paper. However, given that an Abstract is designed to 'sell' your research, you might decide not to mention the limitations until the Discussion (18.12).

13.18   How can I ensure that my Abstract has maximum impact?

There are three main ways to do this. Firstly, put the information in the best possible order (13.3–13.8). Secondly, highlight the importance of what you are saying (Chapter 8). And thirdly, be as concise as possible (13.19).

13.19 Why and how should I be concise?

Below are the first sentences from two different abstracts. How do you think the reviewers reacted when reading them?

S1. Tomato (*Solanum lycopersicum L.*) is a worldwide-cultivated vegetable crop which is affected by many viruses that cause significant economic losses whose detection and identification is of critical importance to plant virologists in general and, in particular, to scientists and others involved in plant protection activities and quarantine and certification programs.

S2. In this paper a high performance "pattern matching" system is presented. The system is based on the concept of Recalled Association (RA), designed to solve the track-finding problem typical of high energy physics experiments executed in hadron colliders. It is powerful enough to process data produced from 90 overlapping proton-proton collisions.

The paper that contained S1 was rejected, the author was informed that 'the paper must be rewritten completely'. The reviewer gave an example of what kind of 'rewriting' was required – basically he wanted all the redundancy removed (he managed to remove 40% of what the author had written!):

S3. Tomato (Solanum lycopersicum L.) is affected by many viruses that cause significant economic losses. Their detection and identification is of critical importance in plant protection and quarantine, and in certification programs.

Moral of the story:

- If the reader or reviewer sees a lot of redundancy in the abstract, then he/she will probably stop reading.

- In your abstract every word must add VALUE.

In addition to being heavily redundant, S1 contains one long 50-word sentence. S2 has the same number of words as S1 but contains three sentences. You might thus think that S2 escaped the reviewer's wrath (anger). The problem is that S2, like S1, contains a lot of redundancy which massively reduces its impact and thus immediately diminishes the reader's desire to continue reading. A better version would be:

S4. A high performance pattern matching system based on Recalled Association is presented. It solves the track-finding problem, which is typical of high energy physics experiments in hadron colliders. It can process data produced from 90 overlapping proton-proton collisions.

S4 is about 20% shorter than the original S2, but no information has been lost. It also puts the key information right at the beginning of the first sentence.

Moral of the story:

- Show respect for your readers by not forcing them to read words and phrases that are the result of your lazy writing.

- Increase the chances of your reviewers accepting your manuscript by simplifying the review process.

- Be obsessed about removing redundancy. I guarantee that redundancy has a very negative impact on all types of writing.

To learn how to reduce redundancy, read the summary of Chapter 5 at least once a day!

13.20 What should I <u>not</u> mention in my Abstract?

You should try to avoid:

- background information that is too generalist for your readers

- claims that are not supported in the paper

- terms that are too technical or too generic – this will depend on your audience

- definitions of key terms

- mathematical equations (unless the whole paper revolves around these equations)

- generic quantifications (e.g. *many, several, few, a wide variety*) and the overuse or unjustified use of subjective adjectives (e.g. *innovative, interesting, fundamental*).

- unnecessary details that would be better located in your Introduction, such as the name of your institute, place names that readers will not have heard of

- references to other papers. However, if your whole paper is based on extending or refuting a finding given by one specific author, then you will need to mention this author's name.

13.21   What kinds of words do referees not want to see in an Abstract?

You should try to avoid words and phrases that add no value for the reader. Typically:

- words that are not concrete, particularly abstract nouns (5.4)

- expressions that are vague (6.7)

Adjectives, too, can create problems – *interesting, challenging, vital, fundamental, innovative, cutting-edge*. What exactly do these words means? Can you be sure that the referee will understand why something is *interesting* and thus agree that is *interesting*? You cannot throw these words into your Abstract hoping that referees will understand your level of excitement. Much better is to avoid these adjectives completely, and to clearly demonstrate why and how something is interesting or challenging.

If you read on a CV that a candidate describes herself as having 'excellent communication skills', do you believe her even if she provides no evidence in her CV of such excellence? No, you don't. You simply think to yourself "everyone says they have good communication skills, it means nothing". The same is true of any claims you make in your abstract – don't simply tell your readers that something is "fundamental", show them how it is fundamental, convince them.

13.22   What are some of the typical characteristics of poor abstracts?

The following abstract, from a fictitious (though containing real data) paper entitled *An innovative methodology for teaching English pronunciation,* has a series of problems.

The English language is characterized by a high level of irregularity in spelling and pronunciation. A computer analysis of 17,000 English words showed that 84% were spelt in accordance with a regular pattern, and only 3% were completely unpredictable [Hanna et al, 1966] . An example of unpredictability can be found in English numbers, for example, *one, two* and *eight*. Interestingly, English spelling a thousand years ago was much more regular and almost phonetic. Words that today have a similar spelling but radically different pronunciation, such as *enough, though, cough, bough* and *thorough*, once had different spellings and much more phonetic pronunciations. In this paper, a pioneering method, developed by the English For Academics Institute in Pisa (Italy), of teaching non-native speakers how to quickly learn English pronunciation is presented and discussed.

The problems are:

- it is not self sufficient. If readers read this abstract in isolation from the paper, they would have no idea about what the author actually did in his / her research, nor what was found

- it looks like the beginning of an Introduction not an Abstract. Apart from the last line it is all background information. This information is interesting and relevant to the topic of the paper. But it is not new information. Basically, it tells the reader nothing about what contribution the author has made to this field of study

- it contains a reference to another author's work, Hanna. This is not common in an Abstract

- it mentions irrelevant details. In an abstract the reader does not really need to know where the research was carried out, particularly in this case where the exact location of the research (Pisa, Italy) is totally irrelevant – it has no impact on the findings

- the pioneering method is not described, nor do we have any idea about why it is 'pioneering'

- the reader has no idea of what results were obtained

The result is that readers in this field – English pronunciation – are likely to skip this article and move on to the next one they find. A better version of the abstract would be:

We have developed a didactic method for addressing the high level of irregularity in spelling and pronunciation in the English language. We combine new words, or words that non-native speakers regularly have difficult in pronouncing, with words that they are familiar with. For example, most adult learners have few problems in pronouncing *go, two, off* and *stuff* but may have difficulties with *though, cough* and *rough*. Through associations – *go/though, two/through, off/cough, stuff/tough* – learners can understand that familiar and unfamiliar words may have a similar pronunciation and can thus practice pronouncing them without the aid of a teacher. Tests were conducted on 2041 adults selected at random from higher education institutes in 22 countries and incorporating five different language families. The results revealed that as many as 85% of subjects managed to unlearn their erroneous pronunciation, with only 5% making no progress at all. We believe our findings could have a profound impact on the way English pronunciation is taught around the world.

The revised version is better because:

- readers are immediately told what the author did. There is no background information because the context is well known

- the methodology is explained and a concrete example is given

- the selection process of the subjects (*adults*) is described

- the results are given

- numbers are qualified (*as many as* 85%, *only* 5%) to help readers understand whether the numbers reflect normal expectations, or are particularly high or low

- the implications are stated

- the word 'pioneering' is avoided – it is left to the reader to decide if the method is pioneering or not

The result is that readers in this field are more likely to be stimulated into reading the rest of the article.

13.23   Social and behavioral sciences. How should I structure my abstract? How much background information?

Here is an abstract from a fictitious social sciences paper entitled *Is it Time to Leave Him?* written by one of my PhD students, Estrella Garcia Gonzalez from Spain. This abstract is designed to prove to you that even if you don't work in a purely scientific field, you can still write an abstract that would fulfill the criteria expected by journals in most formal sciences and natural sciences (as defined by Wikipedia – http://en.wikipedia.org/wiki/Science).

By *sitting-zapping sessions* Estrella means sitting like a zombie in front of the television and constantly changing channels.

> (1) Three red flags were identified that indicate that the time to leave him has come. These red flags are: five burps per day, two sitting-zapping sessions per day, and fives games on the Playstation with friends per week. (2) A large number of women have doubts about the right moment for leaving their partner. Often women wait in hope for a change in their partner's habits. (3) One hundred couples were analyzed, recording their daily life for six months. Women were provided with a form to mark the moments of annoyance recorded during the day. Burps, sitting-zapping sessions and games on the Playstation with friends produced the highest index of annoyance. (4) The probability of eliminating these habits was found to be significantly low when the three red flags had been operative for more than three months. (5) Thus, these numbers provide a good indication of when the time to leave him has come. With these red flags, women will no longer have to waste their time waiting for the right moment.

Below is a series of instructions for writing an abstract based on Estrella's structure. Again, the numbers refer to the numbers in the abstract.

1. Begin the abstract with one or two sentences saying what you did plus one key result, i.e. begin with information that the reader does NOT already know

2. Introduce the background by connecting in some way to what you said in your introductory sentence. The concept of leaving him is introduced in (1) and then referred to again in (2)

3. Use the background information (which the reader may or not already know) to justify what you did, and outline your methodology (and materials where appropriate)

4. Provide some more information on your results

5. Tell the reader the implications of your results

13.24   I am a historian. We don't necessarily get 'results' or follow a specific methodology. What should I do?

If you analyze history abstracts, and other abstracts from humanistic disciplines, they still have a structure that is similar to a scientific abstract.

You have a primary objective (e.g. a theory or perspective that you would like to share, test, analyze or question), a design to your research, some methods and procedures that you used, some outcomes from your research that support your theory/ perspective, and some conclusions or implications derived from these outcomes.

Abstracts from social and behavioral sciences tend to devote more space to background issues and context setting. The 'thesis' is often formulated as a series of questions that inform the reader about what issues will be dealt with in the paper.

In any case your abstract should include the following:

- background information

- your aim and its importance

- your contribution and its value

- what you looked at

- your conclusions and implications

Here is a fictitious abstract from a researcher interested in the history and evolution of languages.

(1) The Quaker movement was founded in the mid 17th century by George Fox. One of the practices used by this rebellious religious group was the use of 'plain speech' and 'simplicity'. This involved addressing all people with the same second person pronoun, in the words of Fox: 'without any respect to rich or poor, great or small'. The modern use of 'you' in the English language (in 10th century England there were 12 forms of 'you') is thus attributed to Fox's egalitarian movement. (2) Was this use of 'you' for addressing all kinds of people, regardless of their social status, specifically initiated by Fox? Or was it simply a part of an organic unplanned

process in the English language of ridding itself of unnecessary devices and formalities? Are some languages more dynamic than others? And does this depend on how 'controlled' they are by official prescriptions? (3) By analyzing 50 English texts from 1012 to 2012, I show that English has successfully eliminated all accents on words, simplified punctuation use, virtually made the subjunctive redundant, and reduced the average sentence length by more than half from around 35 in the convoluted style of the 18th century to 14 words today. (4) Our findings show that English has the potential for being democratic, concise yet profound, and simple to understand. (5) I believe that this has implications for those languages, such as French, Italian, Korean and Turkish, that have conservative academies for safeguarding the 'purity' of their language.

The above abstract covers the following elements, which typically appear in humanistic abstracts. The numbers below refer to the numbers in the abstract.

1. Background information – there tends to be more context setting in humanistic than in scientific abstracts, and this may take up even 50% of the text.

2. Gap in the knowledge – here the author challenges the accepted view on the topic. Using the question format, the author tells the reader what areas of the topic he plans to address. Questions create variety in an abstract.

3. Methodology and results – the author provides some brief information on the data he used to get his findings.

4. Conclusions

5. Implications – having implications in some way justifies why the author did his work, it gives the work relevance, it shows that the work makes a real contribution and was not just carried out for the author's own personal interest

13.25 I need to write a review. How should I structure my Abstract?

As with all abstracts of all disciplines, when you are writing a review you need to tell your audience what your primary objective is. Given that you will not have space to review every paper in the literature, you should then explain your reasons for selecting certain papers. Your 'results' are your findings drawn from analyzing the literature. Finally, for your review to have a real purpose you will want to state your conclusions and what implications they have for further research in your field.

So once again your structure is: aim, methodology (selection process), results, conclusions, and implications.

13.26   I am writing an abstract for a presentation at a conference. What do I need to be aware of?

What do organizers of conferences want to see in an abstract? To answer this question you need to think about why conferences are organized. As an academic, you may think that the primary aim is to bring people from the scientific community together to talk about the state of the art. But conference organizers also want the conference to make money so that they will be able to propose new editions in future years. They will use any profits made (from accommodation, food, services etc) to finance other events or research, and very importantly they are aware that if the conference is a success it will look good on their CV and further their academic career.

To ensure that all these aims are achieved, they want:

- to appeal to as many people as possible (not just researchers in one very specific field) by inviting presenters who can make their work relevant to a broad audience (however for workshops the participants are likely to be much more homogeneous)

- results to be original and interesting

- speakers to be of a high quality

This means that your Abstract should:

1. really fit the conference theme, which in some cases might have a broad spectrum
2. highlight the level of innovation
3. contain interesting results; thus proposals and future plans tend to be less interesting unless they are already attracting a large community
4. be quickly understood and appreciated by reviewers
5. be understandable by non experts – plenary talks in particular have to be more general – the audience can follow the parallel sessions if they wish to be informed of more technical details

The fifth point is becoming increasingly important. A lot of public money is spent on funding research. Those who allocate such funds need to see some kind of 'return' on their 'investment'. For example, imagine you have been given funds for conducting high-energy physics, funders will want you to publicize your results not only in highly specialized physics journals and conferences, but also in related areas such as electronics. Funders want to see how your methods and findings can be applied in other areas.

Conferences are the perfect opportunity to present your work to a wider audience, thus your abstract must:

- not be too technical (i.e. not take for granted that all readers will understand the importance of the work or the technical jargon used to describe it) – note that certain words have different meanings for scientists with different backgrounds

- give examples that the majority of your audience will understand even if they don't have the same background info as you have

- highlight how your innovations and results could potentially be transferred to other disciplines to solve other problems

In high profile conferences you need to write your abstract as if you were targeting a journal paper. The review process is strict and it's a real privilege if you are accepted.

If the conference that you plan to go to is not in its first edition, you can look at abstracts from the previous editions to see their style and tone. In any case, the rules for writing the abstract itself are the same as for a journal, though your style may be slightly more informal.

Finally, show your abstract to someone outside your research group – if they can't understand it, it probably means you need to rewrite it more clearly.

13.27   How do I write an abstract for a work in progress that will be presented at a conference?

Conferences are generally planned up to two years in advance. When you answer the call for papers, your research may not yet be complete, but nevertheless you think that the conference would be a good way to get feedback on your progress. Below is the first draft of an abstract on how students choose the topic for their doctorate. It was written for a conference by Rossella Borri, an Italian PhD student in Political Sciences, whose research at the time of writing the abstract was only in its initial stages. Her initial draft, below, was not suitable for a conference – it is misleading because it is still a work in progress, which is not apparent from the draft.

With its focus on the research cycle, scientific methodology has devoted a great deal of attention to the phase of problem solving. However, the issue of problem choice has been relatively neglected, notwithstanding its relevant epistemological implications. What are the criteria used by PhD students to set their research agenda? To what extent is the research agenda driven by pure curiosity about social phenomena? How much is it a matter of bargaining with various resource limitations? A survey was carried out among PhD students of European universities to examine the criteria used in the choice of their dissertation topics. The analysis sheds light on the way scientific knowledge is crafted, and about the challenges and limitations researchers face during this process.

The abstract would be fine if she had finished her research – which is what most readers would understand. The problem is that it gives no idea of the fact that the research is only at the beginning and that the data from the survey have as yet not been analyzed. It is thus rather misleading and those who go to her presentation at the conference might be very disappointed not to hear the concrete results that the abstract seems to promise. Having shown her abstract to her tutor who warned her of such a possible misinterpretation, Rossella then revised the second part of the abstract by saying:

> We are currently carrying out a survey of 500 PhD students of European universities to examine the criteria employed in the choice of their dissertation topics. Analysis of the data will explore the relationship between factors such as the duration of the PhD programme, the availability of a scholarship or background experience in the field and PhD students' criteria for choosing the specific issue that they wish to study. Initial results from the first 20 surveys seem to indicate the importance of the availability of funding and the potential job prospects rather than preferences driven by pure interest for its own sake. We hope to shed light on the way scientific knowledge is crafted and about challenges and limitations young researchers face during this process.

The abstract now contains the words *currently, will explore, seem to indicate*, and *we hope*, all of which highlight that this is ongoing research. By adding some of the initial results, the audience at the conference will be interested to know whether these results were confirmed when the whole battery of surveys was analyzed.

Your abstract should encourage conference attendees to come and hear you rather than going to a parallel session. If you don't have any results at all, you should either consider going to a later conference when you have something more conclusive to say, or tell readers what you expect your results to show.

13.28   How do I write an abstract for an informal talk, workshop or seminar at an international conference?

Abstracts for the various workshops and seminars held at conferences tend to be a little more informal. The abstract is likely to include the following:

- brief statement of what the speaker intends to say during his / her session

- background or problem

- progress made

The informality means that personal pronouns (*we, I*) are often (but not always) found, plus active verbs. In the examples below (which like all the examples in this subsection are fictitious) S1 and S3 are written in an informal way, S2 and S4 are formal.

S1.   *In this talk I provide* a brief overview of the results of a survey on whether a nation's sense of humour can be revealed by observing posts and feedback on Facebook. *I will be looking in particular* at ...

S2.   *This talk will look at* the process of analysing the principle sources of spam (on a country-by-country basis) and our team's experiences in analysing the various types of spam. *The main focus will be* bogus health services (particularly for men), requests for bank details, prize winners, and fictitious journal and editing services.

S3.   In *our research we are* trying to understand why so few people ever try to question the opinions that they have held for years – are they blinkered or blonkered? [blinkered: with a narrow outlook on life; blonkered: heavily intoxicated with alcohol]

S4.   *The LANGRYNX project seeks to understand* why the position of the larynx does not explain why bilingual people will speak in a lower tone in one language (e.g. Italian) but a higher tone in another language (e.g. English).

Some authors try to make their Abstract more appealing by using bullets. For example:

The talk will:

- explain the method of calculating the relative chances of a 25-year-old male becoming an Olympic athlete or the winner of a national talent show

- report on experiences of our previous probability studies comparing the chances of publishing one's first work of fiction (approximately 1 in 1,000,000) and playing a sport for one's nation (from 1 in 1000 in some countries, to 1 in 500,000 in others)

- demonstrate that most people erroneously associate a higher level of difficulty with becoming a top team athlete than succeeding in the world of music or literature

Note that for consistency each of the bullets begins with the same type of word (in this case the verb in its bare infinitive form) – see *G* 25.13 in *English for Research: Grammar, Usage and Style.*

13.29 How do journal editors and conference review committees assess the abstracts that they receive?

Apart from investigating the scientific merit and validity of the research that is the topic of your abstract, reviewers will be answering the questions below. These questions, along with the answers, were either lifted or adapted from an excellent document by Professor Bill Pugh of Maryland University.

Some of the answers may not be strictly related to your field but are nevertheless still likely to be valid.

Is the work a significant advance over previous work in the area, by the same authors or others? The abstract should give a clear description of the advantages offered by the new technique over previous techniques. Simply describing an interesting new way of doing something that could be done as simply and efficiently by previous techniques won't get an abstract accepted. The best abstracts give a clear description of what their results allow that couldn't be done previously and why that is significant. Examples and measurements are great for this.

If the work involves a specialized application, does it make a more general contribution? Would the resulting paper be useful to people not interested in your specific application?

Does the abstract address the obvious questions raised by the research? For example, if an abstract claims to describe "an efficient, practical algorithm'" for something, it should give empirical timings, asymptotic analysis or both. If the techniques described require solving a problem that is NP-Complete or undecidable in general, the abstract should discuss the difficultly of solving the problem. It may be that in practice the problems that arise in the author's application can be solved efficiently; but if the abstract doesn't discuss it, the committee doesn't know if the author is even aware of the potential problem.

Is the abstract well presented and understandable? Is the abstract too long? The word limit is to encourage authors to write abstracts that can be absorbed quickly, not to save trees.

13.30 Summary: How can I assess the quality of my Abstract?

To make a self-assessment of your Abstract, you can ask yourself the following questions.

➤ Have I followed the journal's instructions to authors? Have I followed the right structure (i.e. structured, unstructured) and style (*we* vs passive)?

➤ Have I covered the relevant points from those below?

    o background / context

    o research problem / aim – the gap I plan to fill

    o methods

    o results

    o implications and/or conclusions

➤ Is everything mentioned in the Abstract also mentioned in the main text? Is the information consistent with what is presented in the paper?

➤ Whenever I have given my readers information, will it be 100% clear to them why they are being given this information? (You know why, but they don't.)

➤ Can I make my Abstract less redundant? If I tried to reduce it by 25% would I really lose any key content?

➤ Have I used tenses correctly? present simple (established knowledge), present perfect (past to present background information), past simple (my contribution)?

➤ Have I checked the spelling? Have I shown it to other people so that they can find any typos that I may have missed?

➤ Have I chosen my keywords carefully so that readers can locate my Abstract?

➤ Have I shown it to a colleague who is not familiar with the details of my research to see how much they can understand and can identify the value of the research?

Chapter 14

Introduction

Factoids

Below is a list of products that highlights the elapse of time (in years) between a product's conception, and its development and introduction onto the market. The table is adapted from an article in *The New York Times* by Stephen Rosen.

	CONCEPTION	REALIZATION	INTERVAL
television	1884	1947	63
photography	1782	1838	56
radar	1904	1939	35
heart pacemaker	1928	1960	32
antibiotics	1910	1940	30
zippers	1883	1913	30
radio	1890	1914	24
ballpoint pen	1938	1946	16
stainless steel	1904	1920	16
nylon	1927	1939	12
roll-on deodorant	1948	1955	7

© Springer International Publishing Switzerland 2016
A. Wallwork, *English for Writing Research Papers*,
English for Academic Research, DOI 10.1007/978-3-319-26094-5_14

14.1   What's the buzz?

1) Read this extract from an editor's letter to an author whose Introduction was considered by the editor as 'unsatisfactory'.

> The Introduction of your paper is not just a historical summary. It is a constant comparison between what OTHERS have done and what YOU did or are proposing to do.
>
> Present the novelty of your approach and results in the context of what has already been done. Citing key papers without stating how specifically you build on them is insufficient.
>
> Describe, with at least one sentence, (i) what others have done, as far as relevant for the direction of your paper, and (ii) how your contribution is original and distinguishes itself from previous work.

2) Now answer the questions.

- Compared to the other sections in a paper, how difficult is it to write the Introduction? Why?

- How important is the Introduction? What should it include?

- How do you decide which papers to cite and which to omit?

****

The Introduction presents the background knowledge that readers need so that they can appreciate how the findings of the paper are an advance on current knowledge in the field. A key skill is to be able to say the same things that have been said many times before but in a different, interesting, intriguing way.

This chapter tells you how to write the Introduction, excluding the Review of the Literature which is covered in the next chapter.

- First, you need to have a thorough knowledge about everything that has been previously written on the topic and decide what is important for the reader to know.

- Then, you have to give the reader the tools for understanding the meaning and motivation of your experiments.

- Finally, tell your readers how you plan to develop your topic. Give them a roadmap to follow - show them what your line of argument is.

14.2 How should I structure the Introduction? Can I use subheadings?

An Introduction generally answers the following questions. You can use the answers to these questions to structure your Introduction.

- What is the problem?

- Are there any existing solutions (i.e. in the literature)?

- Which solution is the best?

- What is its main limitation? (i.e. What gap am I hoping to fill?)

- What do I hope to achieve?

- Have I achieved what I set out to do?

If your Introduction is more than a couple of pages, subheadings will make it much more 'digestible' for the reader.

14.3 How does an Introduction differ from an Abstract?

There is some overlap between an Abstract and the Introduction. However, a frequent problem is that authors may cut and paste from their Abstract into their Introduction, which can be very repetitive for readers.

Below are the first two sentences from the Abstract and Introduction from a paper (or 'Letter' as it is called in the journal where this study appeared) entitled *Fragmentation of Rods by Cascading Cracks: Why Spaghetti Does Not Break in Half* by Basile Audoly and Sébastien Neukirch. These sentences highlight the distinct ways that an Abstract and Introduction should be written.

ABSTRACT When thin brittle rods such as dry spaghetti pasta are bent beyond their limit curvature, they often break into more than two pieces, typically three or four. With the aim of understanding these multiple breakings, we study the dynamics of a bent rod that is suddenly released at one end.

INTRODUCTION The physical process of fragmentation is relevant to several areas of science and technology. Because different physical phenomena are at work during the fragmentation of a solid body, it has mainly been studied from a statistical viewpoint [1–5].

The Abstract immediately tells the readers the specific topic of the paper and then what the author's goal is. Instead, the Introduction sets the context in very general terms.

The abstract then continues as follows.

ABSTRACT We find that the sudden relaxation of the curvature at this end leads to a burst of flexural waves, whose dynamics are described by a self-similar solution with no adjustable parameters. These flexural waves locally increase the curvature in the rod, and we argue that this counterintuitive mechanism is responsible for the fragmentation of brittle rods under bending.

As you can see, the Abstract gives no further background information, but highlights what the authors found in their research. An absolute minimum number of words have been used. This gives the Abstract substantial impact by telling readers only what they need to know to enable them to decide whether to read the whole paper. As is standard for Abstracts, no references to the literature are made.

On the other hand about 50% of the rest of the Introduction is dedicated to helping the readers see that the general trend given in the first two sentences is being countered by another line of research. In this case, references to the literature are made. Readers are alerted to the alternative trend by the link word *nevertheless*.

INTRODUCTION Nevertheless a growing number of works have included physical considerations: surface energy contributions [6], nucleation and growth properties of the fracture process [7], elastic buckling [8, 9], and stress wave propagation [10]. Usually, in dynamic fragmentation, the abrupt application of fracturing forces (e.g. by an impact) triggers numerous elementary breaking processes, making a statistical study of the fragments sizes possible. This is opposed to quasi-static fragmentation where a solid is crushed or broken at small applied velocities [11].

The concluding sentence of the Abstract is:

ABSTRACT A simple experiment supporting the claim is presented.

This eight-word sentence is expanded considerably in the Introduction, by describing more about what the experiment consisted in, and the result it gave. Note: the text reported below is the rest of the Introduction in its entirety.

INTRODUCTION Here we consider such a quasi-static experiment whereby a dry spaghetti is bent beyond its limit curvature. This experiment is famous as, most of the time, the pasta does not break in half but typically in three to ten pieces. In this Letter, we explain this multiple failure process and point out a general mechanism of cascading failure in rods: a breaking event induces strong flexural waves which trigger other breakings, leading to an avalanche-like process.

I suggest you use a similar comparison between Abstracts and Introductions taken from your chosen journal, to see:

- what parts from Sects. 14.5 and 14.7 are covered in the Introduction. In the spaghetti paper, Parts 1–8 are condensed into eight sentences, Parts 9 and 10 are not mentioned

- how they are structured differently

- what elements from the Abstract the Introduction expands on

- how sentences from the Abstract are paraphrased in the Introduction

- what information is covered in the Abstract but not in the Introduction, and vice versa

- the relative word counts. This will give you an idea of the proportionate length of the Introduction compared to the Abstract. In the spaghetti paper the Abstract is 116 words, and the Introduction 201 words, so the Introduction is approximately twice as long. This is quite typical

14.4 How long should the Introduction be?

There is no definitive answer to this question.

Find the most cited papers in your field, and note the proportion of space given to the Introduction relative to the other sections. Adopt the same proportion.

I have noticed that the longer the Introduction in relation to the rest of the paper, the lower the level of innovation. Often authors write a huge introduction to hide the fact that they have very little to say about their actual research. Reviewers are aware of this trick!

Think about introductions in other areas of life - in a 10 minute oral presentation at a conference would you want eight minutes of introduction? In a 20 minute TV interview with a famous personality, would you want 10 minutes of introduction before the personality even utters a word? I know that presentations and interviews cannot be directly compared to research papers, but the basic idea is that both viewers and readers want the same thing: the meat.

14.5 How should I begin my Introduction?

Below is an example of the structure of a typical Introduction. It consists of a sequence of ten parts, each with a specific role. Your Introduction will not necessarily include all ten parts nor sequence them in the same order.

Your aim is to include only enough background information to allow your reader to understand why you are asking the questions you are, in what context they appear, and why your hypotheses, predictions or expected results are reasonable. It is like a preview to the rest of the paper. Thus, nearly every Introduction, irrespective of the discipline, would incorporate those parts marked with an asterisk (*).

The proportion of space given to each part (particularly with regard to the review of the literature) will obviously vary from discipline to discipline, and from paper to paper.

You could begin with one or more of the first four parts listed below.

FUNCTION	AUTHOR'S TEXT
1 definition of the topic plus background	An XYZ battery is a battery that... The electrodes in an XYZ telephone battery are made of a composite of gold and silver, coated with a layer of platinum. The gold and silver provide structural support, while the platinum provides resilience.
2 accepted state of the art plus problem to be resolved	The performance of the battery can be strongly affected by the number of times the battery is recharged and the duration of each individual recharge. The battery is subject to three possible failure modes. ...
3 authors' objectives	A research program has recently been started by the authors in collaboration with a major battery manufacturer, with the goal of developing new design models for XYZ batteries. Analytical techniques are needed that can predict ...
4 introduction to the literature	Computational techniques have been extensively applied to the study of the lifetime of XYZ batteries, in particular with regard to the number of times a battery is charged. However, little research to date has focused on the length of each individual recharge.

Below is an analysis of Parts 1–4 of the Introduction. In brackets is a very approximate indication of how many sentences you will probably need for each part.

PART 1 DEFINITION OF THE TOPIC PLUS BACKGROUND (1–3)

This introductory phrase may not be necessary in your paper. Here the definition of the XYZ battery indicates to the reader that this is the background topic (i.e. the general context) of the paper. This is the place to include notations, technical definitions, and explanations of key words.

The second sentence gives information that readers should already be familiar with and suggests why the topic is important and of interest. It will help readers to understand why you are investigating this area and how you hope to extend the knowledge. It sets the context for the information that will follow in (3), which may be less familiar for your readers. Readers want to quickly learn what the specific topic of your research is, they are much less interested in being reminded how important the general area of research is.

PART 2 ACCEPTED STATE OF THE ART PLUS PROBLEM TO BE RESOLVED (2–4)*

In the example text, XYZ batteries is the general context. The authors now move from this general context to the specific area of their research: XYZ batteries in telephones, and more specifically, the problems inherent in such batteries. This is the gap that the authors want to fill and that the readers should be most interested in. This part should state in simple and clear language exactly what the problem is, why you chose it and why you claim it is important.

PART 3 AUTHORS' OBJECTIVES (1–2)*

Here the authors outline their major objectives, i.e. how they intend to fill the gap. Parts 6 and 7 (see next page) could be incorporated here. This part also serves as a transition into the review of the literature.

PART 4 INTRODUCTION TO THE LITERATURE

This introduces the background literature that the authors intend to refer to in order to motivate their particular research. It makes a reference to current insufficient knowledge of the topic.

This may be in a separate section with its own heading (Review of the Literature – see Chapter 15), or after the Results in a clinical paper, or incorporated into the Discussion.

14.6 My research area is not a 'hard' science. Are there any other ways of beginning an Introduction?

Clearly, not all disciplines would use the structure outlined in the previous subsection, though they would still cover some of the same main points. An alternative, and quite common approach, is to set the context and research goal in a series of questions.

Here is an example from a dissertation entitled *The Effects of Feedback and Attribution Style on Task Persistence* by psychology student Chris Rozek. Persistence means the ability to adhere to a task, to persevere with something rather than giving up.

> Persistence is an attribute valued by many. What makes some people persist longer than others? Are internal factors, such as personality traits, or external situational factors, such as feedback, responsible for persistence? Could the answer include a combination of both? These are the questions this experiment attempted to answer.

The general topic is mentioned in the very first word (*persistence*) of a very short sentence (seven words). This enables the reader to immediately focus on and understand the context (corresponding to Point 2 in the structure of an Introduction given in Sect. 14.5). Within this context, the second sentence, in the form of a question, outlines the issue that Chris plans to address in his paper (Point 3). His next sentence poses the typical attributes associated with persistence (similarly to Point 5). The question *Could the answer include a combination of both?* hints at what the likely findings of his paper are (Point 7). The final sentence highlights that Chris will cover all the aspects he has mentioned so far. His Introduction then continues with a literature review (Point 6) and concludes with his final hypothesis (similarly to Point 9).

Chris has neatly covered a lot of points typically mentioned in an Introduction. He has achieved this in very few sentences and with a format (questions) that immediately involves the reader by encouraging them to formulate their own answers and thus to continue reading.

14.7   How should I structure the rest of the Introduction?

The Introduction outlined in the previous subsection continues as follows:

FUNCTION	AUTHOR'S TEXT
5 survey of pertinent literature	More recent research has occurred in the field of laptop and jPud batteries. Evans [15] studied the lifetime in 5G jPud batteries. Smith [16] and Jones [18] found that ... However their findings failed to account for ...
6 authors' contribution	To the best of our knowledge there are no results in the literature regarding how the length of each recharge impacts on the silver and gold in the electrodes.
7 aim of the present work	The aim of the present work is to construct a model to perform a comprehensive investigation of the effect of recharging on the electrodes, and to find a new proportion in the amount of metals used. The assumptions of Smith [16] and Jones [18] are used as a starting point ...
8 main results / conclusions	The results of the model are encouraging and show that ...
9 future implications	This new model will be able to ...
10 outline of structure	Section 2 introduces the concept of ...

Below is an analysis of Parts 5–10.

PART 5 SURVEY OF PERTINENT LITERATURE

This part reviews the literature in the author's precise field. As in the previous part, it often draws attention to problems that have still not been solved. For example, you may think a particular study did not investigate some necessary aspect of the area, or that the authors failed to notice some problem with their results.

You only need to describe what is necessary for the specific purposes of your paper. Much of this literature will then be used for comparative purposes in the Discussion.

The length of the literature review (i.e. Parts 4 and 5) ranges from a paragraph to several pages. See Chapter 15 for details on how to write it.

PART 6 AUTHORS' CONTRIBUTION (1–2)*

Here the authors make a very clear statement of how what they describe in the paper represents an advance on current knowledge (i.e. the knowledge outlined in parts 2, 4 and 5).

PART 7 AIM OF THE PRESENT WORK (1–2)*

This statement of the goal to be reached is essential in any Introduction. It should be in a separate paragraph and expressed so that the referee (and readers) are 100% clear about the objectives of your research and the expected outcome. You will need to tell readers what method you used and possibly why you chose this method.

PART 8 MAIN RESULTS OF THE PRESENT WORK (1–4)

Although your main results will be given in other sections of your paper (typically in your Abstract, Results, Discussion and Conclusions), many authors also announce them here to show how the background situation plus their contribution have led to particular results.

PART 9 FUTURE IMPLICATIONS OF THE WORK (1–2)

Some authors prefer to delay mentioning implications to the Discussion or even to the Conclusions. However, mentioning implications here gives readers an instant idea of the possible importance of your work, which may be useful for them as they read the rest of the paper.

PART 10 OUTLINE OF STRUCTURE (3–4 VERY SHORT SENTENCES)

This may not be necessary if the structure of your paper is completely standard for your chosen journal, and thus readers will already know in what order the various elements of your research will be presented. See Sect. 14.12 on how to write the structure.

14.8 What tenses should I use?

In this section, the example sentences S1, S3 and S5 are taken from Audoly and Neukirch's paper (14.3), and S2, S4 and S6 from Rozek's paper (14.6 and 15.4).

The PRESENT SIMPLE is generally used to begin the Introduction in order to describe the general background context, i.e. what is known already.

S1. The physical process of fragmentation is relevant to several areas of science and technology.

S2. Persistence is an attribute valued by many.

The PRESENT PERFECT is then used to show how the problem has been approached from the past until the present day.

S3. Because different physical phenomena are at work during the fragmentation of a solid body, it has mainly been studied from a statistical viewpoint [1–5].

S4. Persistence has most often been studied in terms of cultural differences.

During the review of the literature, several tenses are used (Sect. 15.7).

At the end of the Introduction, the PRESENT SIMPLE is used again when the authors state what they will do in the rest of their paper (*we explain, I hypothesize*).

S5. In this Letter, we explain this multiple failure process and point out a general mechanism of cascading failure in rods: a breaking event induces strong flexural waves which trigger other breakings, leading to an avalanche like process.

S6. Because of these findings, I hypothesize that subjects with internal attribution styles (as measured by the APCSS), higher levels of perfectionism, and any form of feedback will show greater task persistence.

In S5 Audoly and Neukirch use the PRESENT SIMPLE to report their findings (see the underlined verbs). Not all authors use the PRESENT SIMPLE in this context because a general convention (but not rule) is that when you present your findings you use the past simple - the idea is to use the PRESENT SIMPLE for what is already accepted in the literature, and the PAST SIMPLE for your new contribution.

In S6 Rozek uses the FUTURE SIMPLE to talk about his claim / conclusion. This usage of the future tends to be confined to where authors set out to prove a hypothesis, rather than to give hard results.

14.9 How long should the paragraphs be?

Your aim is to allow your reader to quickly digest the background information that forms the basis of your research.

An Introduction should thus not be one long paragraph or a series of very long paragraphs. This problem is typical of Introductions and Discussion, and it is vital to break the paragraph up (see Chapter 3: Paragraphs).

Your paragraphs should range between 75 and 175 words. Try not to regularly exceed 150 words, but feel free to use fewer than 75 words if you want your paragraph to stand out in order to make a key point.

The idea of a series of shorter paragraphs (rather than one long paragraph) is that the series highlights the logical progression (argumentation) of what you are saying - how various ideas are connected and follow on from each other.

This gradual build up of ideas and evidence easily gets lost in a long paragraph.

The moments to begin a new paragraph in the Introduction are when you:

- change topic, or you look at a different aspect of the same topic

- move from talking about one step / phase / period to another

- mention another author and this author has a slightly different take (i.e. view, perspective) on what you have been talking about so far

- want to talk about the consequences of what you have just been describing

- talk about the aim of your study / paper

- talk about the structure of your paper

If you print your Introduction you will immediately see the undesirable effect of having long paragraphs. They are not inviting for the reader.

14.10 What are typical pitfalls of an Introduction?

The Introduction is often the least interesting for you to write, as you may feel it is only incidental to your research.

In an attempt to save time, researchers often skip over whole periods and papers that led to their research and may simply cite a series of references with a throwaway comment such as: *these were great efforts preceding our work.*

However, it is at some point necessary to present the novelty of your approach and results in the context of what has already been done. Citing key papers, but without stating how specifically you build on them, is insufficient.

It is not necessary to "do better" or "more" than them, but (i) describe, with at least one sentence, what others have done, as far as relevant for the direction of your paper, and (ii) describe how your contribution is original and distinguishes itself from previous work. You can do this by:

- listing the shortcomings of previous approaches with a clear analysis of how your proposed approach is an improvement. Match each shortcoming with the advantage that your approach offers

- introduce a new approach, algorithm, procedure, set-up, experiment etc and validate it

If a reviewer calls for you to add more details to your Introduction, by writing a sentence such as "The authors ignore over 30 years of xxx community efforts in relation to yyy", then you cannot simply put additional references.

By covering previous work, you will be able to highlight what the great potential improvements are that your approach could bring. If you do that, your own approach will then be sufficiently introduced and justified. Some of the manuscripts you review will help yours because they raise questions that you can address. Of course, other researchers have probably pursued similar avenues, and those papers also need to be cited in this regard.

A key issue is to make it clear whose work you are talking about: yours or another author's. To learn how to do this see Chapter 7.

Note: Much of the above subsection was based on the comments made by an anonymous referee to a paper I edited.

14.11 What typical phrases should I avoid in my Introduction?

Referees have to read a lot of papers. While this can be a very rewarding task, it can also be quite tedious when many Abstracts and Introductions seem to begin in the same way. Thus, some writing experts advise avoiding stock phrases (i.e. typical phrases that everyone uses) at the beginning of the introduction. For example: *Recent advances in ... The last few years have seen ...* Instead they recommended beginning in a more direct way.

14.12 How should I outline the structure of the rest of my paper?

Check with your journal's instructions to authors with regard to whether an outline of the structure is required. If it is, or if you notice that all the papers in the journal have one, then your aim should be to describe this structure as concisely as possible (as in the RV).

ORIGINAL VERSION (OV)	REVISED VERSION (RV)
The paper is structured as follows: in Section 2 *a survey of the works related to X is provided.* In Section 3 the method that we propose for the analysis of X is shown. In Section 4 the tool that automatizes this methodology is presented and in Section 5 its components are described. In Section 6 *the experience in the application of the tool to industrial case studies is reported and discussed* and finally, *in Section 7, conclusions are provided and future works described.*	Section 2 *surveys* the works related to X. Section 3 *outlines* our method for analyzing X. In Section 4 the tool that automatizes this methodology is presented, and in Section 5 its components are described. Section 6 *discusses some industrial case studies* using the tool.

The RV is approximately half the length of the OV, 45 words rather than 84. This is achieved by:

- deleting unnecessary sentences. Some journals and reviewers advise that there is no need to have an initial sentence saying *The paper is structured as follows.* Simply beginning a new paragraph at the end of the Introduction is enough to alert the reader that you are now going to talk about the structure

- using active verbs (*surveys*) rather than only passive (*a survey ... is provided*). For the sake of variety, the RV also includes some passive forms. But you could, if you wish, use active forms throughout and this would further reduce the length of the paragraph

- removing other redundancy. For example, the phrase *the experience in the application of the tool to industrial case studies is reported and discussed* is unnecessarily verbose

- remove the obvious - most papers end with a concluding section (Section 7 in the OV), you don't need to mention this

Note that the word section, when accompanied by a number, should have the initial s capitalized. Examples:

S1. This is covered in *Section* 4.
S2. More details will be given later in this *section*.

14.13 Summary: How can I assess the quality of my Introduction?

To make a self-assessment of your Introduction, you can ask yourself the following questions.

➢ Does my Introduction occupy too high a proportion of the entire paper and does it contain too many general statements that are already widely known?

➢ Are the rationale and objectives defined? Is it clear what problem I am addressing or trying to solve and why I chose my particular methodology?

➢ Is the background information all related to the objective of the paper?

➢ Is it clear what the reader can expect in the rest of the paper (i.e. main results and conclusions)?

➢ Does my Introduction act as a clear road map for understanding my paper?

➢ Is it sufficiently different from the Abstract, without any cut and pastes? (some overlap is fine)

➢ Have I mentioned only what my readers specifically need to know and what I will subsequently refer to in the Discussion?

➢ Have I been as concise as possible?

➢ Have I used tenses correctly? PRESENT SIMPLE (general background context, description of what will be done in the paper), PRESENT PERFECT (past to present solutions), PAST SIMPLE (my contribution, though this may also be expressed using the PRESENT SIMPLE or FUTURE SIMPLE)

Chapter 15

Review of the Literature

Factoids: Getting (ex)cited

The following factoids are taken from a Nature news feature entitled 'The top 100 papers'.

The measure of a paper's importance is often seen in terms of the number of times it is cited in the works of other scientists. In 1964 the Science Citation Index (SCI) was set up. The index is now owned by Thomson Reuters and the expanded version covers 6,500 top journals in 150 disciplines, from 1900 to the present.

*****

To rank in the top 100 of the Thomson Reuters' Web of Science (which holds over 58 million items), a paper needs to have been cited over 12000 times.

*****

Many famous papers are not ranked in the top 100. The majority that are ranked, relate to what are now very frequently used experimental methods or software programs.

*****

The record holder in terms of citations (over 305,000) is held by biochemist Oliver Lowry, whose 1951 paper describes an assay to determine the amount of protein in a solution.

*****

The area that appears to get the most citations is the laboratory techniques of biologists (6 in the top 10 most cited papers).

*****

In Google Scholar's Top 100 released in late 2014, the top 10 works (6 books, 4 papers) were all published before 1993; and in the top 100, only three were published in the 21st century.

*****

Google Scholar's most cited paper (around 225,000 citations) was published in *Nature* and is entitled: *Cleavage of structural proteins during the assembly of the head of bacteriophage T4.*

© Springer International Publishing Switzerland 2016
A. Wallwork, *English for Writing Research Papers*,
English for Academic Research, DOI 10.1007/978-3-319-26094-5_15

15.1 What's the buzz?

The extracts below come from the 'review of the literature' section. *Alopecia areata* is the medical term for male baldness (i.e. when a man has lost hair from his head). Although the extracts are fictitious, all the causes and treatments (apart from bananas) listed can be found on 'reputable' sites on baldness.

Analyse how the three paragraphs are structured. What function does each sentence serve within the paragraph?

1. Smith et al (2016) reported that *alopecia areata* may be cured by massaging the scalp with substances such as honey, lemon juice, black pepper and egg yolk. *However*, the application of mango pulp with mustard seeds had only an 18% success rate. We prove that the placement of frozen banana skins for 3-minute periods over the bald patch has a success rate of more than 30%, in fact …

2. In 2017, Jones et al carried out tests using coconut milk, *but* only with a relatively small sample (75 subjects). In our experiments, we used a much larger sample (600 males, average age 44.6), using a blend of almond oil and castor oil.

3. In a previous paper [23] we found that emotional anxiety and intake of fast food were the primary causes of alopecia areata. *In this paper, we make a further contribution* by showing that although the consumption of vitamins is considered to be a possible cure, in reality that avoiding certain vitamins not only cures *alopecia areata* but also *alopecia capitis totalis*.

The key to the review of the literature is not to provide a shopping list of past papers. Instead your aim is to state:

1. what others have done or what you did in a previous paper
2. the downside / limit of what they did or why you decided to further the work you did in a previous paper (these limits / additions are highlighted in italics in the sentences above – *however, but, we make a further contribution*)
3. your solution / improvement

See 11.3 for an example of a review of the literature.

Now complete the gaps in relation to your own research.

Smith et al (2016) approached the problem of _____

by doing _____ .

Our approach is to _____ .

In fact, the advantage of our solution is _____ .

It is a novel approach because _____ .

****

The key skill when writing the Review of the Literature is to provide readers with just the right amount of literature regarding the sequence of events leading up to the current situation – not too much to make it tedious, nor too little so that the context of your research is not meaningful to them. The background information is useful because it allows you to:

- Systematically elaborate the achievements and limitations of other studies

- Relate your new facts and data to these studies

The amount of detail you need to give varies immensely from discipline to discipline. In some disciplines you may be required to have a very strong theoretical framework for your study, thus requiring two or more pages.

In other disciplines just one paragraph may be enough. So another skill is to take into account readers who are up to date with your research area and thus not to delay giving the new information for too long.

15.2   How should I structure my Review of the Literature?

A Literature Review generally answers the following questions, and generally in the following order. You can use the answers to these questions to structure your Literature Review.

1. What are the seminal works on my topic? Do I need to mention these?
2. What progress has been made since these seminal works?
3. What are the most relevant recent works? What is the best order to mention these works?
4. What are the achievements and limitations of these recent works?
5. What gap do these limitations reveal?
6. How does my work intend to fill this gap?

15.3 Do I need to cover all the literature? And what about the literature that goes against my hypotheses?

Unless you are writing a review paper, then you do not need to cover absolutely all the literature. You need to cover the literature that justifies your research and relates to it – both positively and negatively.

By 'negatively' I mean any literature in your specific field that is not in agreement with your hypotheses, approach, and findings. Your aim is <u>not</u> to have a reviewer make a comment such as:

> The authors' literature review was limited to those papers that supported their hypotheses rather than covering all the literature related to the study.

Remember that your mission as a researcher is not to blindly follow just one path in order to reach your specific objective and prove your point. You have to be open to other possibilities and show your readers that there are other possible approaches and other possible conclusions.

15.4 How should I begin my literature review? How can I structure it to show the progress through the years?

Below is an extract from the Introduction to a paper entitled *The Effects of Feedback and Attribution Style on Task Persistence* where psychology student Chris Rozek begins his review of the literature (see 14.6 for how he begins the Introduction).

> Persistence has most often been studied in terms of cultural differences. Blinco (1992) found that Japanese elementary school children showed greater task persistence than their American counterparts. School type and gender were not factors in moderating task persistence. This left culture as the remaining variable.
>
> Heine et al. (2001) furthered this idea by testing older American and Japanese subjects on responses after success or failure on task persistence. Japanese subjects were once again found to persist longer (in post-failure conditions), and this was speculated to be because they were more likely to view themselves as the cause of the problem. If they were the cause of the problem, they could also solve the problem themselves; although this could only be accomplished through work and persistence. Americans were more likely to believe that outside factors were the cause of failure.
>
> These cultural studies hinted that task persistence may be predictable based on attribution style. A later experiment showed that attribution style and perfectionism level can be correlated with final grades in college-level classes (Blankstein & Winkworth, 2004).

The first sentence of the first paragraph introduces the main topic (cultural differences), and the rest of the paragraph briefly reviews a major study on this topic. The implications of this study (culture as the remaining variable) are summarized at the end of the paragraph.

The first sentence of the second paragraph then moves on to the next (in chronological terms) major study. Chris summarizes Heine's work in a way that involves the reader: he uses the verb *speculated* and then continues the next sentence using *if* which gives an example of this speculation.

The first sentence of the third paragraph summarizes the findings of the first two paragraphs in order to introduce some more recent findings.

Note also his use of tenses. In his first sentence, which is a very general overview, he uses the PRESENT PERFECT. Then when he talks about the work of specific authors and makes a summary of each step in the chronology of the literature he uses the PAST SIMPLE.

Chris's structure is thus:

1. introduction to topic
2. support from the literature
3. mini summary
4. introduction to next topic. And so on.

This technique works very well because it tells a story – it is a logical build up to the reason behind Chris's investigation that readers can easily follow. In fact, the final sentence to his Introduction begins: *Because of these findings, I hypothesize that …* Chris has gradually prepared his readers for the focus of his work: his own personal hypothesis regarding persistence.

15.5 What is the clearest way to refer to other authors? Should I focus on the authors or their ideas?

There are various styles for making reference to other authors. The four styles below contain the same information, but the focus is different.

STYLE 1   *Blinco [1992] found* that Japanese elementary school children showed …

STYLE 2   *In [5] Blinco found* that Japanese elementary school children showed …

STYLE 3   A *study* of the level of persistence in school children *is presented by Blinco* [1992].

STYLE 4   A greater level of persistence has been noticed in Japan [5].

In Style 1, the author, Blinco, is given as much importance as what he (i.e. Blinco) found. You might choose this style for one of three reasons: (i) it is simply the easiest style to use and the most readable for readers, (ii) you may want to focus on the author more than what he/she found, (iii) you may want to compare two authors (e.g. *While Blinco says X, Heine says Y*).

Style 2 is similar to Style 1, but in this case perhaps you are talking about more than one paper by Blinco, so the paper is the most logical first element in the sentence.

In Style 3, what Blinco found is more important than the fact that Blinco found it. This is a very typical style, but inevitably involves using the passive, which then leads to longer and heavier sentences.

In Style 4 Blinco is not mentioned at all, but only a reference to his paper in parentheses.

The style you use will depend on your journal's "Style Rules", but is likely to contain an element of flexibility. In fact, Chris Rozek's Introduction in Sect. 15.4 uses two styles:

> Heine et al. (2001) furthered this idea by testing …

> … can be correlated with final grades in college-level classes (Blankstein & Winkworth, 2004)

He does this to:

- Change the focus from author to findings

- Create variety for the reader

15.6 How can I talk about the limitations of previous work and the novelty of my work in a constructive and diplomatic way?

Sometimes in the Literature Review you want your readers to note the strong features of your work and the limitations of previous works by other authors. If what you propose has never been done before, you can begin your sentence as indicated by the words in italics below.

> *As far as we know*, there are no studies on …

> *To [the best of] our knowledge*, the literature has not discussed …

> *We believe that this is the first time* that principal agent theory has been applied to …

If you want to mention the limitations of previous works you could adapt one or more of the following sentences:

Generally speaking patients' perceptions are *seldom* considered.

Results often appear to *conflict* with each other …

So far X *has never been applied* to Y.

Moreover, no attention has been paid to …

These studies have *only* dealt with the situation in X, *whereas* our study focuses on the situation in Y.

To learn more about how to highlight your contribution and discuss the limitations of others see Chapters 8 and 9, respectively.

15.7 What tenses should I use?

The PRESENT SIMPLE (S1) or PRESENT PERFECT (S2) are generally used to introduce the literature review.

S1. In the literature there *are* several examples of new strategies to perform these tests, which all *entail* setting new parameters [Peters 2001, Grace 2014, Gatto 2018].

S2. Many different approaches *have been proposed* to solve this issue.

Use the PRESENT PERFECT again to refer to ongoing situations, i.e. when authors are still investigating a particular field. Even though specific past dates are mentioned in S3 and S4 below, these dates are part of a series of dates that describe situations that researchers are still working on today and will continue in the future.

This means that PAST SIMPLE <u>cannot</u> be used in any of these three cases.

S3. <u>Since</u> 2016 there have been many attempts to establish an index [Mithran 2017, Smithson 2018], but <u>until now</u> no one has managed to solve the issue of ….

S4. <u>As yet</u>, a solution to Y has not been found, although three attempts have been made [Peters 2001, Grace 2014, Gatto 2018].

S5. <u>So far</u> researchers have only found innovative ways to solve X, but not Y [5, 6, 10].

In S3–S5 note the underlined words. These are adverbials of time that are typically used with the PRESENT PERFECT because they indicate something that began in the past (i.e. when research first began in this area) and continues into the present.

The PRESENT PERFECT is also used when talking about research that was carried out at some indefinite time in the past, or when the moment it was carried out is of no relevance for the purposes of the present paper.

S6. It *has been shown* that there is an inverse relation between the level of bureaucracy in a country and its GDP.

S7. Other research [Green, 2018] *has proved* that bureaucracy can have a negative impact on incentivizing companies to adopt environmental measures.

Although in S6 there is no reference, the author is implying that the 'inverse relation' was not found by him/her, but by another author. In any case, it is always advisable to put a reference. If the present tense had been used ('it is shown') then the reader would think that the author is talking about the present paper.

S7 indicates a case where an explicit date is given in the reference (i.e. 2018), but for the author of the present paper it is the finding (i.e. bureaucracy's negative impact) that is the key point rather than the date this finding was reported in the literature.

You must use the PAST SIMPLE when:

- The year of publication is stated within the main sentence (i.e. not just in brackets)

- You mention specific pieces of research (e.g. you talk about initial approaches and methods that have subsequently probably been abandoned)

- You state the exact date when something was written, proved etc.

In S8–S10 below we are talking about completely finished actions, so the PRESENT PERFECT cannot be used.

S8. The first approaches used a manual registration of cardiac images, using anatomical markers defined by an expert operator along all images in the temporal sequence. Then in 1987, a new method was introduced which …

S9. This problem was first analyzed in 2014 [Peters].

S10. Various solutions were found in the late 1990s [Bernstein 1997, Schmidt 1998].

In all other cases, the simplest solution is to follow the style of the examples below.

S11. Lindley [10] investigated the use of the genitive in French and English and his results agree with other authors' findings in this area [12, 13, 18]. He proved that …

S12. Smith and Jones [11, 12] developed a new system of comparison. In their system two languages are / were compared from the point of view of … They found that ….

S13. Evans [5] studied the differences between Italian and English. He provides / provided an index of.. He highlighted that …

In S11–S13 the first verb introduces the author and is typically used in the PAST SIMPLE. Other similar verbs are, for example: *examine, analyze, verify, propose, design, suggest, outline.*

Note that the first verb in S11–S13 could also be in the PRESENT SIMPLE. However, generally when the PRESENT SIMPLE is used the construction is slightly different (S14): first the reference and then the author.

S14. In [5] Evans studies the differences ....

In any case, even in S14 the SIMPLE PAST (*studied*) would be fine.

The second verb in S11–S13 describes what the authors found. In S9 *agree* is logical because Lindley's findings still agree today with the findings in the papers referenced at the end of the sentence. In S12 and S13, both PAST SIMPLE and PRESENT SIMPLE are possible. However, it is common to use the PRESENT SIMPLE when describing how a system, method, procedure etc. functions. In S12 the PRESENT SIMPLE underlines that Smith and Jones are still using their system and that it is still valid. The use of the PAST SIMPLE (*were compared*) in S12 would probably imply that Smith and Jones' system is not in use anymore and it was just a step in this road of research that has subsequently been superseded.

The third verb in S11–S13 indicates what the author managed to do (*find, obtain, prove, demonstrate, highlight*), and typically such verbs are used in the PAST SIMPLE (*found, obtained* etc.). Again, however, some authors use the PRESENT SIMPLE in such cases.

Use the PRESENT SIMPLE to discuss previously published laws, theorems, definitions, proofs, lemmas etc. Such published work is generally considered to be established knowledge and the use of the PRESENT SIMPLE reflects this.

S15. The theorem *states* that the highest degree of separation is achieved when ...

S16. The lemma *asserts* that, for any given strategy of Player 1, there is a corresponding ...

15.8 How can I reduce the amount I write when reporting the literature?

Redundancy is often high in the review of the literature, as highlighted in the OVs below.

ORIGINAL VERSION (OV)	REVISED VERSION (RV)
1 Long sentences *are known to be* characteristic of poor readability [Ref].	Long sentences *are* a characteristic of poor readability [Ref].
2 *In the literature* the use of long sentences *has also been reported* in languages other than English [Ref].	Long sentences *are* not exclusive to English [Ref].
3 The use of long sentences *has been ascertained* in various regions of Europe during the Roman period [Ref].	Long sentences *were used* during the Roman period in various regions of Europe [Ref].
4 The concept of author-centeredness *has been suggested as playing* a role in the construction of long sentences [Ref].	Author-centeredness *may play* a role in the construction of long sentences [Ref].
5 *Several authors have proposed* that in scientific writing the occurrence of a high abundance of long sentences *is* correlated to … [Ref].	In scientific writing the occurrence of a high abundance of long sentences *may* be correlated to … [Ref].

The OVs are not bad English, and if you use them occasionally they are absolutely fine. However, if you always refer to the literature in this way you will create a series of unnecessarily long sentences with considerable redundancy. This makes it hard for the reader to immediately identify the key points of the literature.

Nearly all the words in italics in the OVs could be removed. This is because the reader knows from the reference ([*Ref*]) at the end of the sentence that you are discussing another author's work or one of your previous papers. See Chap. 7 on how to make a clear distinction between your current work, your previous work and the work of others.

However, if you do remove the words in italics, you still have to indicate whether something is known to be true (OVs 1–3), or is simply a suggestion or a proposal (OVs 4–5). For things that are known to be true today (RVs 1–2) you can use the PRESENT SIMPLE, and for things that are known to be true regarding the past (RV 3) you can use the PAST SIMPLE. To indicate that something has been suggested or proposed, you can use *may* (RVs 4–5). Because you have put the reference, your use of *may* indicates a general feeling in the community and not exclusively your feeling.

15.9 Summary: How can I assess the quality of my Literature Review?

To make a self-assessment of your Literature Review, you can ask yourself the following questions.

➢ Have I shown that I am familiar with the state of the art.

➢ Have I mentioned only what my readers specifically need to know and what I will subsequently refer to in the Discussion?

➢ Have I avoided only mentioning the literature that supports my hypotheses?

➢ Are the papers I have mentioned in a logical order? Is it clear why I have chosen these papers and not others?

➢ Have I selected a disproportionate number of papers from my own country?

➢ Have I ensured that there are no papers cited in the bibliography that are not cited in the paper, and vice versa?

➢ Have I followed my journal's instructions regarding how I make references to the literature? Where possible have I done this in a variety of ways?

➢ Have I removed any redundancy when reporting the literature?

➢ Have I used tenses correctly? PRESENT SIMPLE (descriptions of established scientific fact), PRESENT PERFECT (at the beginning of review to give general overview; for past-to-present evolutions), PAST SIMPLE (when specific dates are mentioned within a sentence; for the verbs that introduce an author's findings)

Chapter 16

Methods

Factoids: Ancient and medieval medical methods

Miscellaneous health problems: the Egyptians used the dung (faeces) from various animals and insects (e.g. donkeys, dogs, gazelles and flies). Today it is known that the microflora found in some types of animal dung contain antibiotic substances.

*****

Bubonic plague (14th century): in order to avoid death, sufferers were ordered to confess their sins in the presence of a priest.

*****

Generic illnesses: a blood-sucking worm was placed on the affected part (leaching), a vein was cut in order to drain a substantial quantity of blood (venesection), or a hole was bored in the skull (trepanation).

*****

Hemorrhoids: body parts were burned (cauterization) to remove the hemorrhoid. Cauterization was also used to close an amputation and to prevent severe blood loss.

*****

Pain relief during surgery: as an anesthetic a mixture of lettuce juice with the contents of the gall bladder from a castrated boar (a wild pig) was used along with opium, henbane (a plant with psychoactive properties), hemlock juice (a highly poisonous plant), vinegar and wine.

*****

Superhuman powers: mixtures containing mercury, sulfur and arsenic were supposed to give the patients the ability to walk on water and even to become immortal.

© Springer International Publishing Switzerland 2016
A. Wallwork, *English for Writing Research Papers*,
English for Academic Research, DOI 10.1007/978-3-319-26094-5_16

16.1 What's the buzz?

1) For which of the following research projects do you think it would be the most difficult to write a Methods section? What difficulties would be involved? Which one would you most like to study?

> Calculating the speed at which Santa Claus would have to travel to visit all the children in the world.

> Elucidating why fire-walkers don't burn their feet while walking on fire.

> Determining the minimum size for Noah's Ark assuming two animals of every known species plus sufficient foodstuff for six weeks.

> Studying why attractive people become even more attractive when wearing glasses.

> Proving that a particular homeopathic medicine works.

> Investigating the hypothesis that mankind would have developed differently if the dinosaurs had not become extinct.

> Understanding whether a seven-month child is more or less intelligent that a seven-year old cat.

> Devising an apparatus that would enable someone to weigh their own head.

2) What is the key problem with this extract from the Methods section? What other problems are there? The extract describes a methodology for defusing a bomb that is contained inside a box.

> *First, the lid at the top of the box should be carefully removed, provided that it has been ascertained that there is no trigger device. Second, the three wires at the side of the explosive device should be identified before proceeding with step three: the cutting of the green wire. Finally, the red wire should also be subjected to a cutting process after the blue wire has been disconnected.*

****

This section of a paper has several different names including: 'Methods', 'Methods and Materials', 'Experimental', 'Method Description and Validation'. Hereafter, I will refer to it as the Methods section.

In most journals the Methods section follows the Literature Review, in others it follows the Conclusions.

The secret of writing this section is to be able to describe the materials you used in your experiments and/or the methods you used to carry out your research, in a way that is sufficiently detailed to enable others in your field to easily follow your method and, if desired, even replicate your work. A key skill is to make sure the descriptions are complete and yet are also as concise as possible, for example by referring to other works in the literature, including your own, that make use of the same or similar methods.

Another key skill is to write extremely clearly, with generally not more than two steps described in one sentence, and in a logical order. This will then enable your readers to easily follow your description.

Researchers generally agree that the Methods is the easiest section to write because your methods are likely to be clear in your mind, so it may be a good point for you to begin writing your manuscript.

16.2   How should I structure the Methods?

The Methods section should answer most of the following questions, obviously depending on your discipline:

- What / Who did I study? What hypotheses was I testing?

- Where did I carry out this study and what characteristics did this location have?

- How did I design my experiment / sampling and what assumptions did I make?

- What variable was I measuring and why?

- How did I handle / house / treat my materials / subjects? What kind of care / precautions were taken?

- What equipment did I use (plus modifications) and where did this equipment come from (vendor source)?

- What protocol did I use for collecting my data?

- How did I analyze the data? Statistical procedures? Mathematical equations? Software?

- What probability did I use to decide significance?

- What references to the literature could I give to save me having to describe something in detail?

- What difficulties did I encounter?

- How does my methodology compare with previously reported methods, and what significant advances does it make?

You should provide enough quantitative information (concentration, temperature, weight, size, length, time, duration etc.) so that other researchers can replicate what you did.

Describe everything in a logical order to enable readers to easily follow what you did. This will usually be chronological (but see Sect. 16.7), i.e. the order in which you conducted the phases of your tests. It may also help the reader if you use sub-headings to explain the various stages of the procedure, which you can then use again (perhaps with modifications) in the Results.

Your experiments, sampling procedures, selection criteria etc. may have more than one step. It helps your readers if your description of each step follows the same logical order.

Ensure that you cover every step required. Because you are very familiar with your method, you may leave out key information either thinking that it is implicit (and thus not worth mentioning) or simply because you forget.

16.3   What style: should I use the active or passive? What tenses should I use?

The passive is good style in this part of a research paper because the focus is on what was done rather than who did it. Thus you can ignore any expert advice that tells you that the passive should always be avoided. It should be avoided (7.4), but only where it is not necessary (7.3). In the Methods the passive is both necessary and appropriate.

Most Methods sections are written in the PAST SIMPLE and/or PRESENT SIMPLE. The choice will depend on your discipline (and whether it is applied or theoretical), your chosen journal, and what actions you are describing.

The PAST SIMPLE is required when you describe actions that you did, both before and during your experiments (in the lab, in the field, while conducting surveys etc). Thus the PAST SIMPLE is likely to be used in most of this section.

Below is an example of the PAST SIMPLE used to describe some preliminary work:

> An explorative research approach *was adopted* using a seven-page survey on opinions and religious background. The findings *were collected* using an internet questionnaire survey. Six hundred religious institutions *were selected* from AMADEUS database, which *were then classified* into three groups based on …

Here are the methods used by an agronomist, again using the PAST SIMPLE:

A test bench (Fig. 1) *was used* in order to evaluate the effectiveness of the flame burner. Steel plates *were treated* with an open-flame burner (Fig. 2).

The PRESENT SIMPLE is required when you describe a standard method, i.e. not one you invented yourself for the specific purpose of the research that you are reporting in your paper.

For example, if your paper is on ways to recycle paper, when describing methods that have been reported in the literature, you will use the PRESENT. But then, when you describe the various phases of your own system for recycling, then you would probably use the PAST.

The PRESENT SIMPLE is also often used when you are presenting your procedure, model, software, device etc. In this case the active form is often used.

Firstly, we *define* x as an exogenous measure of the natural rate of longevity of people.

As in Chakraborty (2017), we *assume* that ... The rule is thus given by the following formula:

Our machine *uses* diesel ... It *has* a 1000 hp engine ...

The application *requires* 10 TB of space ...

If you are in doubt, then look at your chosen journal and check what tense other authors use in the Methods section.

16.4   How should I begin the Methods?

How you begin will very much depend on your discipline. To help you decide, take a look at the Methods section in papers from your chosen journal, and see how authors start this section.

Typical ways include:

(a) Making a general statement about your method.

The method described here is simple, rapid, sensitive and …

(b) Referring to another paper.

The materials used for isolation and culture *are described* elsewhere [20].
Materials *were obtained* in accordance with Burgess et al.'s method [55].

(c) Stating where you obtained your materials from.

Bacterial strains …*were isolated* and kindly supplied by …
Agorose for gel electrophoresis *was purchased* from Brogdon plc (Altrincham, UK).

(d) Explaining how you found your subjects, i.e. begin with the setting.

Subjects *were chosen* from a randomly selected sample of …
Participants *were selected* from patients at the Gynecology Faculty of the University of …

(e) Indicating where (i.e. a geographical region) your investigation was focused.

Our empirical investigation focused on Tuscany, a central region of Italy, …
The study *was carried out* in four boulevards in Athens (Greece) and …

(f) Referring the reader to a figure which shows the experimental set-up.

To highlight the advantages of the system, Fig. 1 shows the …

(g) Starting directly with the first step in your procedure.

Frontal cerebral cortices were dissected from …
Core-cell composite materials were prepared by colloidal assembly of …

16.5 My methods use a standard procedure. Do I need to describe the methods in detail?

No. You can alert the reader that the method is 'standard' and is described in another paper or in some manufacturer's instructions to their product (make sure you give a clear reference to the related paper or the instructions).

If you use a phrase such as *based on methods previously described*, then you need to make it clear whose these methods are: yours or someone else's. If they are yours, then it would be less ambiguous to write:

S1. based on methods described in *our* previous paper [56].

Even though you might use a standard procedure, you will probably have adjusted it in some way and you should mention these modifications:

S2. Our methods followed the procedures outlined in [Wallwork, 2017] *with the two minor modifications:*

S3. Our procedure is as according to [Wallwork, 2017] *with the following exceptions:*

Finally, if your entire methodology is novel and this novelty is the basis of the whole paper, then you might consider writing a separate paper dedicated exclusively to this new methodology.

16.6 My methods in the paper I am writing now are (almost) identical to the methods I published in a previous paper. Can I repeat them word for word?

If you simply duplicate what you wrote in a previous paper, the editor may consider this to be plagiarism (11.1 and 11.2).

Simply putting a reference to the original paper where your methods are described is probably not enough as (i) it will make your Methods section look very short, (ii) it is not very helpful for readers. A better solution is to write:

S1. Full details of the methods used can be found in our previous paper [45]. In brief, ...

S1 highlights that you should:

- put a reference to where the reader can find the full version of your methods

- clearly state that the reference is to a paper written by your research group (*our previous paper*)

- begin a summarized version with the phrase *In brief*. This phrase alerts the reader that what he/she is going to read now is not the full version of your methods

Also, this gives you the opportunity to talk about any modifications you may have made to your original methods.

Clearly, your current paper should be about a different topic from the paper where the original methods were published.

16.7   Should I describe everything in chronological order?

The basic idea is to present everything in your experiments, trials, procedures etc. in a way that will make best sense to your reader. The fact that you did something before or after something else, may not be relevant for your reader, so in such cases chronology is not important.

However within a sentence or paragraph, readers should feel they are moving forward chronologically.

S1.   * The sample, which was filtered and acidified at pH 2, was mixed with X.

S2.   * The sample was filtered and acidified at pH 2 and then mixed with X.

S3.   The sample was filtered and acidified at pH 2, and then mixed with X.

S4.   The sample was filtered and acidified at pH 2. It was then mixed with X, which enabled the resulting solution to stabilize at ...

In S1 the main idea is that the sample was mixed with X, but we seem to be going backwards (to the filtering and acidification) before we go forwards again to the mixing. S2 resolves this problem by removing the *which*-clause and presenting the steps in sequence. However, S2 uses *and* twice, which means the reader may be initially confused with regard to which two items are connected with each other (*filtered + acidified*, or *acidified + mixed*). This is resolved in S3 by the addition of a comma after *pH 2*. However the clearest version is S4, which simply begins a new sentence.

S1 is an example of a very short sentence that could be rewritten more clearly. Often such sentences are much longer, so the technique given in S4 (rather than S3) may be the best solution.

16.8 How many actions / steps can I refer to in a single sentence?

A frequent problem in the Methods is that the description reads like a manual, where each individual detail or action is described in a single sentence. Given that you are describing a procedure rather than making a complex analysis, it is perfectly acceptable to have two actions in one sentence.

Below is the first paragraph from a medical paper in which the author describes how she selected the participants for her survey on depression. The word 'practice' means an association of medical doctors who offer a service to the public. The 'list size' is the number of patients the practice has.

ORIGINAL VERSION (OV)	REVISED VERSION (RV)
A first postal invitation to participate in the survey was sent to 26 practices in South Yorkshire. A total of five practices indicated their willingness to participate. Multidisciplinary focus groups in four diverse practices were purposively identified. The identification entailed using a maximum variation approach. This approach was based on socio-economic population characteristics and ethnic diversity. These characteristics were taken with reference to census data.	Following a first postal invitation to participate sent to 26 practices in South Yorkshire, five responded positively. Multidisciplinary focus groups in four diverse practices were purposively identified using a maximum variation approach, based on socio-economic population characteristics and ethnic diversity (by reference to census data).

The OV is in correct English and is perfectly acceptable provided that this style is not used continuously throughout the Methods. If it is used continuously, the reader will soon find it tedious, particularly as each sentence begins in the same way (i.e. with a noun).

The technique of the RV is simply to combine two steps into a single sentence, with no extra effort on the reader's part in terms of understanding.

On the other hand, you do not want to have too much information in the same sentence. In the OV below, the reader would find the information much more difficult to assimilate than in the RV, even though the information given is exactly the same.

ORIGINAL VERSION (OV)	REVISED VERSION (RV)
The four practices, which had been previously identified as having list sizes between 4750 and 8200, comprised firstly an inner city practice (hereafter Type 1) with an ethnically diverse population for which the team frequently required translators for primary care consultations, secondly, two urban practices with average levels of socio-economic deprivation (Type 2), and thirdly, a mixed urban/rural practice (Type 3).	The four practices had a list size ranging between 4750 and 8200. They comprised: • an inner city practice with an ethnically diverse population, where the team frequently required translators for primary care consultations • two urban practices with average levels of socio-economic deprivation • a mixed urban/rural practice

In the first three lines of the OV, two pieces of information are included, where the additional information is placed between commas (in italics below):

> The four practices, *which had previously been identified as having list sizes between 4750 and 8200*, comprised firstly an …

This kind of construction should not be used too often as it separates the subject (*practices*) from the verb (*comprised*) – see Sect. 2.6. Readability is generally increased when the subject and verb are close together, as in the RV. The next lines of the OV then continue with a list of three items. It is much easier if these items are put into three different sentences.

16.9   Can I use bullets?

The second RV in 16.8 uses bullets to list the three types of practices. This makes it easier to read and also provides variety in the layout. However, refer to your journal's style guide to check whether bullets are permissible.

You only need to number your bullets if each bullet describes a step that is part of a chronological sequence.

16.10 How can I reduce the word count?

The style of the first RV in 16.8 is to present more than one action per sentence. This reduces the number of words that are required – the RV is more than 20% shorter than the OV.

Other ways to reduce the word count are:

- assume your readers have basic knowledge of the techniques used in your field, you can thus delete any superfluous information

- cite a reference rather than detailing the procedure again if any of your methods are fully described elsewhere (in one of your papers or someone else's)

- use tables and figures to summarize information

- be concise – see Chapter 5

16.11 How can I avoid my Methods appearing like a series of lists?

It is important to be concise in the Methods. But conciseness does not mean writing a series of lists (as in S1). This style may be appropriate on a presentation slide, but should be avoided in a paper. What you write should always sound natural if read aloud. S1 does not sound natural.

> S1. Processes which often occur in lipids include: oxidation, hydration, dehydration, decarboxylation, esterification, aromatisation, hydrolysis, hydrogenation and polymerization. Factors that affect the chemistry of these materials include: heat (anthropogenic transformations), humidity, pH, and microbial attacks.

S2 still contains the same *processes* and *factors* as S1, but the way these are introduced sounds more natural – even though it requires more words.

> S2. Several processes often occur in lipids, including oxidation, hydration, dehydration, decarboxylation, esterification, aromatisation, hydrolysis, hydrogenation, and polymerization. In addition, the chemistry of these materials can be affected, for example, by heat (anthropogenic transformations), humidity, pH, and microbial attacks.

16.12 How can I avoid ambiguity?

In Robert Day's informative and amusing book *How to Write and Publish a Scientific Paper*, several real examples of ambiguous sentences from Methods sections are given. Here are two of them:

S1. *Employing a straight platinum wire rabbit, sheep and human blood agar plates were inoculated …

S2. *Having completed the study, the bacteria were of no further interest.

In S1 it seems that the rabbits were made of platinum wire, and in S2 it seems that the bacteria were responsible for completing the study. You may think that the real interpretations are very obvious, but the fact that Robert Day mentions them means that some referees and readers will also find them amusing and/or aggravating. One solution is to improve the punctuation as in S3, Although a comma has been added after *wire*, S3 is still not.

S3. Employing a straight platinum wire, rabbit, sheep and human blood agar plates were inoculated with …

In S3 a comma has been added after *wire*. But the sentence is still not immediately clear because the use of a series of commas initially makes it seem like a list of things that were employed. S4–S6 are much clearer.

S4. Rabbit, sheep and human blood agar plates were inoculated with …by employing a straight platinum wire.

S5. Employing a straight platinum wire, we inoculated rabbit, sheep and human blood agar plates with …

S6. Rabbit, sheep and human blood agar plates were inoculated with …This was carried out using a straight platinum wire.

S2 could be rewritten as:

S7. Once the study had been completed, the bacteria were of no further interest.

For more on such problems of ambiguity, see Chap. 6.

16.13 How should I designate my study parameters in a way that my readers do not have to constantly refer backwards?

In the second OV in 16.8 the author has designated the three types of medical practices as Type 1, Type 2 and Type 3. This enables her to save time whenever she has to refer to one of the practices. It saves her time, but not the reader. Later in the Methods (or even in the Results or Discussion), whenever readers see, for example, Type 1 they will have to refer backwards to remember which practice Type 1 refers to.

Although I generally recommend being concise, in this case conciseness is annoying for readers. It is much easier for readers to read *inner city practice* than *Type 1*.

Another timesaver for the author is to use an invented acronym. So in this case, the author could have written *ICP* for *inner city practice*. But the same problem arises: the reader is forced to remember what *ICP* refers to.

So the solution is to use the abbreviated forms (i.e. *Type 1* and *ICP*) immediately after you have defined them, i.e. within the same paragraph or at most in the next paragraph. Then, if for a few paragraphs they are not mentioned again, when you do mention them again give the full form in brackets. For example you can write:

> ... *used with Type 1 (i.e. inner city practice).*

and proceed as before (i.e. it is OK to use abbreviated form within the same and next paragraph).

16.14 What grammatical constructions can I use to justify my aims and choices?

You often need to be able to explain why you made certain choices in the light of what they subsequently enabled you to do.

To introduce your choices, you can use the following constructions:

> *In order to <u>validate</u>* the results, we first had to ...

> *In an attempt to <u>identify</u>* the components, it was decided to ...

> *To provide a way of <u>characterizing</u>* the samples, an adaptation of Smith's method [2011] was used.

For the purpose of <u>investigating</u> the patients' previous medical history, we …

Our aim was to <u>get</u> a general picture of …

This choice was <u>aimed</u> at getting a general picture of …

The examples highlight that there are many ways (not all mentioned here) to express your aims and intentions. The important thing is to choose the right verb form (see the underlined verbs in the examples): the infinitive (*to test*) or the *-ing* form (*of testing, at testing*).

However, all the examples could be expressed much more simply using the infinitive form alone (e.g. *To validate the results. To identify the components. To characterize the samples*).

Another way to talk about your choices is to use the verb *to choose*. But note the construction:

This equipment was *chosen for* its low cost.

This equipment was *chosen (in order) to* save money.

16.15 What grammatical construction is used with *allow, enable* and *permit*?

There are several verbs in English that mean 'give the capability of' and highlight for your readers what your initial choices subsequently helped you to achieve.

Allow and *enable* are the most commonly used in research papers and are particularly common in the Methods section. Outside computer science, *allow* and *enable* can generally be used interchangeably. Another verb is *to permit*, which is used less frequently as it often has the meaning of an authority giving someone the permission to do something. All three verbs require the same specific construction. In the examples below I have just used *allow*, but in all these examples from a grammatical point of view *allow* could be replaced with *enable* and *permit*.

GRAMMATICAL CONSTRUCTION	EXAMPLE
allow <u>someone</u> or something to do something	This equipment allowed <u>us</u> to identify X.
allow someone or something to be + past participle	This equipment allowed X to be identified.
allow + noun	This equipment allowed the identification of X.

All three examples mean exactly the same thing. The first is the shortest and most commonly used. It is also the one that gives rise to the most mistakes. This is because *allow, enable* and *permit* require an agent before the infinitive. Hence the use of *us* in the first example is obligatory.

Allow, enable and *permit* involve long constructions but can often be eliminated, generally without any change in meaning. If you find yourself using *allow* and *enable* very frequently, then consider using the alternatives given below. In some cases you may feel that the RV is slightly different in terms of meaning from the OV, in such cases it is best to stick with the OV.

ORIGINAL VERSION (OV)	REVISED VERSION (RV)
Limiting the Xs *allows* the complexity of Y *to be reduced* and permits *the user to control* the deduction process.	Limiting the Xs *reduces* the complexity of Y, and *facilitates control* of the deduction process.
The analysis *allowed the characterization of pine resin* as the main organic constituents in the sample to be achieved.	The analysis *showed that pine resin* was the main organic constituent in the sample.
This model *permits the analysis* of X.	This model *can analyze* X.
	With this model *we can analyze* X.
	With this model, X can be determined
The use of these substrates *enabled us to highlight* the presence of several nucleases.	The use of these substrates:
	highlighted the presence of ...
	meant that we were able to highlight the presence of ...
	offered a means *to highlight* the presence of ...

Note that in the RVs, the verb *let*, which means the same as *allow, enable* and *permit*, has not been used because in most journals it is considered too informal.

16.16 How can I indicate the consequences of my choices and actions?

In 16.14 we saw how (i) to indicate the rationale behind your choices, then in 16.15 (ii) what this choice enabled you to do. Now we will look at how to describe the consequences of (i) + (ii).

Here are two examples that give two alternative endings (*thus / thereby and consequently / next*):

S1. An evaluation of this initial data demonstrated that X=Y,
     thus giving an insight into the function of Z.
     thereby providing a basis for investigating the function of Z.

S2. An evaluation of this initial data demonstrated that X=Y.
     Consequently the next step was to investigate the function of Z.
     The *next* step was *thus / therefore / consequently* to investigate …

In S1 the sentence is in two parts divided by a comma after *Y*. Note how *thus* and *thereby* require the *-ing* form after them. The *-ing* form alone, without *thus* and *thereby* could be ambiguous (Sect. 6.5).

In S2 the first sentence ends with Y. The first word in the next sentence is *consequently*. It would be possible to put *thus* and *therefore* (but not *thereby*) at the beginning of the sentence too but their most natural position is after the verb *to be* (Sect. 2.12). Other alternative words are *hence*, which is most generally used in mathematics, and *so*, which is generally considered too informal for research papers.

16.17   What other points should I include in the Methods? How should I end the Methods?

The Methods section is often the shortest section in a paper. However, in some studies the methods are the main contribution of the paper. In such cases, subsections with subheadings (e.g. *sampling procedure, experimental set up, testing the model*) may help readers to understand the various stages or various components.

Your first subsection may be a general overview of the methods chosen, how they relate to the literature and why you chose them.

Then in each subsequent subsection you:

1. preview the part of the procedure / method you are talking about
2. detail what was done and justify your choices
3. point out any precautions taken (this also helps you gain credibility as a researcher who carries out his / her work accurately and thoroughly)
4. discuss any limitations in your method or problems you encountered
5. highlight the benefits of your methods (perhaps in comparison to other authors' approaches)

If your Methods section is short and does not require any subsections, then you could end it with one or more of Points 3–5 above. If it is long, then you could end with some conclusions regarding the limitations and benefits (Points 4 and 5) of your overall methodology.

16.18   How can I assess the quality of my Methods section?

To make a self-assessment of your Methods section, you can ask yourself the following questions.

➢ Are enough details given? Have I really described my Methods in a way that is easy for readers to follow and which would enable them to retrace or replicate my work? Have I ensured that I have covered every step? Is my structure clear and complete?

➢ Have I justified the choices I made (particularly when the choices might not be obvious)?

➢ Have I written everything clearly in reasonably short sentences, with no unnecessary semicolons? Have I been as concise as possible?

➢ Have I used references to previous works rather than repeating descriptions that readers could easily find elsewhere?

➢ Do the individual sentences in each paragraph contain too many, too few, or just the right manageable number of steps? Have I ensured that my sentences don't sound like lists?

➢ Have I thought about the way readers prefer to receive information? (no ambiguity, no back referencing, everything in chronological order)

➢ Have I checked my grammar (infinitive, gerund, *allow, thus* etc.) with regard to how I outline how and why I made certain choices?

➢ Have I checked my journal's guidelines on how to use numbers?

➢ Have I used tenses correctly? PAST SIMPLE (in the passive form to describe what I did), PRESENT SIMPLE (descriptions of established scientific fact or processes, software applications, standard devices etc)

Chapter 17

Results

Factoids: Misleading results?

1796: Samuel Hahnemann, a German physician, creates homeopathy as a system of alternative medicine. There has never been any conclusive scientific evidence that it works other than as a placebo.

1945: Scientists warn that fluoride in drinking water is poisonous and many local governments around the world ban it. However in low concentrations (one part-per-million) flouride reduces dental decay.

1962: Rachel Carson, a US marine biologist, forecasts that birds will die out and humans will contract cancer due to increasing exposure to the insecticide DDT. No plausible biological mechanism was identified and research failed to support the claims. DDT was nevertheless banned and millions may have died unnecessarily from malaria.

1968: Paul Ehrlich, US ecologist and demographer, publishes his book *The Population Bomb*, where he writes: 'The battle to feed humanity is over. In the 1970s, the world will undergo famines. Hundreds of millions of people are going to starve to death'.

1979: A small epidemiological study reports an association between hypothesised exposure to electromagnetic fields and childhood leukaemia. Thousands of studies have failed to establish a link between actual exposure and any health effect.

1996: Scientists speculate that a variant of Creutzfeldt-Jakob disease (CJD) might be contracted from eating beef from cattle with BSE, and forecast that the disease would kill 10 million people by 2010. This led to the slaughter of 8 million cattle in Britain.

2005: David Nabarro, Senior United Nations System Coordinator for Avian and Human Influenza, warns that an outbreak of avian influenza could kill anywhere between 5 million and 150 million people.

2015: Data apparently shows that the 'vanishing' of polar ice is not the result of runaway global warming.

© Springer International Publishing Switzerland 2016
A. Wallwork, *English for Writing Research Papers*,
English for Academic Research, DOI 10.1007/978-3-319-26094-5_17

17.1   What's the buzz?

Look at these football results from the World Cup.

Vatican City 0 Vanuatu 1	Germany 7 Brazil 1
Malta 2 Liechtenstein 1	Italy 4 Senegal 4
Monaco 0 Maldives 2	South Korea 2 England 1

Think about the answers to these questions.

1. Which ones are readers most likely to be interested in? Why?
2. Which results would you just put in a table, and which in both a table and in the main text?
3. If you were Brazilian, would you avoid mentioning the result?

Moral of the story: Don't tell the reader ALL your results – just the most relevant and / or the most unexpected. Unless you were actually born in one of the countries listed in the first column (six of the smallest countries in the world), you are highly unlikely to be interested in reading details about them. However, they could still be listed in a table, but with no need for comment in the main text.

The results in the second column represent your three big results, i.e. your three most important findings. Such results should be i) put in a table, and ii) commented about.

Even if a result goes against what was expected (e.g. the Germany vs Brazil result), you should still include it.

****

Not all journals require a separate Results section, often it is integrated with the Discussion, under the section title Results and Discussion.

If you have a separate Results section then the standard procedure is to present them with little or no interpretation or discussion.

The key skill is first to decide what results are representative, and then to organize them in a sequence that highlights the answers to the aims, hypotheses or questions that you set yourself at the beginning of the paper. In many disciplines this involves the use of figures and tables, which are commented on in the text. In other disciplines, findings are only reported in text form.

You should also mention any important negative results here.

From an English point of view the key skill is in reporting your results simply and clearly. If the referees of your paper cannot understand your results, then your contribution to the current knowledge base will be lost.

Bear in mind the following comment that a reviewer wrote on one of my client's papers:

> At times this paper reads like a thesis. The authors seem to have included all their results, with the consequence that I am not sure which findings are significant and which are not. However, I also suspect that some contradictory findings have not been included. So although I generally recommend brevity, this should not include leaving out key findings that do not support the authors' line of logic.

This chapter is designed to help you avoid that problem.

17.2   How should I structure the Results?

The Results should answer the following questions.

1. What did I find?
2. What did I not find?
3. What did I find that I was not expecting to find? (e.g. that contradicts my hypotheses)

A typical structure is to follow the order you used for the protocols or procedures in your Methods. You then use figures and tables to sequence the answers to the above questions.

Alternatively, before you begin writing, arrange your figures (tables etc.) in the most logical order for your readers. This order should support the initial aim or hypothesis that you stated in your Introduction. Then associate key findings with each of your figures, excluding any results that are not relevant in supporting your research hypothesis. Note that 'not relevant' does not include results that contradict your hypothesis.

The rest of the section then consists in commenting on these figures one by one. Maeve O'Connor in her book *Writing Successfully in Science*, recommends the following structure.

1. Highlight those results (including those from controls) that answer your research question
2. Outline secondary results
3. Give supporting information
4. Mention any results that contradict your hypothesis and explain why they are anomalous

Very important: Whatever structure you use, throughout your results section you MUST make it clear when you are talking about your findings and not the findings of others. To learn about this extremely important aspect see Chapter 7.

17.3 How should I begin the Results?

There are two typical ways to begin the Results. The first is to give a general panorama of your surveys, experiments etc. without repeating the details you gave in the Methods section, as in the three examples below:

Overall, the results presented below show that ...

The three key results of this empirical study are: ...

The following emergent themes were identified from the analysis: ...

The most common way is to simply go directly to your results, often by inviting readers to look at one of your figures or tables, either in the first sentence or very shortly after:

Figure 1 shows the mass spectra obtained from an analysis of the two residues. The first residue reveals a .. (Fig. 1a)

A total of 34 wheat genotypes (Table 1) were screened for ... Responses to increased sunlight varied significantly (Figure 1) ...

An analysis was made to look for ... To do this, the average times of x and y were compared ... Figures 1–3 show the differences between ...

17.4 What tenses should I use when reporting my Results?

Your results are things that you found before you started writing the paper. They therefore relate to past events, consequently the PAST SIMPLE is used to report them, often in a mixture of the active and passive forms.

You may occasionally wish to use the PRESENT SIMPLE. This is the case when you are taking the reader through your results as if you were a professor at the whiteboard and your reader was a student in the class. If you opt for this style, which – where possible I would avoid, it needs to be absolutely clear that you are talking about your own results and not someone else's (see Chapter 7).

17.5   What style should I use when reporting my Results?

When describing your results you may opt for an impersonal style. This style, in the mind of some editors, serves to add an element of objectivity to your findings. For instance, instead of saying

S1.   We found that doctors viewed the NHS as having failed to provide adequate services.

You could say:

S2.   There was a perceived failure of the NHS to provide adequate services.

However, both S1 and S2 are accepted styles. S3 is an another example of an impersonal style.

S3.   Three levels of feedback were looked at for differences on task persistence. Differences between positive, negative, and no feedback conditions, were minimal and showed no significant findings ... There were larger differences both between genders and in the interaction between gender and feedback conditions. Tables 1 and 2 show the averages for these gender differences. Figure 6 shows ...

In S3, note how the author uses the passive (*were looked at*) rather than the active (*I / we looked at*). This usage may either reflect the author's wish to remain in the background and let his results speak for themselves, and / or because he is following his journal's requirements. However, he uses the active when referring to figures and tables (*Figure 6 shows*).

17.6   Is it OK if I use a more personal style?

Here are some extracts from a Results section in a paper by economist, Andrea Mangani, regarding differences in content between online and print newspapers in Italy. The extracts highlight a much more personal style of reporting results:

Collecting the data was quite difficult ... On the other hand, the statistical analysis is rather simple. Table 2 shows ... Notice that the difference between online and print variety increases during the daytime; this means that the diversity in online content tends to decrease from 09.30 to 17.30. We wondered whether the smaller degree of online variety depended on ...

This kind of writing is less formal and helps the reader to become more involved in the research process. Andrea tells readers not of his difficulties in collecting the data, but the ease with which he managed to analyze these data. He draws his readers' attention to the significance of his data (*Notice that ...*). His readers are also involved in his thought and decision processes (*we wondered whether*). The result is a paper that reads a little like a story, and is much more enjoyable to follow and therefore easier to digest.

Two more things to note:

- Andrea uses the PRESENT SIMPLE when interpreting his data (*online content tends to decrease*). This is very common when referring to data that clearly indicate a certain trend.

- Although Andrea was the sole author of the paper and conducted the research entirely by himself, he refers to himself as *we*. This is quite common in some journals where the use of the first person singular (*I*) is considered too informal.

Andrea's reader-friendly style may also be appropriate in the Discussion section.

17.7   Should I report any negative results?

Yes! Of course!

Dr Ben Goldacre, a campaigner against the suppression of negative data in medical papers, says:

> When you get a negative result, it feels as if it's all been a bit of a waste of time. It's easy to convince yourself that you found nothing, when in fact you discovered a very useful piece of information: the thing that you were testing doesn't work.

In a book published in 1988 and entitled *What do you care what other people think?* Nobel Prize winner, Richard Feynman wrote:

> If you are doing an experiment, you should report everything that you think might make it invalid – not only what you think is right about it: other causes that could possibly explain your results.

To learn how to deal with negative results see Chapter 9.

17.8 How can I show my readers the value of my data, rather than just telling them?

Ken Lertzman, a Professor of Ecology at the Simon Fraser University, gives the following advice in an excellent document available for download.

> Rather than telling the reader that a result is interesting or significant, show them how it is interesting or significant ... show the reader what they need to know to come to their own conclusion about the result.

Ken gives two examples to highlight the difference:

S1.   *The large difference in mean size between population C and population D is particularly *interesting*.

S2.   While the mean size generally varies among populations by only a few cm, the mean size in populations C and D *differed by 25 cm*. Two hypotheses could account for this, ...

In S1, the adjective *interesting* means something very definite for the author, but not for the reader who has not been given the tools to assess why the *mean size* is *interesting*. Such descriptive adjectives (*interesting, intriguing, remarkable*) are rarely helpful.

You need to give your readers sufficient information for them to be able to say to themselves: "wow that is interesting!" This is what S2 does by highlighting specific details (*differed by 25 cm*).

Adverbs such as *interestingly, intriguingly, remarkably* also suffer from the same problem. However, they can be used effectively if used at the beginning of a sentence, in order to attract attention to a key finding. So S2 becomes S3:

S3.   *Interestingly*, while the mean size generally varies among populations by only a few cm, the mean size in populations C and D *differed by 25 cm*. Two hypotheses could account for this, ...

However this technique should be used only once or twice in the whole paper, otherwise it loses its effect.

If you have a Discussion section, then you do not need not to interpret your data in the Results.

S1 and S2 are taken from the biology website of Bates College in Maine, USA.

S1.   The duration of exposure to running water had a pronounced effect on cumulative seed germination percentages (Fig. 2). Seeds exposed to the 2-day treatment had the highest cumulative germination (84%), 1.25 times that of the 12-h or 5-day groups and four times that of controls.

S2.   The results of the germination experiment (Fig. 2) suggest that the optimal time for running-water treatment is 2 days. This group showed the highest cumulative germination (84%), with longer (5 d) or shorter (12 h) exposures producing smaller gains in germination when compared to the control group.

In S1 the authors highlight the trend / difference that they want the reader to focus on, no subjective interpretation is given. S1 is thus suitable for a Results section. On the other hand, in S2 the reference to optimality is a conceptual model to which the observed result is then tied. S2 is the most suitable for the Discussion.

17.9 How should I comment on my tables and figures?

Dr Lertzman (see 17.8) has similar ideas about 'showing not telling' with regard to figures and tables:

> When writing Results sections you should use the tables and figures to illustrate points in the text, rather than making them the subject of your text.

Following his advice, S1 should be rewritten as S2.

S1.   *Figure 4 shows the relationship between the numbers of species A and species B.

S2.   The abundances of species A and B were inversely related (Figure 4).

In S1 the author is merely telling readers what they can already see in the figure. S1 forces readers to make their own interpretations, which may be interpretations that you don't want them to make.

S2 is much more helpful, because it focuses on the meaning that can be inferred from the figure. S2 saves readers from making any mental effort and at the same time guides them towards the interpretation that you want them to have.

Compare S3 and S4, and S5 and S6: note how S4 and S6 don't force the reader to read the obvious.

S3*.   We can see from Table 2 that in the control group, values for early adolescence (13–15) were 6.5. On the other hand, values for mid adolescence (16–17) were 6.7.

S4.   Values for early adolescence were lower than for mid adolescence: 6.5 versus 6.7 (Table 2).

S5*.   Figure 1 shows that levels of intolerance are 9, 15 and 20 during early, mid and late adolescence, respectively.

S6.   Levels of intolerance are highest during late adolescence (Figure 1).

Lack of conciseness is a frequent problem when describing data in figures and tables (Sect. 5.16). Avoid phrases such as *can be seen* and *we can see*. Simply put the figure or table reference in brackets at the end of the sentence. S5 also repeats information that should already be contained in the table, i.e. the respective age ranges for the three stages of adolescence.

17.10   What more do I need to know about commenting on tables?

Below is a table from Wikipedia showing some statistics on the famous World Cup semi-final in which Brazil lost to Germany.

A typical mistake is to repeat information from the table. For example:

S1*.   As shown in the table, the total number of goals scored was one on the part of the Brazilian team and seven by the German team. The Brazilians achieved 18 shots, whereas the Germans accounted for a lower number of shots, namely 14.

The type of commentary in S1 adds no value to the reader. It tells them nothing that they could not have deduced for themselves. When commenting on a table, your job is to:

- interpret / discuss the results

- bring to the reader's attention anything that is particularly meaningful or significant

- add further details that help to explain the results or which enable them to be compared with previous results

For example, you could write:

S2.   Although a close match was expected – both teams had reached the semi-final undefeated – the result was a shocking loss for Brazil (see Table 1). For what was the first time in football history, Germany scored four goals in the space of six minutes. Despite achieving a greater number of shots, having 4% more possession and committing less fouls, and having only two shots less on target, the Brazilians were humiliated. This result recalls the 1952 final when Brazil were defeated by Uruguay.

Note that given that this is the Results section, you should reserve detailed interpretations for the Discussion section.

Table 1 Match statistics

Statistic	Brazil	Germany
Goals scored	1	7
Total shots	18	14
Shots on target	8	10
Ball possession	52%	48%
Corner kicks	7	5
Fouls committed	11	14
Offsides	3	0
Yellow cards	1	0
Red cards	0	0

17.11   What about legends and captions?

A typical mistake is to repeat word for word the caption / legend to your figures and tables within the main text. Legends should have a number. They should be as short as possible and be sufficiently detailed to enable your readers to understand the figure or table without having to read your text. It is vital that you pay attention to legends as some readers may only look at your figures and tables, without even reading the paper itself!

Note that when referring to a figure in the text, the word "Figure" is abbreviated as "Fig.", while "Table" is not abbreviated. Both words are spelled out completely in descriptive legends (see 27.1 and 27.2 in *English for Academic Research: Grammar, Usage and Style*).

The rest of this subsection is taken directly from the biology website at Bates College – a special thanks to Greg Anderson for allowing me to reproduce it. Although Greg's advice relates to biologists, much of it is true for other hard sciences as well.

Every figure and table included in the paper MUST be referred to from the text. Use sentences that draw the reader's attention to the relationship or trend you wish to highlight, referring to the appropriate Figure or Table only parenthetically:

> Germination rates were significantly higher after 24 h in running water than in controls (Fig. 4).

> DNA sequence homologies for the *purple* gene from the four congeners (Table 1) show high similarity, differing by at most 4 base pairs.

Avoid sentences that give no information other than directing the reader to the Figure or Table:

> Table 1 shows the summary results for male and female heights at Bates College.

Like the title of the paper itself, each legend should convey as much information as possible about what the Table or Figure tells the reader:

- what results are being shown in the graph(s) including the summary statistics plotted

- the organism studied in the experiment (if applicable),

- context for the results: the treatment applied or the relationship displayed, etc.

- location (ONLY if a field experiment),

- specific explanatory information needed to interpret the results shown (in tables, this is frequently done as footnotes)

- culture parameters or conditions if applicable (temperature, media, etc) as applicable, and,

- sample sizes and statistical test summaries as they apply.

How much methodology and results are reported in the legends is journal specific. Hot-off-the-press journals like *Science* and *Nature* limit the body text so that virtually all of the Methods are presented in the Figure and Table legends or in footnotes. Much of the results are also reported in the legends.

17.12 My research was based on various surveys and interviews. How should I report quotations from the people we interviewed?

Generally speaking:

- there is no need to translate / report word for word what your interviewees said

- your transcript should simply enable the reader to understand the core points the interviewee made

- even if the sentence uttered by the interviewee was not complete, if appropriate you can complete it if it was obvious what he/she wanted to say

- remove any tangential / irrelevant phrases

- remove any filler words – *I mean, in other words, that is to say, you know, um, er*

However, you should ignore all the above points if the whole purpose of the interview was to report the exact words that were said, e.g. for some linguistics research.

The quotes you provide need further discussion – otherwise the reader is left to make their own interpretations and to try to make sense of the quotation.

17.13   What else do I need to be careful about when reporting data?

Look at the following text entitled *Postdocs and the science of being expendable*, which reports on the difficulties encountered by postdoctoral researchers when entering the labor market. Can you see a problem?

> Postdoc status is highly inflated: its supposedly "academic and cultural value" is not mirrored by the real price "investors" are willing to pay for it. The current system is designed to get cheap AND specialized labour. The average annual salary for neo postdoctoral researchers is about \$44,000 in the US, while stipends vary greatly in European countries with an average of 1,500 euros/month for Italian scientists vs 4,560 euros/month pay for their Dutch counterparts.

The problem is that the author has given an annual value in dollars, followed by two monthly values in euros. This makes it hard for the reader to make a comparison (it would have been helpful to have the equivalent annual salary for postdocs in Europe, which is significantly less than in the US and is, at the time of writing, €30,000).

Also, is the author comparing two identical situations? Are *neo postdoctoral researchers* the same as *scientists*? And are a *salary* and *stipend* the same thing? How can the reader be sure?

Finally, a very punctilious editor might comment that a symbol (\$) is used when referring to the US dollar, but not when referring to the euro.

17.14   Summary: How can I assess the quality of my Results section?

To make a self-assessment of your Results section, you can ask yourself the following questions.

➢   Have I expressed myself as clearly as possible, so that the contribution that my results give stands out for the referees and readers?

➢   Have I limited myself to only reporting the key result or trends that each figure and table conveys, rather than reiterating each value?

➢   Have I avoided drawing conclusions? (this is only true when the Results is an independent section)

➢   Have I chosen the best format to present my data (e.g. figure or table)? Have I ensured that there is no redundancy between the various figures and tables?

➢   Have I ensured that my tables of results are comprehensive in the sense that they do not exclusively include points that prove my point?

➢   Have I mentioned only what my readers specifically need to know and what I will subsequently refer to in the Discussion?

➢   Have I mentioned any parts of my methodology (e.g. selection and sampling procedures) that could have affected my results?

➢   Have I used tenses correctly? PAST SIMPLE for your findings (in the passive form), PRESENT SIMPLE (descriptions of established scientific fact)

Chapter 18

Discussion

© Springer International Publishing Switzerland 2016
A. Wallwork, *English for Writing Research Papers*,
English for Academic Research, DOI 10.1007/978-3-319-26094-5_18

18.1   What's the buzz

(1) Compare these two discussions of the same finding from a fictitious paper which examines the level of intelligence amongst PhD students. In which case is the key result highlighted most effectively?

DISCUSSION A An in-depth study (Smith et al, 2016) of the intelligence quotas of doctoral students researching in the fields of engineering, robotics, biosciences, agriculture and veterinary sciences revealed that such students had a level of intelligence, which on average, was equal to a value of 8.115% above the norm. In the present work, with a larger sample (i.e. 5000 students as opposed to the 500 students analysed in the study by Smith et al) it was found that students in the same disciplines (i.e. engineering, robotics, biosciences, agriculture and veterinary sciences) had an intelligence quota of 9.996% below the norm.

DISCUSSION B Smith et al (2016) found that PhD students in engineering, robotics, biosciences, agriculture and veterinary sciences had above average intelligence (just over 8%). Our study totally contradicts Smith's finding. Using a sample that was ten times larger, our experiments proved that such PhD students have very limited intelligence (a surprising 10% below the norm), and would in fact be more suited to cleaning toilets than carrying out research. This radical finding may help governments reduce the amount of funding given to post-graduate university education.

Discussion B is designed to be humorous for the purposes of this book. However it reveals some important points:

- important findings get lost in long sentences (the sentence length in Discussion A is around 50 words, in B less than 20)

- a short sentence attracts attention (e.g. the 6-word sentence in B)

- you should make clear comparisons and contrasts with literature data

- readers need to be alerted when you are about to announce something important (e.g. *Our study totally contradicts Smith's finding*)

- clear writing with no redundancy is easier to read, easier to immediately understand the importance, and easier to remember

- the occasional use of emotive words (*surprisingly, radical*) may help to give more impact

- using the active and personal forms is more dynamic (e.g. *Our experiments proved* versus *it was found that*)

The primary aim of a discussion is to highlight the level of innovation of your research. Basically, it justifies why you wrote the paper. Thus, along with the Abstract, it is generally the most important section in the paper.

In the Discussion / Conclusions it is essential to:

- be clear what YOU did and what other authors have done

- highlight your UNIQUE contribution

- discuss LIMITATIONS of your findings

- state what the applications and implications of your research are

(2) Think about the answers to these questions.

1. What is your most important finding?
2. Why is it so fantastic?
3. How does it compare with similar findings made by other researchers? What are its advantages and disadvantages?

Write one paragraph highlighting your finding. This task should help you focus on what really is important about your research.

****

People read papers in different ways. Readers in a hurry may read the title and then just look at the figures! Many begin from the part that they find the most interesting, which is often the Discussion.

Most authors find discussing their results to be the most difficult part of the paper to write. When referees reject a paper, it is very often due to a poorly written Discussion. As one of my PhD students commented:

> It is a 'grey zone' where I have to express my point of view without a specific or logical 'grid'. Writing the introduction is easier because you can be really helped by the articles that you have read.

Although there is no *grid* (i.e. template) in which to insert your own text, there is a general pattern or structure to most Discussions. This chapter is designed to teach you various strategies to simplify the process of discussing your results. You will learn how to structure the Discussion and how to ensure that what you write will satisfy the typical requirements of the referees.

The secret is to sound both convincing and credible at the same time. You can do this by being positive about your own limitations, and constructive when discussing what you believe to be the limitations of others.

Another skill is to interpret your results without repeating them.

18.2 Active or passive? What kind of writing style should I use?

In the Discussion, you will constantly be comparing your work with other authors'. In your head you know what you did, and you know what other authors have done. But the reader doesn't. You need to make a very clear distinction, so that in every sentence the reader is 100% clear about whose work you are referring to (Chapter 7).

Passive sentences do not reveal the author of the action and so the reader will not understand if you are referring to your findings or another person. So, to avoid ambiguity, where possible use active sentences.

The table below shows five examples. The first two make it 100% clear to the reader whose work is being talked about. The other three are in order of decreasing clarity. In the final example the reader has no idea whose work is being discussed – this is a very typical mistake in papers and is a very dangerous way of referring to the literature.

EXAMPLE	COMMENTS
In 2018, *we confirmed* that complex sentences reduce readability [25].	*We* clearly indicates that you are referring to your own work.
In 2018, *Carter suggested* that complex sentences could also lead to high levels of stress for the reader [36].	*Carter*, who is another author, is the subject of the verb. Thus it is clear to the reader that this is not your work.
In 2018, *it was suggested* that complex sentences could also lead to high levels of stress for the reader [Carter, 36].	The passive form means that the reader is not sure until the end of the sentence if it was you or another author. A long literature review or Discussion full of sentences like this is very heavy and annoying for the reader.
In 2018, *it was suggested* that complex sentences could also lead to high levels of stress for the reader [25].	Readers cannot know who made the suggestion unless they go to Ref. 25 and see if it was you or someone else.
In 2018, *it was suggested* that complex sentences could also lead to high levels of stress for the reader.	There is no reference. Readers cannot be sure if you made the suggestion or someone else.

18.3 How should I structure the Discussion?

The Discussion should answer the following questions, and possibly in the following order. You can thus use the answers to structure your Discussion. This gives you a relatively easy template to follow.

1. What are my most important findings?

2. Do these findings support what I set out to demonstrate at the beginning of the paper?

3. How do my findings compare with what others have found? How consistent are they?

4. What is my personal interpretation of my findings?

5. What other possible interpretations are there?

6. What are the limitations of my study? What other factors could have influenced my findings? Have I reported everything that could make my findings invalid?

7. Do any of the interpretations reveal a possible flaw (i.e. defect, error) in my experiment?

8. Do my interpretations contribute some new understanding of the problem that I have investigated? In which case do they suggest a shortcoming in, or an advance on, the work of others?

9. What external validity do my findings have? How could my findings be generalized to other areas?

10. What possible implications or applications do my findings have? What support can I give for such implications?

11. What further research would be needed to explain the issues raised by my findings? Will I do this research myself or do I want to throw it open to the community?

Whatever your discipline you will need to answer all the questions above, with the possible exception of Question 8 (your findings may only be very preliminary). Whether you answer Questions 8–11 will depend on whether you have a separate Conclusions section, if so, the Conclusions may be a more appropriate place.

It may make sense for you to organize your Discussion following the same sequence as you presented your findings in the Results section. In this case, you discuss each survey, study or experiment, and interpret it within the overall scenario of the problem.

If you are a medical researcher, you will need to follow closely the appropriate guidelines (e.g. CONSORT, PRISMA, MOOSE, STROKE). Even if you are not a medical researcher these guidelines are still incredibly useful and you can find links to them at bmj.com.

18.4 What is a 'Structured Discussion'?

Some journals, particularly medical ones, not only have structured abstracts (13.10) but also have structured discussions. The British Medical Journal (BMJ) reports the following on its website:

Please ensure that the discussion section of your article comprises no more than five paragraphs and follows this overall structure, although you do not need to signpost these elements with subheadings:

- Statement of principal findings

- Strengths and weaknesses of the study

- Strengths and weaknesses in relation to other studies, discussing important differences in results

- Meaning of the study: possible explanations and implications for clinicians and policymakers

- Unanswered questions and future research

Again, by having a clear structure, authors are forced to express themselves more clearly, with obvious benefits for the reader.

The above subsections equally apply to most other disciplines (if you replace *clinicians* with 'others in my field'). In any case, check out your chosen journal's website to see if they have similar recommendations on how to structure the Discussion.

18.5   How should I begin the Discussion?

Below are four possible beginnings for the Discussion of the paper given in 14.6.

1. Remind readers of your goals, preferably in a single sentence:

   One of the main goals of this experiment was to attempt to find a way to predict who shows more task persistence.

2. Refer back to the questions (hypotheses, predictions etc.) that you posed in your Introduction:

   These results both negate and support some of the hypotheses. It was predicted that greater perfectionism scores would result in greater task persistence, but this turned out not to be the case.

3. Refer back to papers you cited in your Review of the Literature:

   Previous studies conflict with the data presented in the Results: it was more common for any type of feedback to impact participants than no feedback (Shanab et al., 1981; Elawar & Corno, 1985).

4. Briefly restate the most important points from your Results:

   While not all of the results were significant, the overall direction of results showed trends that could be helpful to learning about who is more likely to persist and what could influence persistence.

You could begin with any of 1–4 above, or perhaps use them all in combination. Next, you give readers a very brief statement of what you can conclude from your findings. You can then use this statement as a starting point for interpreting your findings and comparing them to what is already known in the literature.

Some experts recommend that you tell a story to help you build up your theory, where your variables, data or findings are like characters in a book. Your job as the author is to explain how these 'characters' relate to each other, and how each one has (or has not) its logical place.

18.6   Why and how should I compare my work with that of others?

Dr Greg Anderson and Dr. Donald Dearborn of Bates College (Maine, USA) give the following advice to their students:

> You may find crucial information in someone else's study that helps you interpret your own data, or perhaps you will be able to reinterpret others' findings in light of yours. In either case you should discuss reasons for similarities and differences between yours and others' findings. Consider how the results of other studies may be combined with yours to derive a new or perhaps better-substantiated understanding of the problem.

A good structure for doing this is:

1. Make a general statement regarding your findings
2. Mention another author's work that relates directly to your findings
3. Make a link between her/his work and your work
4. Clearly state how your work differs from her/his work
5. State the conclusions that can be drawn from your results in light of these considerations

The following text is an example of how to compare your work with others in the Discussion. It comes from a paper entitled *Exploring Stock Managers' Perceptions of the Human Animal Relationship on Dairy Farms and an Association with Milk Production* by Catherine Bertenshaw and Peter Rowlinson.

The authors did a postal survey of 516 UK dairy (i.e. milk) stockmanagers (i.e. farmers) about how they believed humans could affect the productivity, behavior and welfare of cows and heifers (young female calves that have not given birth). Nearly half said they called their cows by name – such cows had a 258 liter higher milk yield than those who that were not called by their name. About 10% said that a fear of humans resulted in a poor milking temperament.

Below is the beginning of the Discussion section:

(1) Our data suggests that UK dairy farmers largely regard their cows as intelligent beings, capable of experiencing a range of emotions. Placing importance on knowing the individual animal and calling them by name was associated with higher milk yields.

(2) Fraser and Broom [1997] define the predominant relationship between farm animals and their stock managers as fear.

(3) Seventy-two percent of our commercial respondents thought that cows were not fearful of humans, although their reports of response to an approaching human suggest some level of fear, particularly for the heifers. With both cows and heifers this would appear to be greater in response to an unfamiliar human. Respondents also acknowledged that negative experiences of humans can result in poor behavior in the parlor.

(4) Hemsworth et al. [1995] found that 30–50% of the variation in farm milk yield could be explained by the cow's fear of the stockperson, therefore recognizing that fear is important for animal welfare, safety, and production.

In (1), Catherine begins with an overall summary of her key finding and its implications. In (2) she mentions a previous study (by Fraser) in the same topic area and thus connects her findings with the literature.

Fraser's study gave contrasting results to what Catherine reveals in (3). However, in (3) Catherine also tries to account for some of what Fraser's found (*although ... heifers*) and in (4) finds further confirmation of Fraser's findings in another study.

Catherine thus adopts a diplomatic approach in which she questions the findings of other authors in a constructive way. She uses their results either to corroborate her own results, or to put her results and their results in a new light.

Another useful skill that Catherine uses throughout her Discussion, is that she constantly clarifies for the reader whether she is talking about her findings or those of other authors (Sects. 7.3–7.7), or whether she is just talking in general,

(5) The elaborated responses reported in *our postal survey* contribute some examples of the capacities of cattle, and this contextual human insight may be useful for developing hypotheses for further study.

(6) Most respondents (78%) thought that cows were intelligent. (7) However, a study by Davis and Cheek (1998) found cattle were rated fairly low in intelligence. They suggested that the ratings reflected the respondents' familiarity with the animals. (8) The stock managers in our survey were very familiar with their cattle and had a great understanding of the species' capabilities, through working with them daily. (9) Stockpersons' opinions offer valuable insight into this subject, which could enable more accurate intelligence tests to be devised; for example, to test whether cows can count in order to stand at the feed hopper that delivers the most feed.

(10) Hemsworth and Gonyou (1997) doubt the reliability of an inexperienced stockperson's attitudes towards farm animals. *Our* survey found an experienced workforce (89.5% >15 years).

In (5) Catherine concludes a paragraph by suggesting a future course of action. (6) is the first line of the next paragraph, so it is clear that the *respondents* are her respondents and not another author's.

In (7) she uses *however* to indicate that she is going to give some contrasting information. Her use of *they* clearly refers back to Davis and Cheek.

In (8) Catherine then clarifies for the reader that she is now focusing on her study. She does this again using *our*. If she had not inserted the phrase "in our survey", the reader would not know which stock managers she was talking about. Not making this distinction is an incredibly common error in Discussions and leads to total confusion for the referee and readers. In the literature *our* is often used, even if the style of the rest of the paper is impersonal (i.e. the passive is used, rather than *we*). Using *our* can be crucial in differentiating your work from others.

In (9), like she does in (5), Catherine makes a mini summary of what she has said in the rest of the paragraph. Her use of the SIMPLE PRESENT (*offer*) shows that she is talking about all stockpersons – not just those in her study or in Davis and Cheek's study. She also recommends a course for future action.

In (10) Catherine begins a new paragraph to indicate that she is now going to cover another subtopic. Good use of paragraphs is essential in signaling to readers that you are moving on to discuss something different. Catherine begins with a reference to the literature to establish the new subtopic, and then immediately moves on to her findings to make a contrast between inexperienced and experienced workers.

The rest of her Discussion is structured in a similar manner, in which she provides more conclusive evidence that calling a cow by its name, rather than the problem of fear, is more likely to affect milk production. In each case, she makes it 100% clear to her readers why she has mentioned another person's work and how it relates to her work.

For more on this critical point see Chapter 7 in this book, and 10.3 and 10.4 in *English for Academic Research: Grammar, Usage and Style*.

18.7 How can I give my interpretation of my data while taking into account other possible interpretations that I do not agree with?

In a paper that won him an Ignobel Prize, Magnus Enquist made a case for the fact that chickens are able to discriminate between good looking and ugly human beings. Here is an extract of the Discussion section of his paper, *Chickens prefer beautiful humans*.

> (1) We cannot of course be sure that chickens and humans processed the face images in exactly the same way. (2) This leaves open the possibility that, while chickens use some general mechanism, humans possess instead a specially evolved mechanism for processing faces. (3) We cannot reject this hypothesis based on our data. (4) However, there are at least two reasons why we do not endorse this argument. First, it is not needed to account for the data. We believe that the existence of a task-specific adaptation can be supported only with proofs for it, rather than with absence of proofs against. Second, the evolutionary logic of the argument is weak. (5) From observed chicken behaviour and knowledge of general behaviour mechanisms we must in fact conclude that humans would behave the same way with or without the hypothesised adaptation. There would thus be no selection pressure for developing one.

His strategy for anticipating possible objections to his argument is to:

1. admit that he might be wrong – sentence (1)
2. put forward an alternative interpretation (2)
3. reiterate that his data could be used to confirm this alternative interpretation (3)
4. give reasons for not agreeing with this alternative interpretation (4)
5. propose his own conclusion (5)

18.8   How can I bring a little excitement to my Discussion?

Like a verbal discussion, you can make your Discussion quite animated – you can allow yourself to use stronger language and make stronger assertions than you might do in other parts of the paper. You are basically trying to 'sell' your data, but at the same time considering both sides of the issue.

A colleague of mine who is frequently asked to referee papers in his field recommends:

> Be upfront about your findings and achievements. In my work as a referee I often have difficulty in understanding how significant the authors feel their work is, and why their findings add value. This is because authors are not explicit enough – they don't signal to me (and the reader) that they are about to say, or are now saying, something important. The result is that their achievement may be hidden in the middle of a nondescript sentence in a nondescript paragraph ... and no one will notice it.

By *upfront*, he means do not be too modest about your findings, and by *nondescript* he means phrases that do not stand out from the rest of the text. If you really want your contribution to be seen and appreciated, then you cannot use the normal flat phrases that you might use, for example, when describing your materials or methods.

One way to add some passion to your writing, is to use qualitative adjectives (e.g. *convincing, exciting, indisputable, undeniable*) or quantitative adjectives (*huge, massive*). Typical powerful nouns that suggest a major step forward are: *breakthrough, advance, leap*. These adjectives and nouns can also be used in combination (e.g. *a substantial insight, a massive advance*).

However, such adjectives and nouns should be used <u>very rarely</u>, otherwise they lose their effect.

Here are some real examples:

- S1. These observations provide *compelling evidence* that a *massive* black hole exists at the centre of NGC4258.
- S2. It can be stated that these experiments have provided *undeniable evidence* of an autonomic link-up of the limbic area.
- S3. The latter finding is *particularly important* in the sense that it cannot readily be explained socioculturally, thus presenting a *new and convincing argument* for brain-based etiology of this disorder.
- S4. Major changes in the business processes and the organizational models are, *of course, indisputable reasons* for *drastic* decisions regarding the information systems used by the organization.

S5. *To date no work has been published* on the role of circulating miRNAs in breast cancer—an area where, if feasible, their use as *novel* minimally invasive biomarkers would be an *incredible breakthrough* in our management of this disease.

S6. The possibility of contributing to change the way we communicate with machines is a *very exciting proposition*.

My comments below imagine that the authors are describing their own findings or are discussing their own reasoning. However, this does not necessarily reflect how these sentences were in fact used by the authors.

The claim made in S1 is very strong and will certainly attract attention. It could be made softer (weaker) by preceding it with a preliminary statement, as in S2 (*It can be stated that*).

In S3 the authors back up their claim regarding the finding being *particularly important*, by illustrating its importance. There is no point in saying that something is important, without telling your readers why it is important.

S4 adds emphasis to the adjective *indisputable*, by preceding it with *of course*. This makes the claim appear as if it has already been accepted by the community. The adjective *drastic* adds extra power to the sentence.

S5 would work well as a final sentence in the Discussion, or in the Conclusions. Basically, it serves to show how the authors' work in one field could be extended to another field where, to date, it has never been used before.

S6 would be a great final sentence to a paper. It leaves readers feeling upbeat, i.e. optimistic and encouraged. It also leaves referees with a positive final impression of your paper, which may even affect their willingness or not to recommend the acceptance of your paper.

It is best to use this kind of emotive language wisely, and very infrequently (otherwise it loses its effect). Also, such language may not be considered appropriate in your discipline or in your chosen journal – so check with other papers in your journal.

To learn more on highlighting your contribution, and softening strong claims, see Chapters 8 and 10, respectively.

18.9 How can I use *seems* and *appears* to admit that I have not investigated all possible cases?

It is crucial to be totally honest and non-misleading as to the status of results.

Let's take the example of a mathematical proof. There may be some cases that you have not checked, i.e. you are making an intuitive claim or guess based on what you have checked so far.

In such cases you can use *it appears to be* or *it seems*. Such phrases say exactly the truth, i.e. that something is true for the cases you have checked. You are telling the reader that you intuitively suspect or expect that it could be always true, but you don't claim it. That is what 'appears' means. You make no assertion as to the probability because you have not computed or assessed a probability.

> *It appears that* stochastic processes for which $x = y$ can produce finite dimension values.

> This completes the proof of Theorem 1. Note how this enables us to determine all the Xs and Ys at the same time. Thus *it seems that* some natural hypotheses can be formulated as ..

However, you must make it 100% clear to the reader that, for example, you have not checked all cases, that your sample size was small, and that some external factors may have influenced your results.

18.10 What about the literature that does not support my findings – should I mention it?

Yes. Your aim is to be transparent. And don't forget that the reviewers will quickly spot that you have only mentioned other works that support your own – this is one of the main jobs of a reviewer.

18.11 How can I show the pitfalls of other works in the literature?

There are three areas to call into question regarding the work of other authors.

- Hypotheses that have never really been tested. You want to test them.

- Other studies have only been conducted very generally or in one specific field. You want to apply this research to a new area.

- Other studies have limitations. You are trying to overcome these limitations.

The important thing when criticizing others' work is not to undermine their credibility. The idea is that if you treat others with respect, they will treat you with respect.

18.12 Should I discuss the limitations of my research?

Yes!

It is essential that you inform readers of any limitations to your research or any failures or contradicting data. There is no need to consider these aspects of your research to be totally negative. Your readers will appreciate learning about what went wrong, as this may help them with their own research.

However, don't end the Discussion or Conclusions with your limitations. You want your paper to end on a positive note, so in your final paragraph(s) talk about the benefits and wider applications of your research.

To learn how to describe and discuss your limitations, see Chapter 9.

18.13 What typical problems do researchers in the humanities have when writing the Discussion?

Below is an extract from a reviewer's comments on a social sciences paper. The words in italics are mine.

> The authors *overstate the findings*, making large *leaps* to what the implications of the study are which really only show that knowledge influences attitudes and behaviour influences willingness to behave. ... In fact, most of what is included in the discussion is an *overstatement* of the results *with no support from the literature*, and thus should be deleted with a new discussion written that focuses on the actual findings and what they mean. Another issue I have with this paper is that there is *no presentation in the results* of what was actually found. ... If this had been explored in this paper, I believe the paper would have been strengthened and then the authors would have had more ability to draw conclusions about what programs or policies would be useful for ...

In sciences such as chemistry, physics and biology, researchers usually have relatively clear findings that they can present and explain, and for which they can hypothesize implications.

In the humanities, findings are not so clear and are often based on subjective questionnaires and the impressions of the researchers in relation to these questionnaires. Don't fall into the trap of drawing bigger conclusions than are in fact reasonable.

The reviewer above is suggesting the following approach:

- state your findings clearly, i.e. what you really found and not what ideally you would have liked to have found

- on the basis of these findings, discuss what you believe the implications of these findings are (for example, for policy makers, managers, and others who might be doing research in a similar field)

- support your discussion by making comparisons with the literature (i.e. the literature that you presented in the Introduction) – and not just the literature that supports your views!

18.14   How long should the Discussion be?

Find the most cited papers in your field, and note the proportion of space given to the Discussion relative to the other sections. Adopt the same proportion.

18.15   How can I be more concise?

After the Abstract, the Discussion is generally the most important section in the paper. This is where you highlight for the reader what you have achieved and what it all means in the context of the state of the art. So it is very important that you present this information as concisely as possible. Compare these two versions of the same sentence:

> S1. Furthermore, PCB 180 *has been reported* to share several toxicological targets with dioxin-like compounds [Ref. 1]. Hence, *it appears reasonable to assume* that PCB 180 may affect the AhR pathway in pituitary apoptosis. In fact, the involvement of the AhR pathway in the regulation of apoptosis *has been recently reported* [Ref. 2]. The contents of the PCB were in agreement with *the results of* Chad et al [Ref. 3] and similar to *those reported by* Jones [Ref. 4].

> S2. Furthermore, PCB 180 *shares* several toxicological targets with dioxin-like compounds [Ref. 1]. Hence, PCB 180 *may* affect the AhR pathway in pituitary apoptosis. In fact, the AhR pathway *may be* involved in the regulation of apoptosis [Ref. 2]. The PCB contents *were in agreement with* Chad et al [Ref. 3] and similar to Jones [Ref. 4].

S2 is a third shorter than S1, but with no loss of detail. If your Discussion was originally three pages long, then in theory you could save one page by removing redundancy (Chapter 5).

The problem with S1 is that you are forcing readers to read the same phrase (*has been reported*) or a similar phrase (*reported by, the results of*) again and again. Other phrases that you may be able to remove are: *it has been suggested / proposed that ..., it is well known that ...*

Such redundancy may cause the reader to read with less attention, and thus they may miss the important points you are trying to make.

The modal verb *may* in S2 already incorporates the phrase *it appears reasonable to assume that ...*, so the latter phrase is probably redundant. However, if you are deliberately trying to be cautious, then you could write: *we believe that PCB 180 may ...*

You can massively improve the structure and the language you use in your Discussion by analyzing how other authors in your field write their Discussion sections – but only choose papers from high impact journals.

18.16   How long should the paragraphs be?

Your aim is to allow your reader to quickly understand how your results add to the current state of the art.

As with the Introduction (see 14.9), your Discussion should thus not be one long paragraph or a series of very long paragraphs.

The moments to begin a new paragraph in the Discussion are when you:

* change topic, or you look at a different aspect of the same topic

* move from talking about one result to another result

* mention another author with similar or different results

* justify any differences between your work and the literature

* want to talk about the consequences of what you have just been describing

* talk about the limitations of your work

* talk about the implications of your study and any future research lines

* draw conclusions

However, for some of the points above you will certainly need more than one paragraph. Consider having a series of sub-headings within the Discussion, and under each heading you can have one or more paragraphs.

If you print your Discussion you will immediately see the undesirable effect of having long paragraphs. They are not inviting for the reader.

18.17 How should I end the Discussion if I have a Conclusions section?

Discussion sections which also have a Conclusions may end as follows:

- Tell your readers if and how your findings could be extended to other areas. But you must provide evidence of this. If you repeated your experiment in a different context, would you get the same result?

  We only used a limited number of samples. A greater number of samples could lead to a higher generalization of our results ...

  Although this is a small study, the results can be generalized to ...

  Our results may hold true for other countries in Asia.

- Suggest ways that your hypothesis (model, device etc.) could be improved on.

  We have not been able to explain whether $x = y$. A larger sample would be able to make more accurate predictions.

  A greater understanding of our findings could lead to a theoretical improvement in ...

- Say if and / or why you ignored some specific areas.

  Our research only focuses on x, whereas it might be important to include y as well. In fact, the inclusion of y would enable us to ...

  We did not pay much attention to... The reason for this was ...

- Admit what you have not been able to do and as a consequence cannot provide conclusions on.

  Unfortunately, our database cannot tell the exact scale of Chinese overseas R&D investment. Consequently we cannot conclude that ...

- Reiterate your reasons for choosing your topic of investigation in order to convince your readers of the validity of what you have said in the Discussion.

  As mentioned in the Introduction, so far no one appears to have applied current knowledge of neural networks to the field of mass marketing fraud. The importance of our results on using such networks thus lies both in their generality and their relative ease of application to new areas, such as counterfeit products.

18.18   How should I end the Discussion if I do <u>not</u> have a Conclusions section?

Whether or not you have a Conclusions section, your Discussion should end with a summary of the main points you want your readers to remember.

Catherine Bertenshaw concludes her Discussion (18.6) in the classic way by stating:

* what her findings imply

  The attitudinal information from our survey shows that farmers hold cows in very high regard.

* what her recommendations are

  These results create a positive profile of the caring and respectful attitudes of UK farmers to their stock, and this image should be promoted to the public.

* how her research could be continued

  A 56% response rate suggests the respondents are a good representation of UK stock managers. Further on-farm interviews, observations, and animal-centered tests are needed to confirm the inferences made from the data collected in this postal survey.

Many Discussions end in the same way as Catherine's, particularly those that have no Conclusions section. Catherine's paper does in fact have a Conclusions section, but it is only 70 words long and provides an overall summary of her data, and what she thought the implications of her findings might be.

18.19 Summary: How can I assess the quality of my Discussion?

When you have finished writing your Discussion, it is a good idea to make sure you can honestly answer 'yes' to all the questions below. This will enable your peers to make a critical assessment with regard to the strengths and weaknesses of (a) how you carried out your research (b) and how you analyzed your findings. The result will be that you will be seen as a credible researcher.

➢ Is my contribution to the knowledge gap clear? Have I underlined the significance of my findings? Have I related my findings and observations to other relevant studies?

➢ Have I explained what I believe to be new and important very clearly but without exaggerating? Have I ensured that I have not over-interpreted my results (i.e. attributed interpretations to them that cannot actually be supported)?

➢ Have I truly interpreted my results, rather than just reiterating them? Have I shown the relationship (confirmation or rejection) between my results and my original hypothesis? Have I generated new theory rather than simply giving descriptions?

➢ Is there a good balance, rather than a one-sided version? Have I really offered alternative explanations?

➢ Have I clearly distinguished fact from speculation? Will the reader easily be able to understand when I am merely suggesting a possible interpretation rather than providing conclusive evidence for something?

➢ Have I ensured that there is no bias in my research? (i.e. I have not hidden any of my data or any unexpected results, simply because they do not confirm what I was hoping to find)

➢ Have I included those works in the literature that do not corroborate my findings? Likewise, have I avoided distorting the magnitude or direction of the data of the literature that I have selected? (i.e. I have made sure that I have not committed publication bias)

➢ Have I discussed my findings in the context of what I said in the Introduction? Have I exploited my Review of the Literature?

➢ Have I integrated my results with previous research (including my own) in order to explain what I observed or found?

➢ Have my criticisms of the literature been justified and constructive?

➢ Have I ensured that I have not introduced any new findings (i.e. findings not mentioned in the Results)?

➢ Are all the statements I have made in the text supported by the data contained in my figures and tables?

➢ Have I removed any trivial information? Have I been as concise as possible?

Chapter 19

Conclusions

Factoids

The Year 2000 – A Framework for Speculation on the Next Thirty-Three Years written in 1967 by staff members of the Hudson Institute listed 'One hundred technical innovations very likely in the last third of the Twentieth Century', including:

❖ New methods of water transportation (e.g. large submarines and special purpose container ships)

❖ Major reduction in hereditary and congenital defects

❖ Extensive use of cyborg techniques (mechanical aids or substitutes for human organs, senses, limbs, or other components)

❖ New and useful plant and animal species

❖ Pervasive techniques for surveillance, monitoring, and control of individuals and organizations

❖ Some control of weather and/or climate

❖ Human hibernation for relatively extensive periods (months to years)

❖ General and substantial increase in life expectancy, postponement of ageing, and limited rejuvenation

❖ Permanent inhabited undersea installations and perhaps even colonies

❖ Personal "pagers" (perhaps even two-way pocket phones) and other personal electronic equipment for communication, computing, and data processing

© Springer International Publishing Switzerland 2016
A. Wallwork, *English for Writing Research Papers*,
English for Academic Research, DOI 10.1007/978-3-319-26094-5_19

19.1   What's the buzz?

The Conclusions section below was taken from a paper in the field of the Digital Humanities. The paper proposes a way to organize digitized manuscripts and correspondence so that they can be easily accessed by researchers. Note: I have changed some details from the original manuscript in order to make it anonymous.

Read the Conclusions and think of questions that the reviewers of the paper might ask themselves as they are reading. One example question is in italics (i.e. *how?*).

> In this paper we have illustrated the Confucius Linked Dataset, which enriches *How?* the cultural heritage already present on the Web. Our dataset contains previously unpublished information about the world around Confucius, so it will surely constitute an interesting starting point of investigation both for researchers and inquiring people.

By the time they write the Conclusions most inexperienced authors are just desperate to finish the paper and send it to the editor. The result is that Conclusions are often written too quickly and with no clear thought about what they should contain. A typical referee would ask the following questions in italics.

> In this paper we have illustrated the Confucius Linked Dataset, which enriches *How?* the cultural heritage already present on the Web. Our dataset contains previously unpublished information *So why does it merit publication now?* about the world around Confucius, so it will surely *How can you be so certain?* constitute an interesting starting point of investigation *Why?* both for researchers and inquiring people *Who exactly are 'inquiring people'? What are the implications of this work? Can the methodology be applied in other areas of the digital humanities?*

In addition, the Conclusions look too short – less than 50 words. The version below would be more appropriate (125 words). Think about why it is a better version and how it is structured.

> We have illustrated a new approach to digitization, based on multilayered annotation and visualization of a selection of letters written by Confucius. Our methodology radically improves on the current data model (a graph composed of XML nodes), by presenting the knowledge base as a Linked Open Data node accessible via SPARQL. Since the corpus is written entirely in Chinese, future work will aim at enhancing the accuracy of the Chinese lemmatizer. Given that the system architecture is based on: (i) platform independence (ii) component-based design, and (iii) open source software, the technologies and resources developed can be easily tailored to processing any kind of textual resource. In fact, we are currently designing an analogous system for the online presentation of the letters of Chen Tuan.

****

One of my PhD students once remarked to me: *I find the conclusions quite difficult to write, even in my own language. If I wrote everything in the paper, what should I add at the end?* Her question sums up the dilemma that authors have with the Conclusions.

It's not that the Conclusions section is difficult to write, it's just that authors don't know <u>what</u> to write. In fact, several journals do not even have a separate Conclusions sections, authors simply write a concluding paragraph in their Discussion.

Although the Conclusions may not be the last section that readers read, there is a strong probability that they will be the last thing that the referee reads. Consequently, the Conclusions must be clear and concise, and leave the referee with a good impression. If your structure and English are poor this will have a negative impact on the referees and may affect their final decision as to whether to accept your paper or not.

The key skills are in knowing what referees and readers expect to find in Conclusions, not repeating exactly the same phrases and information from your Abstract and Introduction, and in providing a clear and high-impact take-home message for readers.

19.2 Do I have to have a Conclusions section?

As clearly stated in an editorial in *Nature Physics*:

> Conclusions are not mandatory, and those that merely summarize the preceding results and discussion are unnecessary (and, for publication in *Nature Physics*, will be edited out). Rather, the concluding paragraphs should offer something new to the reader.

However, many readers do expect a Conclusions section or your journal may require one. Bear in mind the words of wisdom of Jonathan Shewchuk, professor of computer science at Berkeley:

> Conclusions should synthesize the results of your paper and separate what is significant from what is not. Ideally, they should add new information and observations that put your results in perspective. Here's a simple test: if somebody reads your conclusions before reading the rest of your paper, will they fully understand them? If the answer is *yes*, there's probably something wrong. A good conclusion says things that become significant after the paper has been read. A good conclusion gives perspective to sights that haven't yet been seen at the introduction. A conclusion is about the implications of what the reader has learned. Of course, a conclusion is also an excellent place for conjectures, wish lists, and open problems.

19.3   What tenses should I use?

Many tenses and constructions are used in the Conclusions – the future, condition-als, modal verbs etc. For details on how to use these forms see Chapter 8 in *English for Academic Research: Grammar, Usage and Style.*

One distinction that many authors make is between what they did during the research (SIMPLE PAST) and what they did during the writing process of the manuscript (PRES-ENT PERFECT).

> We *have described* a method to extract gold from plastic. We *used* this method to extract 5 kg of gold from 50 kg of plastic. We *found* that the optimal conditions for this process were ...

The first verb (*have described*) says what the authors have done in the paper, whereas the second and third verbs (*used, found*) say what they did in the laboratory (i.e. a finished action).

The following two sentences are incorrect because they use the present simple instead of the PRESENT PERFECT:

S1.   *In this paper we *consider* the robust design of an extractor for removing gold from plastic.

S2.   *In this study, it *is demonstrated* that by using an ad hoc extractor gold can be easily removed from plastic.

S1 and S2 would be correct in the Abstract or Introduction.

19.4   How should I structure the Conclusions?

The Conclusions section is not just a summary. Don't merely repeat what you said in the Abstract and Introduction. It is generally not more than one or two paragraphs long. A Conclusions section typically incorporates one or more of the following:

1. a very brief revisit of the most important findings pointing out how these advance your field from the present state of knowledge

2. a final judgment on the importance and significance those findings in terms of their implications and impact, along with possible applications to other areas

3. an indication of the limitations of your study (though the Discussion may be a more appropriate place to do this)

4. suggestions for improvements (perhaps in relation to the limitations)

5. recommendations for future work (either for the author, and/or the community)

6. recommendations for policy changes

The order these items appear is likely to be the same as suggested above.

It differs from the Abstract and Introduction as you are making a summary for readers who hopefully have read the rest of the paper, and thus should already have a strong sense of your key concepts. Unlike the Abstract and Conclusions it:

- does not provide background details

- gives more emphasis to the findings (Point 2)

- talks about limitations, which are not normally mentioned outside the Discussion and Conclusions (Point 3)

- covers three additional aspects (Points 4–6)

On his department's excellent website (see References), Dr Alan Chong of the Faculty of Applied Science and Engineering at the University of Toronto, comments:

> Students often have difficulty writing the Conclusion of a paper because of concerns with redundancy and about introducing new ideas at the end of the paper. While both are valid concerns, summary and looking forward (or showing future directions for the work done in the paper) are actually functions of the conclusion. The problems then become (1) how to summarize without being completely redundant (2) how to look beyond the paper without jumping completely in a different direction.

The rest of this chapter is dedicated to solving Dr Chong's first problem. The second problem is not a language issue and simply involves making sure that you avoid developing any new directions in significant detail, and that these future avenues should be clearly linked to the work described in your paper.

19.5   How can I differentiate my Conclusions from my Abstract?

These two sections have completely different purposes. The Abstract is like an advertisement for your paper – it has to <u>attract</u> the reader's attention. On the other hand, the Conclusions section is designed to <u>remind</u> readers of the most salient points of your paper. However, the Conclusions also have to add value. This added value is typically contained in the recommendations, implications and areas for future research.

In any case, it is a good idea to revise the Abstract and Conclusions together, and even shift information from one to the other.

There will be some overlap between the two sections, but this is both accepted practice and inevitable.

The example below shows you how to avoid a 'cut&paste' from your Abstract. It comes from a fictitious paper entitled: *Six key strategies to a meaningful life: the non-believer's worldview*

As you read, compare the structure and the information given.

ABSTRACT	CONCLUSIONS
With no hope of an afterlife, atheists may have difficulty rationalizing their purpose on earth. With the aim of understanding the coping mechanisms of non-believers, we interviewed 150 UK-born couples (125 mixed, 25 same sex; average age 46) who had happily cohabited for more than 15 years. Interviewees were asked ten simple questions regarding their attitudes to the meaning of life. Our results revealed that there are six key strategies in an atheist's pursuit of a happy and meaningful existence: (1) keep everything simple, (2) have fun, (3) cultivate a sense of community, (4) delight in the wonder of nature, (5) find time for creativity, (6) help other people through frequent acts of kindness. Atheists that implement a combination of these six strategies were found to be more equipped than other non-believers to deal with the death of close ones, health problems, financial difficulties, and bad luck.	We found that six strategies are key to atheists having a satisfying life: simplicity, fun, community, a love of nature, and the importance of creativity and of helping others. An additional but not unexpected finding, not considered in the original research aim, was that an unbridled respect for one's partner is fundamental for a long-lasting relationship. In the light of the vacuous and aimless nature of Western society, our findings suggest that the six strategies should be taught in schools as part of children's philosophy or religious education lessons. Comparisons with traditional religions revealed no substantial differences in approach, apart from a believer's blind faith in a benevolent omniscient overlord and the promise of an afterlife (or reincarnation). These commonalities indicate that traditional religions should attempt to be more sympathetic to atheists, and vice versa. Future work will investigate how the promise of an afterlife may undermine the fulfillment of one's true potential on earth.

Now let's look at how the above Conclusions are structured. The numbers in the text refer to the explanations given below.

(1) We found that six strategies are key to atheists having a satisfying life: simplicity, fun, community, a love of nature, and the importance of creativity and of helping others. (2) An additional but not unexpected finding, not considered in the original research aim, was that an unbridled respect for one's partner is fundamental for a long-lasting relationship. (3) In the light of the vacuous and aimless nature of Western society, our findings suggest that the six strategies should be taught in schools as part of children's philosophy or religious education lessons. (4) Comparisons with traditional religions revealed no substantial differences in approach, apart from a believer's blind faith in a benevolent omniscient overlord and the promise of an afterlife (or reincarnation). These commonalities indicate that traditional religions should attempt to be more sympathetic to atheists, and vice versa. (5) Future work will investigate how the promise of an afterlife may undermine the fulfillment of one's true potential on earth.

Analysis:

- Repetition of key findings, paraphrased from the Abstract (1) – this is the only overlap between the Abstract and the Conclusions

- Additional relevant findings (2)

- Recommendations for policy makers (3)

- Implications (4)

- Areas for future research (5)

Not all Conclusions will contain all of the above five points.

19.6 How can I differentiate my Conclusions from my Introduction and from the last paragraph of my Discussion?

The same comments made in 19.5 regarding the difference between the Abstract and the Conclusions, are also substantially the same as for the Introduction, so they are not worth repeating.

If your journal has a separate section for Conclusions, i.e. the conclusions are not included in the Discussion, then it may be best to shift any overall conclusions you may have made in your Discussion into your Conclusions. This means that the final paragraph of your Discussion may just be a conclusion regarding one specific point, rather than an overall summary of the whole paper. See Sects. 18.17 and 18.18 for more on this aspect.

19.7 How can I increase the impact of the first sentence of my Conclusions?

Here are some typical first sentences for the Conclusions section.

> *We have here described a model for understanding* the power of brainwashing in certain 'life-changing' courses ... We have found significant evidence of ...

> *In this paper we have presented* a statistical study of the nature of ... We have shown that it is possible to reason about ...

> *In this paper it has been shown how* critical thinking should become a core subject even in elementary schools ... A novel approach has been introduced to ...

> *In this work it has been attempted to analyze* loop bending in hip hop ... It has been shown that for...

> *The present study is an attempt to understand whether* homeopathic medicines can cure neuroses in dogs.

The parts in italics will have zero impact on either the referee or the reader. They also match the equally uninteresting first sentences often found in Abstracts (13.8).

The last one (*the present study is ...*) even looks like the beginning of an Abstract, and could simply be replaced by *We estimated* (i.e. using the past tense).

Just as professional copy editors advise against beginning a paper with *This paper describes*, they also suggest avoiding ending the paper in the same way (*This paper has described*). This is because such phrases:

- waste a lot of words (5–7 words that tell the reader nothing)

- delay the main topic

- are not memorable for the reader and have no impact

It is not difficult to be more direct and concise, as the following examples show.

ORIGINAL VERSION (OV)	REVISED VERSION (RV)
2. In this study it is concluded that compression plays an important part in ... It was found that ...	Compression plays an important part in ... In fact, it was found that ...
3. This work has demonstrated that a number of compounds present in X are responsible for delaying the onset of ...	A number of compounds present in X are responsible for delaying the onset of ...
4. We have shown that the crystal structure of X reveals that ...	The crystal structure of X reveals that ...
5. It has been suggested in this paper that the localization of X in neurons is a good marker for neuronal viability.	The localization of X in neurons suggests that it is a good marker for neuronal viability.

The RVs have simply removed the initial 5–8 words of the OVs. This means that the main topic of the paper now appears in the first two to four words of the Conclusions. The result is a Conclusions section that is more concise and has more impact.

The RVs versions are considerably more direct and are found in many disciplines, particularly in medicine and biology related disciplines. If you are worried that they are too direct, then you can make them 'softer' by introducing hedgers (Sects. 10.2–10.6). So RV2 becomes *could be responsible*, and RV3 *seems to reveal* (RV4 already contains the verb *suggest*, which in itself is a good hedger).

In RV4 the passive form (*has been suggested*) has been replaced by an active form (*suggests*) while still maintaining an impersonal construction – this may be important if your journal does not allow you to use *we* (Sect. 7.2). In any case, using the passive form in the Conclusions is perfectly acceptable as it allows you to put your main topic at the beginning of the sentence.

A simple method of extracting gold from plastic *has been described*.

The gold found in waste materials *has been demonstrated* to produce more than 100 kg of gold per day from a typical recycling plant.

If the above two sentences had appeared in the Introduction, they might have been ambiguous. Given that they are in the passive there is no subject for the verb, so readers cannot be 100% sure if the author is referring to his/her own work or someone else's. However, in the Conclusions such ambiguity rarely arises because the reader is assumed to have read at least some other parts of the paper and thus knows that these are the authors' conclusions about their own work.

19.8 I don't have any clear Conclusions, what can I do? Should I mention my limitations?

Sometimes it is impossible to leave the reader with clear conclusions regarding the contribution of your work – maybe your method turned out to be inappropriate and your results were not as brilliant as you were hoping for! In such cases simply say what you have learned about the problem and then suggest possible lines of future research. Such a final section is generally entitled Concluding Remarks.

If you don't have any clear conclusions, it is important not to present your findings in an exaggerated light or to say something uninteresting or irrelevant. Readers may still be able to benefit from what you found (or equally important, did not find) – see Chapter 9. In order to present inconclusive conclusions you may benefit from using hedging devices (Chapter 10).

Here are some examples of authors admitting that their work did not achieve all that they had hoped for. In some cases readers are immediately warned of this 'failure' through the use of the words highlighted in italics.

> *Unfortunately*, we could not assess how much of the difference in outcome was due to ..

> When results are compared across different components, the confidence intervals overlap, and we have no conclusive evidence of differences in ...

> *Although* some progress has been made using our model, this incremental approach provides only a partial answer

> *Unfortunately* this trial had too few subjects to achieve sufficient power and had a low ...

> It is also unclear what conclusion should be drawn ...

> *Regrettably*, we did not have the means to ...

To make your Conclusions not sound too negative, you can add some hope for the future.

> *Although* it is too early to draw statistically significant conclusions, two patterns seem to be emerging ...

> *However*, more definite conclusions will be possible when ...

> *Nevertheless*, our study confirms recent anecdotal reports of ...

> *Despite this*, our work provides support for ...

> *In any case*, we believe that these preliminary results indicate that ...

Again, the first words of the sentence alert the reader that you are now going to qualify the negative stuff you said before by offering some optimism. You could also use some conditional sentences to show what might have been possible if you had had different circumstances, or what might be possible in the future.

If we had managed to ... then we might have been able to ...

If we manage to ... then we might be able to.

19.9 How should I relate my limitations to possible future work?

Don't attempt to lessen the negative impact of the limitations of your research (see Chapter 9) by simply claiming that these limitations could be solved in 'future work'. Referees and editors can quickly see through this strategy and thus dismiss your claims as being unfounded or vague. Instead, you need to give some details regarding <u>how</u> they could be solved.

Below I will examine three examples of very poor paragraphs describing limitations and future work. The *italics* are mine.

> EXAMPLE 1 Although we obtained meaningful results, the present study is not without limitations, which *must* be addressed in future research. First, the causal relationships in our test model could be reversed by cross-sectional research. Future studies *may* employ experimental and longitudinal designs to evaluate the causality implied in our model. Second, the samples used in the study are only from Mainland China. *We* should take *care* when *generalizing* these findings to other cultures.

The referees of Example 1 might ask themselves:

1. who is supposed to address the *limitations* - the author or the community?

2. why 'must' they be addressed (*must* sounds very strong)?

3. why has the author used *may* (which indicates a 50-60% probability) in relation to future studies?

4. who does *we* refer to - the author or the community?

5. why should we 'take care' and why should the findings be generalized?

6. what kind of 'care' should we take?

7. if the findings are going to be 'generalized', how might this be done and with what possible outcome?

The main problem with Example 2 is that it seems to have been written in a great hurry and has not been re-read by the author.*How?So why does it merit publication now?How can you be so certain?Why?Who exactly are 'inquiring people'? What are the implications of this work? Can the methodology be applied in other areas of the digital humanities?*

> EXAMPLE 2 Although the *research* setting of the present *research* may be considered of *little interest* from an economic perspective, given the economic performance of the firms in the sample, the relation between the unit of analysis (i.e. learning dynamics) and economic performance is not in the scope of the present *research*. However, this limitation constitutes a trajectory for further *research*.

The word *research* is repeated four times. Repeating key words is a good idea (see 6.4 and 6.5), but *research* can hardly be considered a key word here. In addition, it is not clear whether the phrase that begins *given the economic performance* is linked to the previous phrase or the following one - better punctuation would clarify this point. Finally, it is not a good idea to refer to your own research as being of 'little interest' - if you don't think it is interesting, then the referees certainly won't, and they will consequently not recommend that it be published.

Another issue with Example 2, which is also found in the last sentence of Example 3, is that it is extremely vague and sounds rather pompous. The referees are likely to suspect that this vagueness is the result of the author i) not really knowing how to deal with his/her limitations, and ii) the author trying to disguise his/her lack of confidence and belief in his/own work.

> EXAMPLE 3 The sample is not representative of social finance institutions currently operating in Europe and, therefore, the results *may not* be extended to the entire field of social finance. Nevertheless, it includes innovative SFIs providing social finance in Italy and Ireland which have never been included in previous studies. *This enhanced our research to analyze* alternative financing models and operating structures that may enrich the current debate on social finance.

The last sentence of Example 3 does not make grammatical sense (*this enhanced our research to analyze*). Given that this sentence may be the last sentence that the referees read, it is going to give a bad final impression. In the first sentence, *may not* should probably be *cannot*. Such grammatical errors might well make the referees recommend that the paper be submitted to an English editing service - even if the rest of the paper was written in good English.

An additional problem is that they key finding in Example 3, i.e. social finance for the first time in Italy and Ireland, is lost at the end of a sentence in the middle of the paragraph. If something is important, it should stand out from the text.

So what can you do to avoid these issues?

If you say that your limitations could be resolved in future research, then you need to suggest how such future research might address these limitations:

- If you want to generalize your results to, for instance, another country, then you could state which countries these might be.

- If you state that your sample size was too small and that future work should consider a larger sample, then you need to propose ways of increasing the sample size.

- If something is outside the scope of your current paper, but could be dealt with in a future paper, then you should outline two or three ways of exactly how it might be dealt with.

In summary:

- Don't underestimate the importance of the Conclusions.

- Be as specific as possible. By outlining real concrete possibilities and strategies for the future you will make a much more convincing case to the referees (and readers).

- Re-read everything in terms of checking the correctness of the English (see 20.3).

Imagine you are a very punctilious referee, i.e. someone who shows great attention to detail and will not accept vague unfounded assertions. What questions might referees ask themselves while reading your Conclusions?

19.10 How can I end my Conclusions?

Once you have summarized your work and dealt with any limitations, there are three typical ways to end your Conclusions. You can use one or more of these ways.

The first is to show how your work could be applied in another area.

> Our findings could be applied quite reliably in other engineering contexts without a significant degradation in performance.

> These findings could be exploited in any situation where predictions of outcomes are needed.

> Our results could be applied with caution to other devices that …

Note how the above phrases all make use of *could* as a hedging device (Sect. 10.7).

You might however like to say where they could not be applied for the moment.

> However, it remains to be further clarified whether our findings could be applied to …

> Further studies are needed to determine whether these findings could be applied to components other than those used for …

The second typical ending is to suggest future work. There is some general agreement that the use of *will* refers to your own planned work, and that *should* refers to work that you believe could be addressed by the general community. Thus the following represent the authors' plans:

> One area of future work *will* be to represent these relationships explicitly …

> Future work *will* mainly cover the development of additional features for the software, such as …

> Future work *will* involve the application of the proposed algorithm to data from …

On the other hand, these examples show possible lines of research for anyone in this particular field:

> Future work *should* give priority to (1) the formation of X; (2) the interaction of Y; and (3) the processes connected with Z.

> Future work *should* benefit greatly by using data on …

The third way to end your Conclusions is to make a recommendation. The difficulty in making suggestions and recommendations is just in the grammatical construction.

The examples below highlight a construction that may not exist in your language.

S1. We suggest that policy makers *should give* stakeholders a greater role in …

S2. We suggest that policy makers *give* stakeholders a greater role in …

S3. We suggest that the manager *give* stakeholders a greater role in …

S4. We recommend that stakeholders *should be given* a great role in …

S5. We recommend that stakeholders *be given* a greater role in …

The construction is thus:

> to *recommend* (*suggest, propose*) + *that* + someone or something + *should* (optional) + infinitive (without *to*) + something

The only difference between S1 and S2, and between S4 and S5 is the use and non-use of *should* – the meaning is identical. S3 highlights that the form of the second verb does not change – in fact, it is an infinitive form (or if you are a language expert). This means that in correct English no third person *–s* is required, so *we suggest that the manager gives* is incorrect (but still quite common). S4 and S5 use the passive infinitive (*be*) + past participle (*given*).

Finally, be careful not to make any vague assertions:

> This effort *can therefore be regarded as the first step* towards the development of a marine management tool to study present dynamics and carry out scenario studies.

The reviewer of the paper where the above sentence comes from commented that:

> Short but clear statements on the applicability of your work elsewhere are needed, as well as the use of your work as a management tool. Merely saying this is *a first step* is not good enough.

19.11 How should I write the Acknowledgements?

The Acknowledgements generally include one or more of the following.

1. Sources of funds.
2. People who gave significant technical help (e.g. in the design of your experiment, in providing materials).
3. People who gave ideas, suggestions, interpretations etc.
4. The anonymous reviewers

It is a good idea to let the people that you wish to acknowledge see the exact wording of how you want to acknowledge them – they might think it is too effusive (or occasionally, insufficient).

The style of giving acknowledgements may be quite different from the style of the rest of the paper. For example, you can use the first person (*I, we*).

Keep your acknowledgements as short as possible, they are generally of little interest to anyone apart from those mentioned.

19.12 Summary: How can I assess the quality of my Conclusions?

To make a self-assessment of your Conclusions, you can ask yourself the following questions.

➤ Is what I have written really a Conclusions section? (If it is more than 200–250 words, then it probably isn't – it needs to be much shorter)

➤ If the conclusions are included in the Discussion, have I clearly signaled to the reader that I am about to discuss my conclusions (e.g. by writing *In conclusion ...*)?

➤ Have I given a maximum of one line to comments related to descriptions of procedures, methodology, interviews etc.? (Generally such comments are not needed at all, unless the primary topic of your paper is the methodology itself)

➤ Have I avoided cut and pastes from earlier sections? Do my Conclusions differ appropriately from my Abstract, Introduction and final paragraph of my Discussion?

➤ Are my Conclusions interesting and relevant?

➤ Have I given my Conclusions as much impact as possible and have I avoided any redundant expressions?

➤ Have I avoided any unqualified statements and conclusions that are not completely supported?

➤ Is my work as complete as I say it is? (i.e. I am not trying to get priority over other authors by claiming inferences that cannot really be drawn at this stage)

➤ Have I introduced new avenues of potential study or explained the potential impact of my conclusions? Have I ensured that I have only briefly described these future avenues rather than getting lost in detail?

➤ Are the possible applications I have suggested really feasible? Are my recommendations appropriate?

➤ Have I used tenses correctly? PRESENT PERFECT (to describe what you have done during the writing process), PAST SIMPLE (what you did in the lab, in the field, in your surveys etc.)

In addition, you should look at the summary questions for the Discussion (18.19), as these may also be helpful in deciding whether your Conclusions will have the necessary impact on your readers.

Chapter 20

The Final Check

What the experts say

The following are exact quotes from editors and reviewers of papers submitted by Prof. Charles Fox of the University of Kentucky.

❖ Fox seems to have an enlarged view of the significance of his work.

❖ The explanation is interesting, and worth stating [but] I didn't need to read the paper to get the point.

❖ This is still a most unexciting paper, but it is probably useful to confirm experimentally what everyone knows intuitively.

❖ Fox's productivity in terms of <u>number</u> of papers is impressive [but] there is nothing new in any of his work.

❖ The point is so elementary that it does not require a manuscript of this length to develop it

❖ It is with great regret that I must inform you that your submission … will be accepted, pending revision. My regrets are motivated, of course, by your excessive profile in the literature. Nothing would have given me more pleasure than to reject the paper, but the excellent reviews, and my own opinion of the work, make this impossible.

❖ I went through the paper, trying to find something wrong with the manuscript, because that is what editors do. Then I tried to think of changes I could ask you to make because the other thing editors do is slow up the publication process by requesting revisions. I failed at both of these … Consequently, I have violated all traditions [and recommend] that your manuscript be published exactly as is.

❖ The results are not earth-shattering, but the paper is beautifully written … In fact, the paper is so well-crafted that it may become a classic. … You have done such a good job that I now want to go back and read all your other papers.

© Springer International Publishing Switzerland 2016
A. Wallwork, *English for Writing Research Papers*,
English for Academic Research, DOI 10.1007/978-3-319-26094-5_20

20.1 What's the buzz?

At http://shitmyreviewerssay.tumblr.com/ researchers can leave the negative comments made by reviewers of their papers. Some reviewers can be very insulting (see the factoids to Chapter 11 *Writing a Peer Review* and Section 11.10 in *English for Academic Correspondence*). For example:

> It is clear that this manuscript will not win a beauty contest. There are still many awkward sentences that make me feel like listening to someone that scratches a glass plate with an iron nail.

> The biggest problem with this manuscript, which has nearly sucked the will to live out of me, is the terrible writing style.

However many are probably very true.

(1) Below are samples of reviews taken from the website. Read them all, and then try to put them into categories (e.g. unclear aim of research, poor vocabulary). For your future work, remember these comments – they may apply to your own manuscripts too!

1. I'm sorry, but I'm reading this thinking, we've already heard about that, you're telling us again and now you're telling me I'm going to hear about it again in the next chapter.

2. Considering by the end of the paper I had no idea what was being said, I don't believe the paper was successful in its argument. In fact, it felt like the author was merely saying the same thing over and over again but with synonyms.

3. I could not find any passage in the MS that would explain to me what is the exact novel idea, proposal, argument or hypothesis.

4. The interchangeable use of *evaluate* and *validate* is a concern because it is not clear if authors know the difference between these two verbs.

5. There are not enough headings.

6. I counted 15 uses of 'clear' or 'clearly.' That's one per page. 'Clearly' the results aren't as clear as the author would like them to be.

7. The authors presents a flurry of statistics, but they do not explain why or how those are relevant to the study.

8. It is not clear what the author wants to accomplish.

9. Overall, this paper goes to significant amounts of trouble to accomplish something that is already well established as a technique in a less elegant manner than is currently employed. This paper should not be published.

10. The paper brings to mind the Mark Twain quote: 'I didn't have time to write a short letter, so I wrote a long one instead.'

11. The paper is grossly over referenced, and reads a little like a student trying to impress a supervisor that a lot has been read, rather than a mature and parsimonious use of citations. The conclusions are hardly world shattering.

12. It was agonizing for this reviewer to read a total of nine pages describing the overall methods.

13. Alarming errors, even if they could be easily corrected, gave the manuscript a sense of carelessness that makes me hesitant to recommend it for revisions.

14. This would have been a question of high interest 10 years back.

15. I also would add that while I don't have anything serious to complain about, I also see this work as being pretty straightforward – there is no "big idea" that I see as especially imaginative or creative. Again, it is extremely solid, just not necessarily sexy.

16. There are FAR too many analyses and results. The reader is swamped. It's simply not possible to take it all in. It needs to be pruned.

17. So, what is the point of this?

18. Words are used inappropriately—I count, for example, 13 instances of "unique", but it is used correctly only once.

19. Not sure how to say this diplomatically, but the manuscript is really dull.

20. The abstract says absolutely nothing, and I mean this literally.

(2) Read the sentences below and find the mistakes. Each sentence contains at least one mistake. The mistakes can be (a) grammatical, (b) word choice, (c) punctuation, or (d) spelling and typos.

1. In this contest the underling problem is that form an economic point the process is too costly which would thus make it prohibitive to purchase.

2. This is the first time that such result is found in the filed of Nuclear Physics.

3. The samples were weighted (av. 5 g) and then subjected to Smith's method (Smiht et al, 2017) and each sample was associated to one of three categories.

4. In addiction in the final phase the micro-thin stripes of tissue have been examined under the microsope.

5. The influence of the color of the structure was found to have a greater influence then the type of behaviour.

You can find many more grammar, vocabulary and writing exercises in the following books in the series:

English for Academic Research: Grammar Exercises

English for Academic Research: Vocabulary Exercises

English for Academic Research: Writing Exercises

****

According to Professor David Dunning, professor of psychology at Cornell University:

A full 94% of college professors state that they do 'above average' work, although it is statistically impossible for virtually everybody to be above average.

You too may consider your paper to be above average work, but it is worth checking the coverage (i.e. what referees expect to find) and quality of each section by referring to the final subsection in each of Chapters 12 to 19.

If you have time it is a good idea is to get colleagues to review your manuscript (including the title), and you review their work. Often it is much easier to spot mistakes (grammatical, stylistic, structural etc.) in other people's work than in your own. But you can improve your critical skills of your own work if you become accustomed to critically evaluating other people's papers.

Referees are famous for asking for revisions before accepting a paper. These revisions often involve what you might consider as trivial details, such as typos and spelling mistakes. Such delays cost you time and money and may also mean that another paper on the same topic gets published before yours.

This chapter covers what you should look for when doing this final check. The result is that you will increase the chances of your paper being accepted.

20.2 Print out your paper. Don't just correct it directly on your computer

It is good practice to print out your paper. You are more likely to find mistakes connected with grammar, word order, and structure. Convert your document into a font that you find easy to read (e.g. Arial) and use 'double space' line spacing.

On screen you have much less perception of how your paper will look visually, and may not even notice that a paragraph is more than a page long. In a printed version, such long paragraphs are instantly visible. You thus have the opportunity to break them up into shorter paragraphs that are easier on the eye. Breaking up paragraphs is quick and easy to do (3.13).

Also, ask a colleague to read your printed version. He or she will very likely find mistakes that you have overlooked – in fact, your familiarity with your own work makes it quite difficult to spot errors.

Finally, read your manuscript aloud. You will find mistakes that are hard to find by reading silently – particularly with regard to how a sentence flows and whether there are words missing.

20.3 Ensure your paper is as good as it could possibly be the first time you submit it

Many researchers finish their manuscripts just before (and often after!) the deadline. Due to such pressures of time, they often send their manuscript to the editor without doing a final check. Most manuscripts are written by multiple authors. This involves a lot of exchanges of versions of the manuscripts, with a consequent increase in the possibility of mistakes being introduced. Lots of changes are made at the last minute, and often no one checks them for accuracy in terms of English. One author needs to be responsible for the final check.

Unfortunately, poor English and lack of clarity are one of the most frequent causes of a paper being initially rejected. You will waste several months if you have to resubmit your paper, and in the meantime someone else might publish a paper on the exact same topic!

Bear in mind the following:

- Judge your paper with the same criteria as you would if you had written it in your own native language.

- Double check you have followed the journal's guidelines/instructions for authors.

- Ensure everything is accurate (data, dates, references, bibliography).

- Ensure everything is consistent (US vs GB spelling, punctuation, capitalization) – for more on this see 20.9 and 20.11.

- It takes much longer for editors and reviewers to read badly-written work than well-presented work. They may not react well.

- Rewriting (which includes cutting) can be a very satisfying as well as being an essential process.

- After weeks or months of working on your paper, you will find it hard to spot your own errors – ask a colleague to help you.

- Consider using a professional editing agency to edit and proofread your work – they will also act as a pre-review by highlighting aspects of the paper that may need reworking. However, if you are not in a hurry to have your paper published, it might be worth waiting to hear the referees' comments before submitting your paper to a professional agency, who can then work on your final version.

20.4   Cut, cut, cut and keep cutting

Joseph Addison (1672–1719), English essayist, poet and politician once remarked:

> The English delight in silence more than any other European nation, if the remarks which are made on us by foreigners are true. ... To favour our natural taciturnity, when we are obliged to utter our thoughts, we do it in the shortest way we are able.

Imagine that you have been asked by the referee to reduce your paper by 25%. As you go through the paper, cut as much as you can (without necessarily eliminating any content). This very rarely leads to a poorer manuscript, more often it improves it massively.

On the basis of identical content, there is no referee in the world who would prefer to review a paper of twenty pages rather than fifteen (see 5.20).

Make sure you haven't included any sentences or paragraphs just because they sound good to you or you are particularly pleased with the way you have expressed yourself.

Also consider cutting whole paragraphs and subsections.

A few months into the future you will not even remember what you cut. It may seem desperately important for you to include something now, but really ask yourself: Do my readers need to read this? Will they notice if I have cut it out?

20.5   Check your paper for readability

Website designers follow the principle of 'don't make me think'. This means that everything should be so clear to visitors to their websites, that these visitors intuitively know where to find the information they need. The visitors are not required to think.

Similarly, writers of technical manuals focus on presenting information in an orderly straightforward fashion that requires minimal intellectual effort on the part of the reader – they want the readers to assimilate the information in a relaxed way, they don't want to make their readers tired and stressed.

Richard Wydick, Professor of Law at the University of California, writes:

> We lawyers do not write plain English. We use eight words to say what could be said in two. We use arcane phrases to express commonplace ideas. Seeking to be precise, we become redundant. Seeking to be cautious, we become verbose. Our sentences twist on, phrase within clause within clause, glazing the eyes and numbing the minds of our readers. The result is a writing style that has, according to one critic, four outstanding characteristics. It is "(1) wordy, (2) unclear, (3) pompous, and (4) dull."

You do not want referees and readers to consider your work wordy, unclear, pompous, or dull, so when you make the final check of you manuscript, ask yourself the following questions:

- are my sentences reasonably short? (sentences longer than 30 words are generally hard to assimilate without having to be read twice)

- are my paragraphs reasonably short?

- have I only written what adds value, have I ensured there is no redundancy?

- have I clearly differentiated my work from the work of others so that the referees can understand what I did in relation to what others have done before me?

- have I highlighted my contribution and the gap it fills so that the referees can judge whether my paper is suitable for my chosen journal?

Readability is also affected by the following factors (these are all covered in Part 1 of this book):

- poor layout: large blocks of text are hard to read, whereas short paragraphs with white space in between them are much easier

- ambiguity and lack of clarity: the reader is not sure how to interpret a phrase

- lack of structure: within a sentence, paragraph or section

- too much abstraction: the reader is not given concrete explanations or examples

- lack of consistency

20.6 Always have the referee in mind

The key factor when revising your paper is to have the referee in mind. Here are two quite typical comments related to poor writing skills.

> I often had to defer my interpretation of the meaning of a sentence until I had read it in its entirety. Frequently I got lost in a series of subordinate clauses. The paper would thus benefit from a major revision from a language point of view.

> This paper could be improved considerably if the authors gave more consideration to their readers. At times it was difficult to follow the logical connection of the authors' ideas, and on several occasions I was tempted to stop reading completely.

Referees often make a direct connection between the time and effort that an author makes in presenting information, and how much time and effort the author has spent in doing their research. If the information is presented badly, then the implication is that the research may have been conducted badly too. Also it helps to remember that referees make reports on manuscripts in their free time for no financial reward – they are of much more benefit to you, than you are to them! To learn about how reviewers write their reports see Chapter 11 in *English for Academic Correspondence*.

20.7 Check for clarity in the logical order of your argumentation

In English it is considered good practice to state upfront what will be argued in an article and how. As you re-read your manuscript make sure there is a logical progression of your argument. Don't be influenced by how a paper might be written in your own language. Kateryna Pishchikova, a Doctor of Philosophy in Linguistics, says:

> Russians tend to use long and complicated sentences. They often follow a "detective story" logic according to which the reader has to follow the events or arguments as they unfold and will only learn what the author is trying to say at the end. Overall, complexity, and not clarity, is synonymous with good scientific or specialist writing.

So check that your key findings are not hidden in the middle of sentences or paragraphs.

20.8 Be careful with cut and pastes

If you write your paper in conjunction with other authors you multiply the chances of mistakes and ambiguity. Words such as *it, that, this, one, former, latter* and *which* are potentially dangerous if the words they refer to are subsequently changed by another author. For example, imagine Author 1 writes

... Russia, Canada and the United States. In the former ...

Then, in order to put the countries in alphabetical order, Author 2 modifies it as follows:

... Canada, Russia and the United States. In the former ...

The problem is that *the former* in Author 1's sentence refers to Russia. But in Author 2's sentence *the former* refers to Canada. To avoid such mistakes it is always best to repeat the key word rather than using *it, that, this, one, former, latter* and *which.* In any case, if it is your job to read the final version of the manuscript it is worth taking such problems into consideration.

For more on sources of ambiguity see Chapter 6.

20.9   Make sure everything is consistent

Referees will suggest a delay in the publication if they find inconsistency in your paper. Here is a genuine example from a referee's report. The only thing I have changed is the key words (X and Y).

1. "Figure 1" on page 4, yet "fig 5a" on page 8.
2. page 4: "Figure 1 shows an example of an X graph," yet page 5: Figure 1 caption states "Example of Y". So is it a Y or an X graph?
3. commas after some equations like on page 10, but not after all equations.
4. caption to Fig 4 states "Initial Size Distribution," yet the illustration is of a graph not a size function.
5. sometimes comma after i.e. e.g., and other times not

Here is an extract from another referee's report, which again highlights the importance of what you may consider to be fairly marginal issues:

This work is novel and is worthy of publication. However, the presentation of the work is, quite frankly, unprofessional. There are many sloppy mistakes like spelling mistakes and incorrect references, as well as inconsistency such as changing terminology and differences between captions and inline text.

20.10   Check that your English is suitably formal

There are certain words and expressions that are considered by most journals to be too informal. Check that your manuscript doesn't contain any of the following (note these are just examples and do not represent a comprehensive list):

- contracted forms: *doesn't, can't, we'll* etc.

- informal nouns: *kids* (rather than *children*)

- informal adjectives: *trendy*; prefer *topical*

- informal expressions of quantity / size / appearance: *a lot, big, tiny, nice*

- informal conjunctions and adverbs: *so, till, like*; prefer *thus, until, such as*

- informal phrasal verbs: *check out, get around, work out*; prefer *examine, avoid, resolve*

- *going to* when *will* or the present tense could be used

- use of *you*

See 15.9 in *English for Academic Research: Grammar, Usage and Style.*

20.11   Don't underestimate the importance of spelling mistakes

I cannot overestimate the importance of doing a final spell check as the very last thing you do before submitting your manuscript.

A variation of Murphy's law predicts that last-minute revisions to your work will inevitably contain typos!

Referees have been known to initially reject a manuscript on the basis of incorrect spelling alone (though I suspect that sometimes this is for political reasons!).

In any case, referees do not like to see spelling mistakes, and some may think that there is an implicit relation between not taking time to check your spelling and possibly not checking your data! Make sure you choose the correct version of English – US or UK – corresponding to your chosen journal. Their style guide for authors should in any case tell you which spelling system they require.

Spelling checkers only pick up words that are not contained in their dictionaries. Mistakes and typos like the ones below would not normally be found because they are words that are in the dictionary (though not with the meaning that the author intended).

   The company was *funded* in 2010. (founded)

The samples were *weighted* and *founded* to be 100 g. (weighed, found)

It was different *form* what was expected. (from)

We *asses* the values as being … (assess)

Be careful of: *choose / chose / choice, filed / field / filled, from / form, there / their, then / than, through / trough, use / sue, were / where, with / whit.*

Remember that spell checkers tend to ignore words in CAPITALS. Given that sometimes titles of papers and other headings are in 'all caps', you need to double check them.

An additional problem is that your paper may have been written by various people and the language set for the spell checker may vary throughout the text. It should be the responsibility of the person who sends the paper to the editor to ensure that the language is set on English throughout the paper, and that American or British English have been chosen as appropriate.

Regarding US vs GB spelling, don't worry about *-ize* vs *-ise*, both forms are used by US and GB authors indifferently (it is only Word that has decided that *-ize* is US spelling). However, differences such as *color / colour, modelled / modeled* should be taken into account.

There is a tendency to ignore Word's (and other software's) red underlining of technical words. Just because such words are not in the software's dictionary, does not necessarily mean that you have spelt them correctly.

Spell checkers may not be perfect, but they are very useful. Grammar checkers are also likely to find a few mistakes that you may not have noticed. They will help you find errors connected with subject verb agreement, word order, punctuation (before *which* and *and*, and with hyphenation between words), unnecessary passive forms etc. Obviously the grammar check can only make suggestions, but Word's grammar check found several mistakes in the draft of this book.

To learn more about spelling see Chapter 28 in *English for Academic Research: Grammar, Usage and Style.*

20.12   Write a good letter / email to accompany your manuscript

If your English is poor in your email, the editor may suspect that the English will be poor in the manuscript too. This is not a good start.

To learn how to write effective emails, see Chapter 13 in *English for Academic Correspondence*.

20.13 Dealing with rejections

Most journals reject large numbers of papers. In general, the higher the impact factor of a journal, the higher the risk of rejection. Don't be demoralized – yours is certainly not the first paper to have been rejected! See 12.2 in *English for Academic Correspondence*.

The highest ranked journals also tend to have the fastest turnaround and may thus return your rejected paper quite quickly. The benefit to you is that you are likely to be given a peer review of an excellent standard, which should help you to revise your paper before submitting it elsewhere. See rejection as an opportunity for making your paper even better.

To give you an idea of how difficult it is to publish a paper in a top ranking journal, here are some statistics from the 'Welcome to resources for authors' page of the website of the British Medical Journal (BMJ), one of the world's most prestigious journals.

We can publish only about 7% of the 7,000–8,000 articles we receive each year.

We reject about two thirds of all submissions without sending them for external review.

However there are still advantages of sending your paper to such a journal, even if there is a very high chance of rejection. The BMJ makes very quick decisions (2–3 weeks) so you don't really delay your chances of publishing elsewhere. If they don't even send your paper for external review, it either means your paper is outside the scope of the journal, or that it has some serious flaws in terms of science and/or structure and language. This is a clear indicator that you need to seriously revise your paper. If the BMJ does decide to submit your paper to peer review, the reports you will receive from the reviewers will be very helpful in indicating how your paper can be improved.

See Chapter 12 in *English for Academic Correspondence* to learn how to write to editors.

20.14 Take the editor's and reviewers' comments seriously

There is a tendency to only take into account the editor's and referees' comments that you agree with and to discount everything else. However, if a referee says that he/she cannot understand what you mean, there is a very good chance that readers will have the same problem.

Don't underestimate editors and reviewers when they ask for a 'linguistic revision'. Here is what one editor wrote after the authors revised the technical aspects of their paper but failed to address English language issues:

> This new revision does address many of the concerns regarding the technical substance of the manuscript. Unfortunately, the English writing (which the reviewers raised, and which was explicitly listed as requirement #2 in the review summary) continues to be an issue (in fact, the newly revised portions have the most language issues). There are problems with word order, commas, (missing or incorrect) articles, duplicated or missing words, logical inconsistencies, and general grammar issues throughout.

> There will therefore need to be yet another minor revision, after which point I hope the manuscript will be in an acceptable state.

> Let me stress the fact that improving the writing is *not* optional. If the manuscript comes back with significant remaining language issues, then it will unfortunately have to be rejected.

See Chapter 13 in *English for Academic Correspondence* to learn how to communicate with editors.

20.15   A tip for using professional editing agencies

If you decide to use the services of a professional editing agency, ensure that you request a certificate that certifies that the English of your manuscript has been edited by a native English speaking editor. You can then send this certificate to the editor along with your manuscript.

This should help you to deal with reviewers whose own English is not sufficiently good to judge the quality of your English, but who claim that your 'English needs to be revised by a native speaker' maybe because you have a non-English surname.

Of course, this means that you need to choose a good English editor to do the job, otherwise the reviewer might be right!!

See 13.5 in *English for Academic Correspondence* to learn more about using editing agencies.

20.16   A final word from the author: Let's put a bit of fun into scientific writing!

There's a tendency in the academic world to take oneself and one's discipline very seriously. This seriousness often leads to extremely tedious presentations at conferences where presenters feel obliged to be mega formal. An over inflated sense of importance also leads to papers that lack any sign of the presumed enthusiasm of the researcher for his / her work.

The British Medical Journal is one of the most respected journals in the world, not just in the field of medicine but in science in general. Yet they felt it was perfectly acceptable to publish the following paper: *Orthopaedic Surgeons: As Strong As an Ox and Almost Twice As Clever?*

The objective of the research was *To compare the intelligence and grip strength of orthopaedic surgeons and anaesthetists*, and its Conclusions (as reported in their structured abstract) were: *Male orthopaedic surgeons have greater intelligence and grip strength than their male anaesthetic colleagues, who should find new ways to make fun of their orthopaedic friends.*

The Introduction to the paper reads as follows (I am very grateful to Paddy – Padmanabhan Subramanian – first author of the paper and an Orthopaedic Registrar in London, for allowing me to quote from his paper):

> A humorous anaesthetic colleague recently repeated the following popular saying while an operating table was being repaired with a mallet: "typical orthopaedic surgeon—as strong as an ox but half as bright." Making fun of orthopaedic surgeons is a popular pastime in operating theatres throughout the country. This pursuit has recently spread to the internet; a humorous animation entitled "orthopedia vs anesthesia" had received more than half a million hits at the time of writing. [1] Several comparisons of orthopaedic surgeons to primates have been published, and the medical literature contains suggestions that orthopaedic surgery requires brute force and ignorance. [2–4]

> The stereotypical image of the strong but stupid orthopaedic surgeon has not been subject to scientific scrutiny. Previous studies have shown that the average hand size of orthopaedic surgeons is larger than that of general surgeons. [2, 3] However, a search of the worldwide scientific literature found no studies assessing the strength or intelligence of orthopaedic surgeons. In the absence of a cohort of willing oxen as a control group, and given that the phrase is popular with anaesthetists, we designed this study to compare the mean grip strength of the dominant hand and the intelligence test score of orthopaedic surgeons and anaesthetists.

I am not advocating that everyone should adopt Paddy's humorous approach, but I am suggesting that now and again we should all try to inject a bit of fun into our writing and presentations.

People tend to remember and implement what they have enjoyed reading and learning, but quickly forget torrid tedium.

20.17 Summary of this chapter

➢ Respect the referee. Don't waste his or her time by submitting a poorly written manuscript

➢ Get a colleague to read through your paper or use a professional editing service

➢ Print a hard copy of your manuscript. Don't rely on reading it on screen

➢ Check for all types of mistakes in English: grammar, vocabulary and spelling

➢ Apply the same standards as if you had written your manuscript in your own mother tongue

➢ Cut as much as you can

➢ Check your manuscript for readability and logic

➢ Be careful with problems caused by multiple authors, e.g. cut and pastes

➢ Ensure you have followed the journal's style guide, e.g. for citing the literature

➢ Check for accuracy and consistency

➢ Take editorial comments seriously

➢ As your last task before sending the manuscript to the journal, do a spell check. Don't rely 100% on automatic spell checkers. Spell checkers do not know the difference between *witch* and *which*, *asses* and *assets,* or *tanks* and *thanks.*

20.18 Summary of the entire book: 10 key concepts

1. Preparation is vital. Read as many papers as possible on similar topics from your chosen journal to learn about the expected style, length of the various sections etc.

2. Always have the referees and readers in mind. You are writing for them, not for yourself.

3. Don't equate the length of a paper with its importance. Do everything you can to reduce redundancy (words, sentences, paragraphs, even sections).

4. Keep it simple. Write reasonably short sentences using grammatical structures and vocabulary that you are familiar with. Your aim is to add to the state of the art of your discipline, to communicate your results in the clearest and most accessible way possible. Your aim is not to impress your reader with your wonderful writing style.

5. Don't underestimate the visual impact that your paper has on the readers' eyes. Avoid long blocks of text and very long sentences. Use headings to help readers navigate. Place tables and figures strategically to break up blocks of text.

6. Be very very careful when using pronouns (if possible replace them with the noun they refer to); likewise avoid synonyms for key words – the reader may not know what the pronoun or synonym refers to.

7. Ensure the reader can see your key findings (don't bury them in the middle of a long paragraph) and understand the gap you are filling and the level of innovation. And make it clear whose findings you are talking about – yours or another research group's.

8. Always mention any limitations.

9. Where possible, show how your work could be applied in other fields. Remember that your work is often funded by public money, and the public needs to feel that their money has been invested well.

10. Triple check everything.

And if you can ... Find ways to enjoy writing your manuscripts. If you don't find it a pleasurable experience, how can you expect your readers to enjoy or at least appreciate what you have written?

Acknowledgements

Massive thanks to Gráinne Newcombe for proofreading this new edition and for help with other books in this series.

The following people allowed me to quote their work or gave me advice – thank you!

Alan Chong, Ali Hedayat, Andrea Mangani, Ahmed Nagy, Alyson Price, Anchalee Sattayathem, Anna Southern, Antonio Strozzi, Alistair Wood, Basile Audoly, Beatrice Pezzarossa, Begum Cimen, Bernadette Batteaux, Boris Demeshev, Brian Bloch, Calliope-Louisa Sotiropoulou, Carolina Perez-Iratxeta, Caroline Mitchell, Catherine Bertenshaw, Cesare Carretti, Chandler Davis, Chandra Ramasamy, Chris Powell, Chris Rozek, Congjun Mu, Daniel Sentenac, David Dunning, David Hine, Donald Dearborn, Donald Sparks, Du Huynh, Elisabetta Giorgi, Estrella Garcia Gonzalez, Filippo Conti, Francesco Rizzi, Greg Anderson, Ivan Appelqvist, James Hitchmough, Javier Morales, John Morley, John R. Yamamoto-Wilson, Justin Kruger, Karen McKee, Kateryna Pishchikova, Keith Harding, Ken Hyland, Ken Lertzman, Khalida Madani, Lena Dal Pozzo, Liselotte Jansson, Magdi Selim, Maggie Charles, Magnus Enquist, Marcello Lippmann, Marco Abate, Maria Andrea Kern, Maria Gkresta, Mark Worden, Matteo Borzoni, Melanie Bell, Mercy Njima, Michaela Panter, Michael Shermer, Mike Seymour, Mohamed Abedelwahab, Osmo Pekonen, Paola Giannetti, Peter Rowlinson, Pierdomenico Perata, Richard Wydick, Robert Adams, Robert Coates, Robert Matthews, Robert Shewfelt, Ronald Gratz, Rogier Kievit, Rory Rosszell, Rossella Borri, Sandy Lang, Sara Tagliagamba, Sébastien Neukirch, Stefano Di Falco, Stefano Ghirlanda, Tracy Seeley, Wei Zheng, William Mackaness, and Wojciech Florkowski.

A special thanks to: William Pugh, Robert Coates, Charles Fox, Rogier Kievit, the creators of the Ignobel prizes some of whose award-winning papers I have used in this book (www. improbable. com), NASA's Office of Communication for allowing me to quote freely from Katzoff's article, the content creators of the websites of the British Medical Journal, Nature, and Bates College.

© Springer International Publishing Switzerland 2016
A. Wallwork, *English for Writing Research Papers*,
English for Academic Research, DOI 10.1007/978-3-319-26094-5

Sources of the Factoids and other info

Much of the information contained in the factoids is publicly available on the Internet. Below is more information about the sources for some of the other factoids, quotations, and other statistics. The numbers in brackets indicate the number of the factoid, e.g. (2) = the second factoid or quotation.

Chapter 1

(1) *In Search of the Cradle of Civilization*, Georg Feuerstein, Quest Books, 2001; (2) Thomson Reuters press release 15 May 2007; (3) *Communicative characteristics of reviews of scientific papers written by non-native users of English*, M Kourilova, Comenius University, Bratislava; (4) http://www.theguardian.com/education/2014/sep/09/italy-spain-graduates-skills-oecd-report-education; (5) www.insme.org/documenti/Statistic_Report_part1.pdf 6) http://www.oecd.org/document/30/0,3343,en_2649_33703_35471385_1_1_1_1,00.html

1.1 *Writing for Science*, R Goldbort, Yale University Press, 2006; *How to Write and Publish a Scientific Paper*, R Day, Cambridge University Press, 2006; *Handbook of Writing for the Mathematical Sciences*, N Highman, SIAM, 1998. Highman's book is one of the best books I have read on scientific writing. Any researcher in mathematics should seek out a copy.

1.13 Nicholas Carr, *The Shallows*, W. W. Norton & Company, 2010

Chapter 2

(3) *Can a Knowledge of Japanese Help our EFL Teaching?* John R. Yamamoto-Wilson

© Springer International Publishing Switzerland 2016
A. Wallwork, *English for Writing Research Papers*,
English for Academic Research, DOI 10.1007/978-3-319-26094-5

Chapter 3

(1) Nicholas Carr, *The Shallows*, W. W. Norton & Company, 2010; (2) Leggett A "Notes on the Writing of Scientific English for Japanese Physicists" published in the Nihon Butsuri Gakkaishi (Vol. 21, No. 11, pp. 790–805). This is fascinating stuff for EAP trainers and scientific editors. The full article is available at: http://wwwsoc.nii.ac.jp/jps/jps/topics/Leggett.pdf; (3) www.guardian.co.uk/books/2010/jul/15/slow-reading

3.18 *Clarity in Technical Reporting*, S Katzoff, NASA Scientific and Technical Information Division. Free download at: http://courses.media.mit.edu/2010spring/mas111/NASA-64-sp7010.pdf

Chapter 4

(1) Statistic on Stanford students from: *Consequences of Erudite Vernacular Utilized Irrespective of Necessity: Problems with Using Long Words Needlessly*, by Daniel Oppenheimer, available at: http://web.princeton.edu/sites/opplab/papers/Opp%20Consequences%20of%20Erudite%20 Vernacular.pdf, (3 and 4) John Adair's "The Effective Communicator" (The Industrial Society, 1989 – also available on Google Books).

4.1 *On the Origin of Species*, Charles Darwin, 1859; *Good Style – Writing for Science and Technology*, John Kirkman, Routledge, 2006

Chapter 5

(1)   http://www.businessinsider.com.au/the-worlds-smallest-language-has-only-100-words-and-you-can-say-almost-anything-2015-7; (2) http://www.nature.com/authors/author_resources/how_ write.html (3,4) Nicholas Carr, *The Shallows*, W. W. Norton & Company, 2010

5.1 The first three quotations come from The Penguin Dictionary of Twentieth Century Quotations (1996) edited by M J & J M Cohen. The quote by novelist Barbara Kingsolver comes from a BBC interview with her on June 9, 2010. Bruce Cooper's quote can be found in his excellent book (for those offering editing services) *Writing Technical Reports*, Penguin UK, 1999).

5.20 *The Impact of Article Length on the Number of Future Citations: A Bibliometric Analysis of General Medicine Journals*   http://journals.plos.org/plosone/article?id=10.1371/journal. pone.0049476#pone-0049476-t003

Chapter 6

(1) *The Mother Tongue*, Bill Bryson, HarperCollins, 1990; (2) http://www.mfa.gov.il/mfa/foreign-policy/peace/guide/pages/un%20security%20council%20resolution%20242.aspx

6.6 For more info see: http://www.fact-index.com/u/un/un_security_council_resolution_242.html

6.12 The legal example is based on a real case and is contained in Douglas Walton's paper "New Dialectical Rules For Ambiguity".

6.14 *The Mother Tongue*, Bill Bryson, HarperCollins, 1990

Chapter 7

All the factoids are available in the public domain and were taken from many different sources.

Chapter 8

All the factoids are available in the public domain and were taken from many different sources.

Chapter 9

(1-3, 5-10) I wish I hadn't said that: Experts speak and get it wrong, C Cerf & V Navasky, HarperCollinsPublishers, 2000: (4) http://www.theguardian.com/uk-news/2015/jun/10/nobel-scientist-tim-hunt-female-scientists-cause-trouble-for-men-in-labs

9.1 *Brilliant Blunders: From Darwin to Einstein – Colossal Mistakes by Great Scientists That Changed Our Understanding of Life and the Universe*, Mario Livio, Simon & Schuster, 2014

9.2 *Why People Believe Weird Things*, Michael Shermer, Holt Paperbacks, 2002: http://abacus.bates.edu/~ganderso/biology/resources/writing/HTWtablefigs.html; Pauling quoted in Livio.

9.3 www.bmj.com

9.6 For more on this topic, see Dr Maggie Charles's very useful article "Revealing and obscuring the writer's identity: evidence from a corpus of theses" in Chap. 9 of "Language, Culture and Identity in Applied Linguistics", a book by the British Association of Applied Linguistics.

Chapter 10

(1) *The Ascent of Man* Jacob Bronowski by Little Brown & Co., 1974; (2) Leggett A "Notes on the Writing of Scientific English for Japanese Physicists" published in the Nihon Butsuri Gakkaishi (Vol. 21, No. 11, pp. 790–805).

10.1 George Mikes' book is a fun read, you can find the full text at: http://f2.org/humour/howalien.html

Chapter 11

(3) www.ithenticate.com/; 5) McCabe article: https://www2.bc.edu/~peck/mccabe%20article.pdf

11.1.3 The quotation by Prof Robert Adams was specifically commissioned for this book. The quote from Dr. Ronald K. Gratz comes from his paper "Using Another's Words and Ideas". Gratz's paper is essential reading for those in EAP and editing services, it is available at: www.paperpub.com.cn/admin/upload/file/20089394456141.pdf and at http://www.bio.mtu.edu/courses/bl447/persp/fhbk2/plagrism.htm

11.2 http://cdn2.hubspot.net/hub/92785/file-318578964-pdf/docs/ithenticate-decoding-survey-summary-092413.pdf

To learn what editors think about plagiarism:

http://www.springer.com/authors/book+authors/helpdesk?SGWID=0-1723113-12-807204-0

http://www.elsevier.com/editors/publishing-ethics/perk/questions-and-answers#plagiarism

11.3 Alistair Wood's article was originally published in Science Tribune in April 1997 and is freely available at: http://www.tribunes.com/tribune/art97/wooda.htm.

11.4 and **11.6** see ref. to 11.1.3 above.

Chapter 12

(1-4) winners of Ignobel prizes (www.improbable.com/ig/winners/), (5-6) arxiv.org, 7-12 http://mathoverflow.net/questions/44326/most-memorable-titles

12.2 http://www.nature.com/news/papers-with-shorter-titles-get-more-citations-1.18246; *The relationship between manuscript title structure and success: editorial decisions and citation performance for an ecological journal* http://onlinelibrary.wiley.com/doi/10.1002/ece3.1480/full

12.17 This section was taken from the website of the American Journal Experts (AJE) – a very useful website both for researchers and scientific editors, and was written by Michaela Panter: https://www.aje.com/en/author-resources/articles/editing-tip-crafting-appropriate-running-title

Chapter 13

(1) http://arxiv.org/ftp/arxiv/papers/1110/1110.2832.pdf; (2) The Journal of Emergency Medicine Vol 8 Issue 3 May-June 1990; (3) http://scholar.harvard.edu/files/joshuagoodman/files/goodmans.pdf; (4) http://arxiv.org/abs/0711.4114; (5) http://arxiv.org/abs/1004.2003v2; (6) http://link.springer.com/article/10.1007/s00300-003-0563-3?no-access=true (7) EOS Trans. AGU Vol 72, No 27-53, p456

For more great titles and abstracts see: http://www.quora.com/What-is-the-funniest-research-paper-you-have-ever-read

13.1 http://www.tribunes.com/tribune/art97/wooda.htm

13.8 Style 1) http://www.tribunes.com/tribune/art97/wooda.htm; Style 2) R A J Matthews Tumbling toast, Murphy's Law and the fundamental constants, 1995 Eur. J. Phys. 16 172–176, available at: http://www.iop.org/EJ/journal/EJP; Style 4) Copyright © 1999 by the American Psychological Association. Reproduced with permission. Kruger, Justin; Dunning, David, Unskilled and unaware of it: How difficulties in recognizing one's own incompetence lead to inflated self-assessments, Journal of Personality and Social Psychology. Vol 77(6), Dec 1999, 1121–1134. The use of APA information does not imply endorsement by APA.

13.10 http://www.nlm.nih.gov/bsd/policy/structured_abstracts.html NLM email 28 May 2015 "You may paraphrase the comments made on this webpage.

13.12 http://www.sigsoft.org/resources/pughadvice.htm

Source: www.nature.com/nature/authors/gta/Letter_bold_para.doc

13.13 If you need help in creating a video I recommend Karen McKee, who kindly contributed to much of this subsection You can access her service at: http://thescientistvideographer.com/wordpress/how-to-make-a-video-abstract-for-your-next-journal-article/

13.14 www.nature.com/nature/authors/gta/Letter_bold_para.doc(email 22 May 2015)

13.29 http://www.sigsoft.org/resources/pughadvice.htm

Chapter 14

(1-10) *The Book of Lists*, David Wallechinsky, Irving Wallace, Amy Wallace, Corgi, 1977

14.3 Fragmentation of Rods by Cascading Cracks: Why Spaghetti Does Not Break in Half, was published in Physical Review Letters Vol. 95, 095505 (2005). The full version available at: http://www.lmm.jussieu.fr/spaghetti/audoly_neukirch_fragmentation.pdf

14.6 For the full version of Chris Rozek's paper "The Effects of Feedback and Attribution Style on Task Persistence" see: http://gustavus.edu/psychology/files/ Rozek.pdf

Chapter 15

http://www.nature.com/news/the-top-100-papers-1.16224

15.4 For the full version of Chris Rozek's paper "The Effects of Feedback and Attribution Style on Task Persistence" see: http://gustavus.edu/psychology/files/ Rozek.pdf

Chapter 16

16.1 *The Ultimate Book of Notes and Queries*, ed. Joseph Harker, Atlantic Books, 2002.

16.5 and 16.6 These sections were inspired by a very helpful paper entitled *Be careful! Avoiding duplication: a case study* and published by Journal of Zhejiang University-SCIENCE B (Biomedicine & Biotechnology) Vol. (14)4, Apr 2013, the authors present a case study of an author who was asked to make revisions to avoid self-plagiarism

16.12 *How to Write and Publish a Scientific Paper*, Day R, Cambridge University Press, 2006

Chapter 17

(2-6)   https://www.ipa.org.au/publications/1964/a-history-of-scientific-alarms   (7)   https://en.wikipedia.org/wiki/Influenza_A_virus_subtype_H5N1 (8) http://www.telegraph.co.uk/news/earth/environment/globalwarming/11395516/The-fiddling-with-temperature-data-is-the-biggest-science-scandal-ever.html

17.7 *Bad Science*, Ben Goldacre, Harper Collins, 2008. See also videos on Goldacre's website: www.badscience.net; *What do you care what other people think?* Richard Feynman, W. W. Norton & Company, 2001

17.8, 17.9 Ken Lertzman's "Notes on Writing Papers and Theses" are available for free download at: http://www.jstor.org/stable/20167913?seq=1#page_scan_tab_contents; Bates: see ref. to 17.11.

17.10 http://en.wikipedia.org/wiki/Brazil_v_Germany_%282014_FIFA_World_Cup%29

17.11 Bates College site: http://abacus.bates.edu/~ganderso/biology/resources/writing/HTWtablefigs.html

See also http://textualidade.net/wp-content/uploads/2014/03/Robert-Barrass.-Os-cientistas-precisam-escrever.pdf

17.13 The piece on postdocs was written by Filippo Conti.

Chapter 18

18.4 www.bmj.com/about-bmj/resources-authors/article-types/research

18.6 Greg Anderson's biology website from Bates College in Maine, USA is essential reading, even for those researchers outside the field of biology: http://abacus.bates.edu/~ganderso/biology/resources/writing/HTWtoc.html

18.6, 18.18 Catherine Bertenshaw and Peter Rowlinson's article, "Exploring Stock Managers: Perceptions of the Human-Animal Relationship on Dairy Farms and an Association with Milk Production," appeared in Anthrozoos: A Multidisciplinary Journal of The Interactions of People & Animals, Volume 22, Number 1, March 2009, pp. 59–69(11), Berg Publishers, an imprint of A&C Black Publishers Ltd. Full version: http://www.ingentaconnect.com/content/berg/anthroz/2009/00000022/00000001/art00006

18.8 "Chickens prefer beautiful humans" originally appeared in Human Nature Volume 13, Number 3, 383–389. Full version: http://www.fao.org/fileadmin/user_upload/animalwelfare/ghir-landa_jansson_enquist2002.pdf

18.9 This subsection was based on Professor Shahn Majid's notes for math students, "Hints for New PhD students on How to Write Papers" which can be found at: http://www.findaphd.com/students/life2.asp

Chapter 19

The Year 2000 – A Framework for Speculation on the Next Thirty-Three Years, Herman Kahn and Anthony J. Weiner, Macmillan, 1967.

19.2 http://www.nature.com/nphys/journal/v3/n9/full/nphys724.html; http://www.cs.cmu.edu/~jrs/sins.html

19.3 The University of Toronto's excellent website on writing skills can be found at: http://www.engineering.utoronto.ca/Directory/Student_Resources/Engineering_Communication_Program/Online_Handbook/Components_of_Documents.htm

Chapter 20

These are genuine referee's comments on the papers of Professor Charles Fox: http://www.uky.edu/~cfox/PeerReview/Index.htm

20.1 The reviews come from: http://shitmyreviewerssay.tumblr.com/ Big thanks to Rogier Kievit.

20.1 The Dunning quote comes from *Ignobel Prizes – The Annals of Improbable Research by Mark Abrahams*, Penguin Group, USA. I would like to thank him for allowing me to use it.

20.5 *Plain English for Lawyers*, Richard C. Wydick, Carolina Academic Press

20.16 http://www.bmj.com/content/343/bmj.d7506

Index

This book has been indexed by chapters and subsections. For more information on grammar use, particularly the use of tenses, see the companion volume English for Research: Usage, Style, and Grammar

- Numbers in **bold** refer to complete chapters (e.g. **5** = Chapter 5).
- Words in *italics* refer to the usage of specific words (e.g. *although* 4.9 = how the word 'although' should be used in certain contexts. This information can be found in subsection 4.9).
- Words that begin with a capital letter refer to the typical sections in a paper (e.g. Abstracts, Introduction, Acknowledgements).
- Advice about how to use tenses (e.g. present simple, present perfect, past simple) is all contained under TENSES.

© Springer International Publishing Switzerland 2016
A. Wallwork, *English for Writing Research Papers*,
English for Academic Research, DOI 10.1007/978-3-319-26094-5

CPSIA information can be obtained at www.ICGtesting.com
Printed in the USA
BVOW06s0216220316

441267BV00009B/54/P